BIBLICAL AND THEOLOGICAL INSIGHTS FROM ANCIENT AND MODERN CIVIL LAW

BIBLICAL AND THEOLOGICAL INSIGHTS FROM ANCIENT AND MODERN CIVIL LAW

George Wesley Buchanan

Studies in Religion and Society
Volume 29

The Edwin Mellen Press
Lewiston/Queenston/Lampeter

Library of Congress Cataloging-in-Publication Data

Buchanan, George Wesley.
Biblical and theological insights from ancient and modern civil law / George Wesley Buchanan.
p. cm. -- (Studies in religion and society ; v. 29)
Includes bibliographical references and index.
ISBN 0-7734-9601-7
1. Law (Theology) 2. Christianity and law. 3. Jewish law. 4. Bible and law. 5. Civil law. I. Title. II. Series: Studies in religion and society (New York, N.Y.) ; v. 29.
BT96.2.B825 1992
261.5--dc20 92-27602
CIP

This is volume 29 in the continuing series
Studies in Religion and Society
Volume 29 ISBN 0-7734-9601-7
SRS Series ISBN 0-88946-863-X

A CIP catalog record for this book
is available from the British Library.

The Edwin Mellen Press
Box 450
Lewiston, New York
USA 14092

The Edwin Mellen Press
Box 67
Queenston, Ontario
CANADA L0S 1L0

The Edwin Mellen Press, Ltd.
Lampeter, Dyfed, Wales
UNITED KINGDOM SA48 7DY

Printed in the United States of America

TO MY BORN AGAIN DAUGHTER

MARY COLLEEN BUCHANAN

TABLE OF CONTENTS

CHAPTER ONE 1
RELIGION AND THE STATE 1
INTRODUCTION 1
TRADITION 2
Always the Same 2
Liturgy 3
Parallels 3
LEGAL AUTHORITY 4
Resistance to Change 4
Court 4
Church and Synagogue 5
TEXT AND INTERPRETATION 5
Fact and Fiction 5
The King and the Code 8
Royal Agency 10
Bodies of the King 10
Corporation 11
Legal Identity 13
Legal Transformation 13
Agent of God 17
LEGAL INFALLIBILITY 17
The King 17
The Pope 18
The Status of Judges 19
Civil and Religious Courtrooms 22
CONCLUSIONS 27

CHAPTER TWO 29
TRIALS AND TESTIMONIES 29
THE EARLY JURY TRIALS 29
Family Fights 29
Community Court 30
NEEDS FOR VENGEANCE 31
Families and Nations 31
Punitive Compensation 32
Pain as Satisfaction 33
COURT SYSTEMS 34
Court Variations 34
Open Courts 34
Formal Liturgizing 35
Professional Advocates 35
Corruption in Court 35

PARTICIPANTS 36
The Plaintiff 36
The Defendant 37
RELIGIOUS CONFLICTS 38
THE ARGUMENT 38
Rhetoricians 38
The Art of Rhetoric 38
Outline of the Argument 39
THE INTRODUCTION 39
The Purpose 39
The Judge and the Opposition 40
THE STATEMENT OF FACTS 40
VERIFICATION OF FACTS 41
WITNESSES IN COURT 43
Testimony of Witnesses 43
World Court 43
Role of Witnesses 44
Christian Witnessing 44
Cross-Examining the Witness 45
Evidence 46
Joseph's Robe 46
Biblical Testimony 47
Scripture and Testimony 47
Importance of Evidence 48
Proof and "signs" 48
From the Particular to the General 49
Light and Heavy 50
THE CONCLUSION 51

CHAPTER THREE 53
WORSHIP IN THE COURTROOM 53
INTRODUCTION 53
PRAYERS IN COURT 54
Prayer Terms 54
Prayer and Judgment 55
Judgment Prayer of the Psalmists 56
POSTURES IN PRAYER 57
Facing the Judge 57
Herod's Sons on Trial 57
Humility in Prayer 58
OUTLINES IN PRAYER 61
Before a Court Judge 61
Before a heavenly Judge 62

Collect for Purity 63
Prayer to a King 64
PRAYER LETTERS 66
Comparisons 66
Salutation 67
Address to the Judge 68
The Body 68
Prayer for Relief 69
The Closing 71
CONTROLLING THE JUDGE 71
Trained Oratory 71
Crisis in the Wilderness 72
Abraham's Rhetoric 72
Status of the Judge 72
Mitigating a Sentence 72
CONCLUSIONS 73

CHAPTER FOUR 74
LOVE AND CONTRACTUAL THEOLOGY 74
INTRODUCTION 74
TYPES OF CONTRACTS 74
Secular Contracts 74
Validity of Contracts 74
Biblical Contracts 75
MARRIAGE CONTRACT 77
Husbands and Wives 77
Ancient Contracts 78
Terms of Contract 78
Parties to the Contract 79
Contracts and Oaths 80
Breaking Contracts 80
English Translation 81
BIBLICAL LOVE 82
Love and Marriage 82
Marriage and Divorce 82
National Divorce 82
Divorce and Remarriage 83
Love and Contracts 84
Demands of Love 85
Parties to Contracts 85
CONCLUSIONS 86

CHAPTER FIVE 88
THE DAY IN COURT 88

INTRODUCTION 88
THE HEAVENLY DAY IN COURT 88
The Judgment 88
Preliminary Material 89
Biblical Courts 90
JOSHUA'S DEFENSE 90
GARMENTS AND COURTS 92
Garment Symbols 92
Abraham 92
Eliakim 93
Son of Man 93
Jehoiachin 93
Herod 93
Joshua 94
Jesus 94
Other Instances 94
Legal Implications 95
THE HASMONEAN JUDGMENT DAY 96
Antiochus on Trial 96
The Announcement 96
The Session 97
The Books 98
The Participants 98
The Verdict 99
The Defendant's Death Sentence 99
Court Drama 100
The Revised Version 102
Divine Symbols 102
Jesus and Judas 103
Clouds and Sun Disks 105
The Divine Leader 105
The Clouds and the Son of Man 106
Writings of the Contestants 106
History and the Court 107
The Role of the Plaintiff 107
Theology and Myth 107
CONCLUSIONS TO DANIEL SEVEN 108
Problems 108
Confusion of Kings 108
THE ROUTE OF ANTIOCHUS III 109
CONCLUSIONS 111

CHAPTER SIX 113
CHRISTOLOGY AND CANON 113
INTRODUCTION 113
AGENCY AND APOSTLESHIP 113
Modern Law 113
Legal Agents 113
Messengers and Agents 115
Christianity and Judaism 116
Theology 116
The Deity, Agent, and People 116
Apostleship 117
Apostleship in the Bible 117
Affirmations and Explanations 118
The Necessity of Agents 118
The Agent Moses 119
Traditional Claims 119
Pentateuchal Assumptions 119
Prophets as Agents 120
"Earlier Prophets" 120
The Later Prophets 121
Prophets as Messengers 121
Kings as Agents 127
King Jehoshaphat and Subordinate Judges . . 127
Psalms and the Wisdom Literature 127
The Clay Feet of the Agents 128
Jewish and Samaritan Agents and Canons . . 129
Royal Agency 130
The Word and the Spirit 130
Royal Authority and the Spirit 131
THE AUTHORITY OF THE MESSIAH 132
Jesus the Apostle 132
Jesus the King 133
Jesus as Agent 134
The Sent One 135
Christological Implications 135
Through Christ 135
The Incarnate Word 137
Legal Incarnation 137
The Incarnate Christ 138
Eternal Life 139
Apostolic Implications 140
Acts of the Apostles 140
Legal Perfection 141

CONCLUSIONS 141
INDICES 144
WORDS 144
ANCIENT NAMES 147
MODERN SCHOLARS 149
BIBLICAL REFERENCES 150
NON-BIBLICAL REFERENCES 156
GEOGRAPHICAL LOCATIONS 158

PREFACE

Before 1974 I had been in a court room only twice in my life, and these were occasions that did not require that I understand much about the procedure or logic of court practice. The purchase of a "lemon" for an automobile, however, changed all of that. In Washington, D.C., we bought a car to be picked up in Sweden. We had not driven the car a hundred miles before it needed oil. By the time we had driven it fifteen hundred miles it had used six liters. That was only the beginning of its problems. We took it to many dealers, all of whom said we would have to take it back to the United States where we had bought it. It could not be warranted in Europe. The car broke down and stopped functioning in Lebanon, so we had to give up our research project there. When we reached the United States, the dealer from whom we purchased the car said he was only the agent. The principal was in Sweden, and it was there that we would have to find relief. The principal in Sweden was not at all prepared to do anything to compensate for our misfortune, and consumer laws were not as effective then as they are now. The contract said that all legal transactions would have to be tried according to Swedish law. When I tried to find attorneys to represent me, I was told that I would have to put about ten thousand dollars up front before they would become involved (The car initially cost about $4,200 back in 1973). Since I did not have that kind of money, I had to learn something about law myself.

Fortunately, I had a student who was a retired attorney, Dr. Edgar Martin, esq. who taught me how to begin research in a law library and how to file a law suit. I went to the D.C. court house and observed court cases being tried, just so that I would know something about the way court cases proceed. It was while observing court trials that I heard familiar words, like "prayer," being used and noticed how similar the court liturgy was to the liturgy in a church service. In dealing with the automobile I had to learn the significance of terms like "contract," "legal agent," and "principal." This reminded me of Christian terms like "covenant" and "apostle."

Later my wife and I put a very small down payment on a run-down twelve apartment building in Washington, D.C., where there is rent control but no price control. We quickly learned that our tenants were skilled in suing landlords for frivolous causes. They could obtain free legal counsel, and they knew landlords could not afford to pay the extensive fees lawyers charged and so would settle out of court. The only way we knew to win in this game was to learn to represent ourselves in court and contest every suit. This gave us the opportunity to study law and to observe court practice in action. While this was going on, I was regularly teaching Hebrew Scripture, New Testament, and Rabbinic Literature, so I made the situation curriculum. I continually noticed the relationship between court terms and religious terms, and I gained some insights that clarified biblical and religious concepts that I had never before understood adequately.

I continued to be in contact with my friend, Dr. Edgar Martin, and several other practicing attorneys became my students. While they were learning New Testament exegesis and Rabbinic literature, I continued to learn from them as much as I could about United States law. One of these students was Dr. Noah Mack Smith, esq. Some other personal friends who were practicing attorneys were Dr. Charles Shields III, esq., Dr. Roberta Lamb Swartzendruber, esq. and her husband, Dr. Lydon Swartzendruber. Attorneys Martin, Shields, Smith, and Swartzendruber, and the research physicist, Dr. Lydon Swartzendruber, have all read this entire manuscript at least once and have offered suggestions for improvement. I am also grateful to Justice Blackmun who allowed me to sit in his box and observe the United States Supreme Court in session. I received a National Endowment of the Humanities grant to study biblical law in Cornell U. under the guidance of Prof. Calum M. Carmichael and his seminar. This provided me a helpful opportunity to devote undivided attention to this project, a time for which I am grateful. Prof. J. D. M. Derrett read the entire manuscript, offered much encouragement, and made many very helpful suggestions for its improvement. These have been taken into account with appreciation.

Part of chapter six was published at an earlier stage as "The Function of Agency in the Formation of Canon," Explorations 8 (1990):63-79. It is updated here and used with permission and appreciation.

My greatest appreciation is to my wife, Harlene, who reads all of my manuscripts, improves my style, and supports all of my research. I am not burdened with the illusion that through my brief, amateur studies I have become an expert in modern United States law, or that I have learned all there is to be known about the significance of law to biblical studies. I assume that many others will correct my mistakes and gain still further and better insights than those shown here, but this is an introduction that I hope others will find thought-provoking.

One of the legal concepts that I learned in this project is that the idea of being born again and becoming a new creature is a legal expression. A person could be born only once, physically, but by changing membership, status, nationality, family, or religion he or she could be legally reidentified and therefore become a new creature or "born again." I then realized that my daughter, Mary Colleen, is a born again Buchanan. She had been born in a hospital somewhere in Wisconsin, when I was not present. About two years later she came to live with us and was born again in an Appleton, Wisconsin, court house. Although this ceremony took only a few minutes for the legalities to be completed, the birth pangs she and I suffered took much longer as we learned to cherish and trust one another. She has become such a loyal Buchanan that it is hard to believe she was not born a Buchanan the first time. She has brought me much joy, and I am proud to be her legal father. It is to her that I dedicate this volume.

CHAPTER ONE

RELIGION AND THE STATE

INTRODUCTION

Anyone who attends a church with a divided chancel (one with both a pulpit and a lectern) and a formal liturgical service and also observes court in session frequently will note several superficial similarities between the court session and the worship service. Such a person might ask how all of this came about. Particularly in the U.S.A. is this surprising, because there has been a studied effort to keep the church and state separated, from the framing of our constitution until now. How did these similarities originate? Why is the area around the altar (the chancel) or around the judge's bench (the chancel) kept removed from people who are not specially qualified? Those unordained or not admitted to the bar are normally restricted to the nave of the church or the main part of the courtroom. Why is it that both the minister or priest and the judge wear robes? Both services begin with a call to order. In both situations, the congregation is expected to rise and stand as the leader enters. Prayers are offered in both cases. In both institutions tradition is quoted and arguments are given to make the tradition apply to the situation at hand. Services of various kinds are conducted both in courts and churches according to formal patterns, following specified rituals. Jurists, such as Leiser, Llewellyn, and Hoebel, have no idea where these patterns and rituals originated. They probably never were instituted at the command of any legislature or sovereign.[1] There is even some architectural similarity. A further investigation shows that there is a still deeper relationship that is thought-provoking, even if it is not possible to show exactly how these practices have paralleled one another across the centuries. This chapter will try to discover how much alike these systems are and what difference it makes. Ancient, medieval, and modern practices will be compared without suggesting that parallels indicate direct dependence

---

[1]1 B. M. Leiser, Custom, Law, and Morality (Garden City, 1969),p. 109. Discussing the origin of law, K. N. Llewellyn and E. A. Hoebel, The Cheyenne Way (Norman: U. of Oklahoma Press, c1967), pp. 56-56, say, "Legal historians, with a particular eye on Rome, have tended to lay down too flatly 'the' origin in religion. An understandable counter-emphasis has tended to insist too flatly upon 'the' secular original base of law. The given fact seems to be that, as a body of trouble-easing and conduct-channeling devices, law-stuff begins in three things: first, in any order which a group may have. 'What goes on, what is done,' unspecialized and general, is the matrix. Upon this plays, second, the 'litigant' individual's action, the experimental, the often unpredictable, the that-which-happens-to-get-done-this time. Third, there is the tendency to cluster further problem solution around any machinery or competing bodies of machinery which happen to have arisen any where in the culture, for that purpose. We deny any exclusive, single line of origin, on the evidence."

upon one another. One of the most obvious similarities about these two institutions is the attention both give toward tradition.

TRADITION

Always the Same. In the musical play "The Fiddler on the Roof," the theme "tradition" is played out in many ways. Jews seemed to live out the ritual, following the music of the fiddler on the roof. This was tradition. The fiddler had always done it that way, and Judaism structured a philosophy to justify its existence around the tradition. Like Judaism, Christianity has given a great deal of attention to tradition. The same books of worship and the same ritualistic practices continue in many churches year after year, century after century, with very little change, compared with other aspects of life. People recite the same creeds, sing the same hymns, read the same scripture responsively, and confess the same theological beliefs that their religious ancestors have observed, often without knowing what these practices mean or why they must be continued. These customs are successfully designed to preserve the tradition unchanged. The same is true in the practice of law. The nineteenth century English jurist, H. S. Maine, said, "Ancient law uniformly refused to dispense with a single gesture, however grotesque; with a single syllable, however its meaning may have been forgotten; with a single witness, however superfluous may be his testimony."[2]

This is also true of the church. For example, in orthodox, liturgical churches, some clergy leaders would not consider a eucharist valid if parts of the service were omitted. In a Jewish service, the liturgy that is to be read by the entire congregation frequently includes ancient directions for participation, such as, "Let the people say, 'Amen!'" At one time in the past, the leader read the passage, and at certain places the congregation said, "Amen!" Now, in the United States, lawyers continue to prove cases on the basis of English law. Like modern sermons, legal arguments are still couched in antiquated, Shakespearean English, like "perforce," "herein," "thereto," and "unto." Both the court and the church capitalize many nouns that are not proper, like King, Law, Gospel, Counsel, Judge, Plaintiff, and Defendant. Lawyers heavily salt their presentations with Latin expressions, just as ministers and priests use Greek, Hebrew, Latin, and German. Most ministers and attorneys are not very well versed in these languages, and often mispronounce the words, but both seem to use or misuse them--not

---

[2]H. S. Maine, Ancient Law (London, c1901, 17th), p. 272; (U.S.A.: Dorset, c1986), p. 226. There have been many editions of this book published, and most of them have different paginations. When possible I have given the page numbers for more editions than one. J. M. Lundquist, "What is a Temple," The Quest for the Kingdom of God: Studies in the Honor of George E. Mendenhall (Winona Lake, 1983), p. 206, said, "In the light of the extraordinary disruptions in the ancient world . . . it is important to note that there were areas of equally extraordinary cultural, historical and religious continuity." See also G. E. Mendenhall, "'Change and Decay in all around I see': Conquest, Covenant and the Tenth Generation," BA 39 (1976):152-57.

because they are necessary for communication--but probably because they create an atmosphere or impression of academic competence and traditional continuity.

The Federal Register, law schools, and other authorities and social action groups, like HALT, occasionally make efforts to modernize the language of law so that non-specialists can understand it, but these efforts continue to meet stiff resistance from both attorneys and judges. Biblical scholars continually try to produce modern Bible translations, but they still include antiquated words like "wrought," "behold," "he-goat," "likened unto," and "covenant." Like theologians, lawyers uphold traditional "doctrines" and "dogmas."[3]

Defense lawyers develop arguments in ways that are very similar to those of biblical apologists and Greek rhetoricians. Attorneys exegete laws the way theologians prepare exegesis of traditional texts that are considered sacred. It is not by coincidence that the legal term "apologist" applies both to dogmatic or systematic theologians and attorneys. Together with the traditional language is traditional ceremony and drama, a psychological factor in social control for both institutions. The continuity provides comfort for society's insecurities.

Liturgy. Churches and synagogues have standard forms to follow when conducting weddings, funerals, baptisms, and weekly worship services. Courts also have standard forms by which they write wills, interrogatories, prayers, contracts,[4] and a standard procedure to follow in trying cases. Because of the traditional nature of these institutions, similarities can also be found in antiquity, even though it is not certain how widely these practices have been followed across the centuries. In some way or another there are enough parallels to suspect that these are not all coincidental.

Parallels. There are similarities evident between some current court practices and some ancient court practices. There are also similarities between ancient religious practices and modern religious practices, but the line of development is not direct. In some ways the nineteenth century A.D. American legal and religious practices are more primitive than second millennium B.C. religious and legal practices in ancient Mesopotamia. There are further parallels between ancient court practices and ancient religious practices. Some of these customs are similar, even though the legal practice involved is ancient and the religious custom is modern or vice versa.

These parallels do not show direct borrowing of one institution from the other, but they show that two very traditional institutions have successfully kept some similar traditions unchanged for a long time. In some way they both came

---

[3]Such as the doctrine of sovereign immunity or the doctrine of Stare decisis. See "Jimmy V. Mayle, Appellant v. Pennsylvania Department of Highways," Atlantic Reporter vol. 388 2nd series: 709 and Corpus Juris Secundum vol 82A #298, p. 946.

[4]Such as American Jurisprudence Pleading and Practice Forms (Rochester, 1967).

from similar origins which each has preserved very carefully. Unfortunately the evidence is spotty, and it is not possible to compare these institutions at every point at every age. The parallels that are now apparent will be shown here, side by side and one after another, so that readers may evaluate data and conclusions throughout the paper. The purpose of this study is not to add any new insights into the modern practice of law, but to gather insights from law that might clarify the understanding of the Bible and Christian origins.

LEGAL AUTHORITY

Resistance to Change. Modern law is not as unchangeable as that of the ancient Medes and Persians (Dan 6:8, 1, 15), but lawyers today normally do not try to introduce new laws if it is possible to win a case on the basis of laws that already exist, and if they do introduce something new, they present it as if it were really inherent in the old law. When presenting a case, competing attorneys usually call the judge or jury's attention to the relevant laws and the way each thinks these laws should be interpreted. These interpretations are supported, as well as the lawyer is able to discover, by a survey of the ways these laws have been interpreted by earlier courts. In the United States, this is called "shepherdizing." One of the strong arguments in deciding a case is a legal precedent.

In the course of the deliberations, counsels quote case books and law journals, chapter and verse, in ways familiar to biblical exegetes. This is no new practice. Ancient teachers of rhetoric, like Quintilian, supported their arguments by quoting from earlier rhetoricians, like Aristotle, Demosthenes, and Cicero. From the religious tradition, prophets as early as the eighth century quoted from earlier Pentateuchal laws and precedents from the Psalms. Of course, by New Testament times, arguments were supported from any of the texts from the Hebrew Scriptures that were appropriate. Some were careful to cite precedents from both the Pentateuch and the prophets.

Court. The U.S. Supreme Court holds the constitution of the United States as the primary authority for its judgments. Congress can make laws, but the Supreme Court decides whether or not they are constitutional. There are procedures by which the constitution can be amended. When that happens, the courts must judge on the basis of the new constitution as it exists in its amended state. The amended constitution functions in court, to some degree, the way the scripture has traditionally functioned in the worshiping community.

Galinski noted that there are only 5,845 verses in the entire Torah and most of this is not legal material. It has only 613 precepts. Comparing this to Lord Halsbury's Laws of England, which contains more than forty large volumes, and Code Napoleon, which has nearly three thousand sections, it is apparent that both the U.S. constitution and the legal section of the Torah are remarkably brief.[5] Most people know how the constitution obtained its authority. They also realize that the Bible has a very great authority, without knowing just why. In the New Testament, for instance, Hebrew Scripture was quoted and held to be the words of God (Heb 1:5) or the Holy Spirit (Heb 3:7; 10:15). Where did the Bible get this divine authority? Some clues to the answer may come from the authority of ancient law as well as the concept of legal agency.

Church and Synagogue. Regardless of its brevity, the Torah, like the United States Constitution, forms the basis for later Jewish and Christian direction. Jesus, Paul, and many rabbis argued cases on the basis of passages from the Hebrew Scripture. The authority of these documents was taken for granted and generally recognized and accepted within the Jewish Christian context. The custom of re-pecting the authority of scripture began long before Paul or Jesus and probably originated in relationship to the nation's attitude toward law. For example, the ten commandments are contained in Deuteronomy five. Chapter six begins an exhortation to keep these commandments, "when you lie down, when you rise up, and when you walk by the way" (Deut 6:7). The same exhortatory section concludes with the same admonition, "When you walk on the way, when you lie down, and when you rise" (Deut 11:19). Proverbs 7 contains a six chapter poetic sermon based on these three points from Deuteronomy[6] and became the basis upon which later judgments could be made. From then on Proverbs 2-7 could be treated like a precedent in court, and later rabbis quoted both texts together. In arguing a case, the text from Deuteronomy could be used as if it were the American Constitution, and Proverbs 2-7 was an example of the way Deuteronomy had been interpreted by some later community. Whatever body decided to amend the canon to include Proverbs 2-7 probably did so because it recognized its relationship to the written "constitution" that already existed.

TEXT AND INTERPRETATION

Fact and Fiction. Once literature gained the status of scripture, like the amendment to the constitution, it became the basis on which future arguments could be formed and even the basis on which prophecies could be made. For example Daniel thought of the time Jews spent in Babylon as the "prison" term required for a debtor slave to work off debts. Since most of these terms were of a limited duration, Daniel wanted to know how long the captivity in Babylon was scheduled to continue. The place he looked, of course, was to the scripture (Dan 9:1-2). He evidently went directly to Jeremiah, because Jeremiah had become the authority on the word of God in relationship to the captivity. Jeremiah was the one who predicted it and told how long it would be. Daniel looked to the scripture to find

---

[5]M. Galinski, Pursue Justice (London, c1983), pp. 23-27.

[6]G. W. Buchanan, "Midrashim Pre-Tannaïtes," RB 72 (1965):227-39.

his solution, just as an attorney would have researched a case that decreed a sentence against a certain criminal in which he or she was interested. In the records there Daniel found that Jeremiah (Jer 5:1) had prophesied that the term in Babylon would last seventy years (Dan 9:2).

As soon as that prophecy had been accepted as scripture, later prophets were not free to change the text to make it say one hundred years or more. It was like the constitution, and biblical jurists had to respect its authority and interpret it some way or another. Daniel not only checked Jeremiah but also the Pentateuch. From Leviticus he learned that God promised to pay Israel back seven times for its sin (Lev 6:4, 8). This means Jeremiah's seventy years was not the complete amount. Leviticus required that he multiply seventy times seven to get the full amount. That calculation resulted in four hundred, ninety years (Dan 9:4). This seemed to be the logical conclusion to deduce from the scripture.

Maine was speaking about Roman law, but he might just as well have been dealing with Christian or Jewish interpretation of traditional scripture, when he said 1) that the text of the old code remains unchanged but 2) that over the course of time jurists made explanatory glosses on authoritative written documents. At first these were exclusively collections of interpretive opinions, but gradually, as with English law, all legal language made adjustments to these glosses, and the law as it was enforced actually changed. Roman lawyers would have denied, of course, that this was actually the case. They held that they were merely bringing out the full inherent meaning of the existing law by explaining and deciphering it. In so doing they introduced into law a huge variety of canons of which the original compilers of the law they claimed to be observing would never have dreamed.

In fact the law changed, but in fiction it remained as it always was.[7] Contemporary needs forced this change upon the law, but generally it is not the civilization which expands the law, but it is the law that limits civilization. Social needs and opinions are always ahead of the law; there is always a gulf between the law and progress, with law as the traditional, stabilizing factor. When the collective opinion of the entire society reaches a point where it can no longer be ignored, the law changes, but it is usually explained in terms of the recovery of a lost perfection.[8]

---

[7]Maine, Ancient Law (U.S.A.: Dorset Press, c1986), pp. 22, 26-28.

[8]Ibid., p. 28. A modern example of selective change in tradition took place in a small claims court in Washington, D.C. in 1989. The judge was a woman who wore a traditional robe and followed customary liturgy for beginning the session. Then she told the men of the court room to remove their hats, since it was not raining inside. The etiquette that required men to remove their hats in court and church also required women to wear hats and gloves. This judge was part of an equal rights movement that rejected the traditional pattern. She wanted the right for women to be judges, and she may never have worn a hat or gloves in court or church in her life. This change had begun to take place about thirty years earlier. By the time she spoke she may have thought it was traditional for women not to wear hats or gloves. In any event she wanted all other parts of the

This is the tradition, and this is precisely the way Daniel changed Jeremiah, and in the process Daniel became the successor to Jeremiah on matters reflecting the end of the "captivity," without anyone discounting the source, Jeremiah, from which Daniel obtained his legal authority.[9] Jeremiah said "seventy years," and this continued to be valid, but it was interpreted to be "four hundred, ninety years," and that interpretation became the standard. As a legal fiction, the later community still adhered to Jeremiah's prophecy, but in fact it accepted instead the interpretation of Daniel, which was seven times that amount.

The movement from fact to fiction also reflects the way Luther changed the tradition of the church by appealing to the authority of Paul, with most later Protestant scholars assuming that Paul really thought that which Luther explained. The Lutheran interpretation of Paul's teachings, however, would certainly have surprised Paul.[10] On the basis of scripture, Christians today are claiming that segregation is a sin. That scripture, however, teaches that it is a sin not to segregate. It is wrong to mix different kinds of species (Lev 19:19; Num 5; Ezra 9-10; 1 Cor 6:1-19; Ezra 10:14-30), and the chosen people are required to keep themselves separated from the heathen. In fact the law of segregation has changed, but in fiction it remains the same.

In pre-Christian Judaism, the most pious of all Jews were monks. When they believed the temple was defiled, they volunteered to keep their monastery as undefiled as the temple was supposed to be at all times, so that the Lord would have a place on the land in which to dwell. To avoid defilement, they bathed before each meal, changed garments when they entered the monastery, and allowed no women in the monastery. Because they believed sexual intercourse, menstrual periods, and male emissions were defiling, monks did not marry. Some, however, compromised so as to continue the race. Those who did, married only girls who were old enough to bear children and had proved this by three menstrual periods. Prospective wives also had to be strictly trained in purity and dietary laws before they could marry a member of one of these orthodox sects. The wife was considered defiled for fourteen days after the beginning of every menstrual period. During this time she was required to avoid touching her husband. On the fourteenth day, she bathed and was believed to be undefiled after the beginning of the fifteenth day. This is the time she was most likely to be fertile, so that she might become pregnant with only one intercourse (defilement).

---

tradition retained, including men removing hats in court. This breach of ancient etiquette made her uncomfortable.

[9]For other biblical additions see G. M. Tucker, "Prophetic Superscriptions and the Growth of Canon," G. W. Coats and B. O. Long (eds.), Canon and Authority (Philadelphia, c1970, pp. 56-70.

[10]On this see further Buchanan, "The Day of Atonement and Paul's Doctrine of Redemption," Novum Testamentum 32 (1990):236-49.

If she became pregnant, there would be no more defilement until the child was born.[11]

This was the rhythm method used for defilement control--not birth control. The goal was not to control the number of children born, but to control the amount of defilement necessary for each child. That goal has long since been forgotten, but the Roman Catholic Church, which inherited these rules from Judaism, continues to uphold the rhythm method as true traditional ethics of sex--but just off-beat. The goal now is to control the number of children born rather than the amount of defilement involved. The claim is still made that sexual intercourse is only for the procreation of children; birth control is permitted; but only by use of the rhythm method, as if it were an ancient law. In fiction the law is the same as it has always been, but in fact it has just reversed itself and is defended with as much religious zeal as if the current law were really fulfilling the original, traditional rule. According to Maine, civil laws change in exactly the same way.

The King and the Code. The stele on which one copy of Hammurabi's famous code was engraved is topped by a bas-relief which shows Hammurabi receiving the commission from the sun-god, Shamash, the god of justice.[12] This code was instituted as the law of the land in the eighteenth century B.C. Hammurabi probably had this code drawn up by the best legalists in his country, but once it was completed, it was held to have been divinely inspired. Ahlström said, "In principle, any king could claim that his god had directed him to take certain actions. As the god's viceroy and administrator, he was the one who revealed the will of his god."[13] Before there were binding rules by which a judge made decisions, people believed that the deity dictated the awards to the king, personally. The Homeric word for divinely dictated judgments is themis θέμις (pl. themistes, θέμιστες. Since the king acted with the authority of the deity and was the human agent of the deity, it was assumed that he also acted on the command of the deity from whom he received themistes.[14] This was the concept of the woman from Tekoa who addressed King David, "Like a messenger (agent) of God thus is my lord the King to hear good and evil, and the Lord your God will be with you" (2 Sam 14:17). When David invited Barzilai to become a member of his court,

---

[11]Buchanan, "Essenes," International Standard Bible Encyclopedia II, pp. 147-55.

[12]T. J. Meek (tr.), "The Code of Hammurabi," J. R. Pritchard (ed.), Ancient Near Eastern Texts (Princeton, c1969), pp. 163-80, fig 58.

[13]G.W. Alström, Royal Administration and National Religion in Ancient Palestine (Leiden, 1982), p. 72. See further G. Widengren, Religionsphaenomenologie (Berlin, 1969), pp. 546-555; A. Bertholet, Die Macht der Schrift in Glauben und Aberglauben (Berlin, 1949), pp. 42-43; and E. M. Hooker, "The Significance of Numa's Religious Reform," Numen 10 (1963):87-132.

[14]Maine, Ancient Law (Dorset, 1986), pp. 3-4.

Barzilai refused, saying he was too old to discern good and evil (2 Sam 19:31-37). He could not become a judge, functioning as an agent of the Lord in a court room.

When the king was believed to have themis for judgment there was no recognized code of laws, like a constitution, for which the king was accountable in making judgments. The bases for these judgments were secrets between the god and the king. Seneca said Nero might have said, "Have I not been chosen to act on earth as vicar of the gods? I am the arbiter of life and death for the peoples. What each man's lot and state shall be is laid into my hands, and what Fortune would bestow on any mortal, she makes known through my mouth."[15] During the Middle Ages the king was thought to be both king and priest, and lawyers and judges were called priests in the temple of justice.[16] Although kings were legally infallible, in actual practice kings had assistant consulting judges and traditional laws to guide them in judgment. One example of this was David in relationship with Nathan.

After David had seduced Bathsheba and had her husband Uriah killed, Nathan came to David to ask his judgment about an apparently hypothetical situation: "'In a certain city there were two men, one was rich and the other, poor. The rich man had numerous flocks and herds, but the poor man had only one little ewe lamb, which he had purchased. It grew up with him and his children. It ate from his food and drank from his cup. It used to lie in his bosom. It was like a daughter to him. Now a traveler came to the rich man as a guest. [The rich man] was not willing to take one of his own flock or herd to prepare for the traveler who came to him, but he took the poor man's lamb and prepared it for the man who had come to him.'[17] David became very angry against the man and said to Nathan, 'By the life of the Lord, the man who did this deserves to die, and he will restore the lamb fourfold, because he did this and because he had no pity.' Nathan said to David, 'You are the man!'" (2 Sam 1:1-7).

This was a cleverly designed parable. David was the highest judge in the land. Nathan was one of his governmental advisors, probably with some authority as a subordinate judge. It would have been normal for him to consult David on legal matters. David responded by citing the legal ruling for stealing a sheep. For that part of the offense, the thief should pay fourfold (Exod 22:1). This ruling is part of a unit of laws (Exod 21:28-22:6) dealing with offenses that could be settled by payment of money, and they are organized around parabolic situations: 1) the goring ox, 2) the pit, 3) the destroying beast, and 4) the fire that extends to a neighbor's property. Rabbis composed an entire tractate of the Mishnah,

---

[15]E. H. Kantorowicz, The King's Two Bodies (Princeton, 1957), pp. 106-124.

[16]Kantorowicz, Two Bodies, pp. 501-502.

[17]For a similar use of parables in court see 1 Kings 20:39-43 and Herodotus, Hist. 1.27, 159, 332.

called Baba Qama, on the basis of these four categories. The goring ox, for instance, was a class of offenses in which someone's beast, slave, or agent violently injured someone else. Some of Aesop's fables constitute legal offenses in which an animal represents a human being. The same was true of Nathan's parable. David evidently knew the laws in their context of Exodus, and when Nathan asked him a legal question about a related situation, he first responded with the ruling given in Exodus 22:1. By staging his question in parabolic form that was similar to the rulings in Exodus 21:8-22:6, Nathan caught David off guard in a very clever way. The parable Nathan told is very dramatic, pointed, and effective. It also suggests that this collection of laws was composed before the time of David, because he was acquainted, not only with the ruling for stealing sheep, but he knew the method of classification to which Nathan's parable applied.[18]

Royal Agency. What was the logic behind these claims? One answer may be the legal authority of a monarch. Kings in antiquity were often believed to be God's apostles or legal agents. Some were called sons of God. Pharaoh was called the son of Re [an Egyptian deity]. Alexander the Great considered himself to be the son of Zeus.[19] Israelites seem to have shared that Near Eastern custom. Both King Solomon and the messianic king, Jesus, were called Sons of God or the Lord. In Rome, as early as 7 B.C. altars were dedicated to the genius of Augustus. This meant that the emperor as Pontifex Maximus could offer sacrifices at these altars and as the genius could also receive them. Caligula required subjects to swear oaths by the emperor to be loyal to the emperor.[20] These were legal fictions that were later spelled out explicitly.

Bodies of the King. One important analysis of kingship was made by Kantorowicz who studied the physical and legal identities of English royalty from A.D. 1100 to the Elizabethan period. During Queen Elizabeth's reign, English judges held that the king had two bodies: 1) a natural body which was subject to all sicknesses, injuries, imbecility of infancy or old age, and all the other defects that happen to the natural bodies of other people. 2) He also had another legal body, the body politic, which could not be seen nor handled. It consisted of policy and government. This body was completely void of infancy, old age, death, and other

[18]The fact that David had consultants and rules with which to govern meant he was a king and not a tyrant. Those who acted without rules or counsel were called tyrants as distinct from kings. It was only legally that judicial officers stood above the populace in terms of righteousness. Courts were called temples, but that did not place them out of bounds to corruption. Judges were called "priests," but they were as corrupt as if they had only secular offices. This does not presume that priests were never involved in corruption.

[19]Nikolaus, "Progymnasmata," L. Spengel, Rhetores Graeci (Leipzig, 1856) III, p. 460.26-29.

[20]Kantorowicz, Two Bodies, p. 7.

natural defects. This body could not be invalidated by any disability in the king's natural body.[21] These two bodies were decided by the courts to be indivisible: "Notwithstanding that these two Bodies are at one Time conjoined together, yet the Capacity of the one does not confound that of the other, but they remain distinct Capacities."[22] This reasoning makes sense only to those acquainted with legal fiction.

Corporation. So far as anyone could see with the naked eye, the king was one human being, but to the legalist there were two bodies present in the king. One of these is a legal body, or corporation, which is treated legally as if it were an existent body, but it is really a legal fiction. The same is true of the church which is called the "body of Christ" (1 Cor 1:1-7). A corporation, like a church, is legally treated like an individual. It can be taxed and sued in court just the way individuals can. Since the king's body politic was a corporation or legal body, it was incorporated with subordinate officials who were legally identical with one of the king's bodies. Therefore they had the authority to determine the king's will. Even if courts and judges made decisions in opposition to the king, they were, nonetheless, the king's judgments, even if he objected to them. Jurists claimed the ability to distinguish between what the king willed and what the king wanted. Even if they judged erroneously, they had the authority to act as if they were infallible on this point, and legally they were.

Jurists agreed that the king's desire was law, but the king's desire was that which he, together with his counsel of advisors, decided. Even if the council overruled the king, their decision was the king's will. This distinction between the physical body of the king and the body politic seems to have been recognized by Alexander the Great in the fourth century B.C. He made a distinction between those who were friends of Alexander and those who were friends of the king.[23] Likewise, Philip II of Macedonia was seated in the theater at Aigai while the images of the twelve Gods were brought into the theater in solemn procession together with the image of Philip as number thirteen.[24]

English lawyers distinguish between "corporations aggregate" and "corporations sole"--both of which are legal fictions. In any corporation, by legal definition, the members can all be changed completely, but the corporation remains the same and is immortal. It never dies. The corporation aggregate is made up of several people or "members" of the corporation or "body," all of whom function at the same time, whereas the corporation sole has the qualities

[21]Kantorowicz, Two Bodies, p. 12.

[22]Ibid., p. 16.

[23]Plutarch, Alexander, c47; Moralia 181.D.

[24]Diodorus, XVI.92, 5. So Kantorowicz, Two Bodies, p. 501.

of a corporation aggregate, but the members of the body are different people who hold office in succession, only one at a time. The offices of the king and the church pastor are examples. The office is the corporation, and as such is perpetual, whereas the individual who occupies either of these offices can be changed. Neither the pastor nor the king ever dies. It was customary in England to refer to the physical death of a king as his demise. He did not die; his legal body was simply transferred to his successor. This means the office of the pastor or the king never ceases, but individual kings and pastors come and go, and there is no time when these offices are not filled.

The king's crown was both visible and invisible. Its authority lay in its invisible quality, so there were two crowns, just as there were two bodies of the king. Loyalty to the crown usually meant loyalty to the invisible crown.[25] In the same way there is the physical body of Christ, the visible corporation, and also the mystical or invisible church, which is immortal. Christ is the head of the church, just as the king is the head of the state or the legal body of the king.[26]

This whole concept of an immortal body is not radically different from the legal status of a Roman citizen. When a citizen died, his or her heir or heirs who succeeded him or her did not receive only his money and lands. The heir or heirs continued the civil life, the legal existence, of the deceased. This removed the fact of death from a legal point of view.[27] Maine argued, "But Ancient Law, it must again be repeated, knows next to nothing of Individuals. . . The life of each citizen is not regarded as limited by birth and death; it is a continuation of the existence of his forefathers, and it will be prolonged in the existence of his descendants."[28]

It is from this point of view easy to understand how Jesus could have been crucified and the body of Christ continue long after his death. He had appointed apostles--legal agents--who were legally identical to him. Only his physical body died at the crucifixion, but his legal body continued in the life of the church, the body of Christ. The body of Christ is a corporation which remains the same even though all of its members are changed. It never dies; it is immortal. This is the creed of modern churches, in one of which the pastor begins the liturgy for receiving members into the church, "Dearly beloved, the church is of God and will continue to the end of time . . ." This is consistent with the doctrine that corporations never die. All the members of the corporation can be replaced, but the corporation is immortal, and the church as the body of Christ is a corporation. In similar language justices Stanford, Saunders, and Brown said of the

---

[25]Kantorowicz, Two Bodies, pp. 336-82.

[26]Ibid., pp. 194-222.

[27]Maine, Ancient Law, pp. 186-90; (Dorset, c1986), pp. 149-51.

[28]Ibid., p. 258; see Dorset, c1986, pp. 152-53.

king: "King is a name of continuance, which shall always endure [emphasis theirs] as the head and governor of the people, as the Law presumes . . . and in this the king never dies [emphasis theirs]."[29]

Legal Identity. Kantorowicz discovered a document written by an anonymous Norman legalist who lived about A.D. 1100. Of the king he said, "We have to recognize [in the king] a twin person, one descending from nature, the other from grace . . . One through which, by the condition of nature, he conformed with other men: another through which, by eminence of [his] deification and by the power of the sacrament [of consecration], he excelled all others. Concerning one personality, he was, by nature, an individual man: concerning his other personality, he was, by grace, a Christus, that is, a God-man."[30] As a private person, the prince was under the law; as a public person, he was above the law. In legal function as judge, he shed blood without guilt,[31] because there was no higher court to declare him guilty. Kantorowicz showed further that the same legal fiction applied in the church and to such officials as popes. Maine said it was the church which gave authority to feudal lords to function as agents of the Almighty God.[32] The historian of English law, Holdsworth, said the church added a new sanctity to the person of the king in England, and through the king, to the authority of the state. The status of the Anglo-Saxon king increased considerably when he became thought of as "the head and representative of the state, defender of the church, and protector of the oppressed, the vicegerent of Christ."[33]

Legal Transformation. The king was, in their judgment, born as a human being, but he became anointed or consecrated as a legal identity. It was as a legal agent that he could be without sin. It was his office that was divine. Like Jesus, the king had two natures, one was physical and the other was legal. This attitude toward public offices is as old as the fifteenth century B.C. At that time an Egyptian vizier told of his ordination: "My abilities were not as they had been: my yesterday's nature had altered itself, since I had come forth in the accoutrements [of the vizier, having been promoted] to the Prophet of Maat."[34] This was a legal transformation that came with his office as the highest judge in the land.

---

[29]From Plowden, Reports, 175b-76. Taken from Kantorowicz, Two Bodies, p. 407.

[30]Kantorowicz, Two Bodies, p. 46.

[31]Ibid., pp. 95-96.

[32]Maine, Ancient Law, p. 399.

[33]W. S. Holdsworth, A History of English Law (Boston, 1927) II, p. 23.

[34]J. A. Wilson, "The Vizier of Egypt," Pritchard, Ancient, p. 213.

These attitudes toward positions and offices are similar to those also accepted in the church. The vizier did not say that he had been born again or had become a new creation, as Christians did when they were accepted into membership of the church, but by saying his nature had changed by this legal installation, he probably intended about the same meaning.

In the time of Henry VII English jurists reasoned the same way as the ancient Egyptian vizier had. They said Henry VII was no longer the same person as he was before the coronation. This ceremony transformed him. "And the reason thereof is, because the Body natural and the Body politic are consolidated into one, and the Body politic wipes away every Imperfection of the other Body, with which it is consolidated, and makes it to be another Degree than it should be if it were alone by itself."[35] Using other words, the jurists argued that the king had become a new creature, legally, when he received the crown. He might also have been said to have been born again, legally. Pre-Christian Jews anticipated a messianic banquet when "[God] gives birth to the Messiah with them" (אם יוליד [אל] א[ת] המשיח אתם) (1Qsa 2.11-12). More freely translated, this means God would produce or provide the Messiah to be with them. Of course, God is the Creator of all beings and would have created the person to become the Messiah in the first place, but he would not have given him birth in full adulthood with the leadership training necessary to become king of Israel. When God would "give birth" to the Messiah, he would take some Jew who had already been born, physically, and present him for anointing. Then the citizen involved would legally be born again as the messianic king of Israel. It is at this occasion that he would have been born of the Holy Spirit. According to scripture, that which was expected to happen when the Messiah appeared had already happened to a certain king whom the Lord addressed at the king's coronation: "You are my son; today I have given you birth" (Ps 2:7).

According to the Fourth Gospel, Jesus told the Pharisee, Nicodemus, that he had to be born again if he wanted to see the Kingdom of God. Both Nicodemus and Jesus knew it was not possible to be born again physically, but the birth of which Jesus spoke was being born of the water and of the Spirit. This required a legal transformation. He had to join Jesus' group which required baptism and reception of the Holy Spirit. Since Nicodemus had already been circumcised he was not required to fulfill that obligation. Legally it is possible to be born when one is old. Physically, Nicodemus was probably born into a Pharisaic home, but legally he could become born again as a Christian (John 3:1-5).

Every proselyte into Judaism was born again and began life anew as a child born that day (Gerim 2:5; Yeb 48b). This second birth, of course, was a legal birth. At Sinai all Israel was made anew like a child born that day; as a legal body or corporation it became a new creature (Song of SongsR 8:2, 5). This took place because Israelites entered the legal process of becoming parties to a

---

[35]Plowden, Reports, p. 238. Taken from Kantorowicz, Two Bodies, p. 11, fn. 9.

contract with the Lord by which they agreed to become his people and he agreed to become their God.

Physically children are usually born in homes or hospitals, in Western society, but they can be born again in court rooms while being adopted by new parents. Those installed or ordained into new offices become new creatures, legally. They are not the same as before; they have new obligations, rights, and authority. This does not change them physically. They still have the same intellectual abilities, the same ages, the same physical ailments, and the same physical appearances. This is only a legal change, but it is very important. Just as legal birth can take place in a court room, it may also take place in a church or a synagogue where legal changes occur by people joining a new legal body or becoming legally adopted into new families. A wedding can take place either in a church or in a court setting, with the officiating leader functioning as an officer of the state, even though he is a minister or priest of the church. Until recently, the wedding involved the legal adoption and rebirth of the bride by a family to which she was not physically born. At that time she became an "in law" member of the new family to which she had been legally born. The ceremony involved the woman receiving a new ring and a new name, identifying her legally with a new family.

There are legal ceremonies through which people are born again into new families or societies. There are also legal ceremonies by which people can die, legally. When a person is expelled from a community, disowned by a family, divorced from a spouse, or has had citizenship papers removed, he or she has faced a legal death, just as acceptance provides legal life. Many times the word "life" occurs in scripture which does not refer to physical life--eating, breathing, and taking up space. People who were physically alive were asked to enter into life (Matt 19:17). When the prodigal son left his father's house to live with the Gentiles (hogs), he was believed to be dead, but when he returned and was accepted he was alive again. The legal resuscitation ceremony involved the father replacing his clothes and putting a ring on his finger (Luke 15:3-4). An early convert either to Judaism or Christianity spoke of this experience as being circumcised by the Holy Spirit. His circumcision had become his salvation; he drank from the living water that did not die. The Lord stripped off his folly like a garment and renewed him with the Lord's garment; he led the new convert to Paradise which was the Lord's land (Ode of Solomon 11). This was a mythical way of describing and interpreting the initiation ceremony.

Those who were expelled from a community were said to have first committed a sin unto death (1 John 5:16). Just as legal admission into some body was called second birth, so expulsion or apostasy was called second death. John of Patmos assured those Christians under trial that those who conquered would not be found guilty of the second death (Rev 2:11), meaning that they would be judged innocent and not be expelled. Second death will have no authority over those who take part in the first resurrection (Rev 20:6). The second death is the lake of fire (Rev 20:14).

The unfaithful ones, who had been false to the contract, idol worshipers, and guilty of other sins that are not forgiven will be thrown into the lake of fire, which is the second death (Rev 21:8). This means those who are finally not accepted into the religious community after the tribulation is over are finally dead so far as the community is concerned. Even though their physical bodies are alive and well, their legal bodies or souls are as dead as if they had been hurled into a lake of burning fire and sulphur. From the standpoint of religious faith, second birth and second death are more important than physical birth and physical death. To this day when an Orthodox Jew leaves his or her religion, or when the Jewish community chooses to alienate one of its members it conducts a funeral for that person, because the person is considered legally dead from the community point of view. According to Matthew, Jesus told his disciples not to fear the one who could kill only the physical body but had no authority over the soul, i.e. legal membership in the community of life. Disciples were told to fear, instead, the one who has authority to throw both body and soul into Gehenna (Matt 10:8). That is the one who could destroy both the physical body and the legal body, thereby causing both the first and the second death.[36]

In antiquity many legal transactions were conducted by ceremony. People acted out a formula by which the legal process was conducted. Failure to include every point would make the ceremony invalid. A promise could not be upheld in court if it had not been accompanied by a proper ceremony. The church has carried over some of these traditional ceremonies through such formal rites as weddings, baptisms, and funerals. In business and law, today, most of these legal acts are handled in writing.[37] The anonymous Norman said that at the moment of the king's consecration, the spirit "leaped" into the terrestrial king and made him "another man" alias vir,[38] just as the spirit of the Lord took possession of Gideon (Judges 6:2), Jephthah (Judges 11:9), and Samson (Judges 14:19; 15:14), and they became leaders. The Spirit came upon Saul after he had been anointed king of Israel (1 Sam 10:1-10). In Acts, those who were baptized and received the Holy Spirit became legally transformed as Christians. There is a close relationship

---

[36]Buchanan, The Consequences of the Covenant (Leiden, 1970), pp. 305-13. N. P. Petersen, "Pauline Baptism and 'Secondary Burial,'" HTR 79 (1986):217-26, relates Paul's language about life and death to ancient customs of burial for the first time to let the flesh decompose and a second time to replace the bones. Petersen was correct in saying the strongest argument against his thesis is that Paul never mentioned a second burial. Paul's language makes better sense understood in legal terms. See also L. H. Schiffman, "Exclusion from the Sanctuary in the Temple Scroll," Hebrew Annual Review 9 (1985):301-20. In Greek thought form, the soul was that which left the body at death. The expression was used metaphorically in early Judaism and Christianity to refer to membership in the contract community. A person might give up his soul to the pagan world to save his soul in the community where life was possible. This meant giving up one's soul for the sake of the community.

[37]Maine, Ancient (10th), pp 268-303.

[38]Kantorowicz, Two Bodies, p. 47.

between reception of the Spirit and legal authority. When Paul was with the Corinthians in spirit, he gave them authority to expel one of their members from the community (1 Cor 5:1-5). When Jesus breathed the Holy Spirit upon the twelve, they became apostles or agents of the Lord (John 20:22-3). Legal transformation and reception of legal authority was usually associated with some legal ceremony--laying on of hands, anointing with oil, change of garments, baptism with water, or becoming ordained or consecrated into some office.

The anonymous Norman said that the emperor was elevated by his consecration, "since so much is he conjoined to Him in power that no other power is more nigh to God, or more sublime than that of the emperor; yea all other power is inferior to his."[39] That is because he had become an agent of God through his coronation.

Agent of God. Israelites claimed that the Lord made their lawgiver, Moses, God to Pharaoh (Exod 7:1). Jezebel had Naboth killed because of the accusation that he had cursed God and the king (1 Kings 1:10). Isaiah prophesied that people would become hungry and curse their king and their God, implying that to curse one was as bad or the same as cursing the other (Isa 8:1). Hosea looked forward to the time when the children of Israel would seek the Lord their God and David their king, as if seeking one meant seeking the other (Hos 3:5). He left no room for seeking just one or the other. God and the king were identified, because the king was understood to be God's agent. As God's legal agent the king, within the limits of his jurisdiction, was legally identical to God. If Moses were Pharaoh's god, this means the normal relationships between a king and his vizier had been reversed.

LEGAL INFALLIBILITY

The King. Kings were factually fallible, but they were legally infallible. No one could take them to higher earthly courts. They were recognized as lawgivers, and they were held to have the "power of attorney" to act in behalf of God over the territory entrusted to them. Therefore, lawgivers, like Hammurabi and Moses, provided laws that were accepted as divinely inspired (i.e. they had received the Spirit) and had divine authority. The vizier of Upper Egypt was the supreme judge of that land. A fifteenth century B.C. vizier, Rekh-Mi-Re, said "[I acted] in conformance with that which he had ordained. He gave me a tribunal under my authority, and there was none therein who could oppose me."[40] In England, as the body politic the king was immortal. At his coronation the king became the

---

[39]Ibid., p. 63.

[40]Wilson, "Vizier," p. 213.

body politic incarnate, and immortality was transferred to him.[41] This means that King Henry VII was still "alive" even though Henry Tudor had been dead for years. It was the king's new, immortal, perfect body that was referred to as "Majesty."[42] In the same way twentieth century judges in the United States are addressed, "Your Honor," ex officio. The honor does not pertain to the personal attributes of the judge. The same is true of the holiness of the pope. This is the honor and holiness that belong to the legal body.

Louis XIV of France said, "I am the state!" When fully practiced, in such a legal system as this the king could kill without legal guilt. The authority of ancient monarchs was later called in England, the "doctrine of immunity." In England it was understood, at least since the middle of the thirteenth century that the king could do no wrong. Of course this meant that legally he could do no wrong. He was exempt from prosecution. He could not have been sued without his consent,[43] which he was not required to give. That which was established as a doctrine in English law had been an understood royal privilege in antiquity. Kings were also judges, and some of the awe and authority kings had was also given to other judges, like Rekh-Mi-Re in Egypt, because they too, as agents of the king who was an agent of the deity, spoke God's words.

The Pope. The pope also was considered a monarch and was therefore officially above the law of the church. At one time the adversaries of Pope Leo III had accused him of such offenses as adultery and perjury. When Charlemagne came to Rome to hear the case, "The synod began with the prelates declaring, 'We do not presume to judge the Apostolic See, which is the head of all the Churches, for we ourselves are all judged by it, and it, according to ancient custom, can be judged by none. In this case too we shall canonically concur with what the pope himself decides.'"[44]

They recognized the pope's legal status. They could register complaints, but they could not bring the pope to trial. "Leo said, 'I follow the steps of those who have gone before and I am ready to cleanse myself from false accusations.'" After that he performed the ritual necessary to cleanse himself from this defilement, and the affair was closed.[45] People might find fault with the pope, but legally they could enforce no punishment, and legally he could pardon and cleanse

---

[41]Kantorowicz, Two Bodies, p. 13.

[42]Ibid., p. 14.

[43]See "Jimmy V. Mayle, appellant v. Pennsylvania Department of Highways," Atlantic Reporter 388, 2d series, p. 710.

[44]F. Gontard, The Chair of Peter, tr. A. J. and E. F. Peeler (New York, c1964), pp. 181-82.

[45]Ibid., p. 182.

from all offenses--even his own! It was his personal sins that needed cleansing and forgiving, but it was his legal body that had the authority to forgive.

Even today, in the United States, at least some judicial decisions constitute something more than the words of individual judges. They are court decisions and are influential in determining the law of the state. When judges give their decisions, they refer to them as the opinions or verdicts of the court. In antiquity, state law was considered divine law, so that books, like Deuteronomy, which, before the Babylonian captivity, were considered to be both civil and religious law, enforceable by the state, were also given the same divine status as codes of other nations. Deuteronomy was intentionally composed with the structural form of a treaty between the Lord and his people. Like other treaties, it began, "These are the words . . . ."[46] and concluded with a list of blessings and curses. Once the Jews moved to Babylon, against their will, their patriotism to the promised land was partly expressed by emphasizing their belief that this was the law that was really divinely inspired and was destined to be used again on the promised land. Motivated by this patriotic drive Jews continued to transmit these sacred texts from one generation to another. Jews looked forward to the time when they might return to the promised land and there live again by such rules as those of the Book of Deuteronomy, the laws of the true state, their promised land, and also the word of the true God.

The Status of Judges. When a modern American judge enters the chancel of the court room, the marshall, clerk, or bailiff still announces his or her arrival something in the manner in which a king was introduced centuries ago, asking all present to stand and maintain a respectful silence. When the judge takes the seat, lawyers do not come near without asking permission to approach the bench where the judge is presiding. Should a person in court act in a way that the judge considers improper, the judge has authority to cite that person for contempt of court. Although this can be appealed, the judge has all the powers of the state to enforce such decisions. Few attempts are made to challenge the power of the judge to punish those who treat the judge or the judgment process depreciatively. Perhaps the reason for this is to protect the respect for the institution. If the judge is insulted, so also is the state that authorizes judicial activity.

The chancel gets its name from the small fence that separates the observers in the court from the judges and, when permitted, the plaintiff, the defendant, and their respective attorneys and witnesses. The chancel is the line that distinguishes the status in court of those of authority from those without legal authority. Also associated with this fence in England is the office of the Lord Chancellor. The chancellor was an agent of the king or queen. One of his important responsibilities was that of judging in behalf of the king or queen. Another possible

---

[46]For other examples see A. Goetz (tr.), "Hittite Treaties," Pritchard, Ancient, pp. 202-205.

explanation for the relationship of the chancel to the chancellor is that the Lord Chancellor received his title because he occupied the bench inside the chancel.[47]

In traditional churches with divided chancels and ancient liturgies there is also a small fence that segregates the congregation from the clergy. This fence is called the communion railing. In churches with closed communion doctrines, communion is served with the priest on the inside and the parishioners on the outside. Only those who have been ordained and authorized to wear the stole are admitted inside this railing. Although some of these rules have recently been relaxed, the fence has been established to segregate the clergy from the parishioners just as the chancel was established to segregate the judge and the attorneys from the citizens. As in a court setting, the segregated area in a traditional church is called a chancel.

Traditionally judges have been given a great deal of respect, because the highest judge in any land used to be the king who was considered God's agent on earth or God's son. The king was respected, not just for his own merit and status, but because he was an agent of the Lord. To be disrespectful to the king was the legal equivalent of showing disrespect to God.[48] Ugaritic literature reflects a Canaanite belief in divine kingship.[49] Egyptian sources show that the pharaoh of Egypt, for example, was called the son of Re, the god of the earth.[50] He was held to have been two gods at the same time, both Horus and Seth.[51] Since this

---

[47]Lord Campbell, Lives of the Lord Chancellors and Keepers of the Great Seal of England (Boston, 1874) I, p. 1. When Alexander Jannaeus was high priest and king of Judah, many people thought he was an illegitimate leader. When he offered sacrifice at the Feast of Tabernacles, where people come to the temple in procession carrying palm branches and citrus branches, people took citrus fruit from these branches and pelted the high priest while he was functioning. After that the high priest had a high fence built to separate himself from the people to protect him from citrus fruit (Josephus, Ant. 13.372-73). If there had ever been any such practical needs in antiquity for the fence to separate the judge from the citizens it does not seem to have been recorded.

[48]Galinski, telling the rabbinic attitude toward the king, said, "All honour had to be paid to the king (2 Kings 15:5; Isa 6:1), and to this end, he could not be chosen from despised occupations (TSan 4:2; 1 Kings 1:23; 2 Sam 7:18; Sotah 40b). He was not allowed, even in humility, to denigrate his royal position, or to overlook offenses or attempted offenses to his dignity and honour (1 Sam 3:31-34; San 19b). Nobody was permitted to use his horse or chariot, or to sit on his throne or seat of judgment, or to make use of his crown, sceptre, regalia or other equipment. Nor was any person permitted to see him in a state of nudity" (San 2:5; 22a). For an explanation of the relationship of Israelite and Jewish attitude toward God and the customary attitude of Near Eastern peoples toward kings, see J. H. Tigay, "On Some Aspects of Prayer in the Bible," Association for Jewish Studies Review 1 (1976):363-72.

[49]I. Engnell, Studies in Divine Kingship in the Ancient Near East (Oxford, 1967), p. 173, et passim.

[50]Engnell, Studies, pp. 4-15.

[51]Frankfort, Kingship of the Gods (Chicago, c1948), p. 19.

is a physical impossibility, it probably means that he was legally, and not physically, identical with those two gods. He was the authorized agent of both gods.

In conformity to this tradition, Solomon, while king over Israel and Judah, was called God's son (1 Chron 17:11-13; 22:30) and was ruler over the Lord's kingdom. Like David (2 Sam 1:1-6), Solomon judged legal cases (1 Kings 3:16-8; see also Deut 17:14-0). According to Enoch the Son of man or the elect one sat on the Lord's throne, functioning as the Lord's agent (Enoch 51:3; 55:4; 61:8; 6:, 5; 69:6-7), and the righteousness of the Son of man was the righteousness of the Head of Days (Enoch 71:14), meaning that the agent was legally identical to the principal. Through the name of this Son of man or Elect One the righteous were saved (Enoch 50:3).

Legend adjusted history to this tradition. Moses was made, not only the great lawgiver, but also a judge of cases (Exod 18:13). As administrator of the court system, he appointed subordinate judges (Exod 18:14-6; Deut 1:9-18). Judges were set over numbers of people. They were not only judges of civil and criminal cases, but they acted as rulers and military leaders. The distinction between a civil judge and a ruler was not very clear. The Israelite rulers in Canaan before the reigns of Saul, David, and Solomon were called by a word which later came to mean "judges," so these judges were treated like kings. The practice developed, therefore, of deferring to any judge in the same manner in which subjects deferred to kings, as agents of God. The modern reverence contemporary Westerners show toward judges is probably the traditional preservation of the attitude ancients had toward God. The worst of all possible sins was blasphemy, which was disrespect of the believer toward God or anything religious--set feasts, scripture, or God's name. This was considered the unpardonable sin against the Holy Spirit.

In England, the king was always considered the fountain of justice, and even after there were rules by which common law courts were governed, there continued to be the office of the Lord Chancellor, who functioned as an agent of the king. He was held to be the conscience of the king and initially was not under the restrictions of law. If he chose to pardon someone, the common law courts could not change his decision. On the other hand, if someone appealed to the chancellor for relief after he had lost his judgment in the common court, the chancellor had the final judgment. He was given authority over the great seal which had the same authority as a signature of the king. He functioned as a judge above the law, because he was an agent of the king. The Lord Chancellor was appointed, and he was not required to have any legal training. It seemed to have been assumed that he was endowed with some kind of divine insight, which earlier peoples would have called themistes. During the Middle Ages chancellors were usually not attorneys but clergymen or statesmen. It was the authority of the chancellor, rather than his ability, that was significant.[52]

---

[52]Campbell, Chancellors, pp. 1-31; see also W. S. Holdsworth, A History of English Law (Boston, 1931) I, pp.395-421.

Early Roman law followed a somewhat similar system. Romans had a list of major offenses, such as adultery, forgery, murder, bribery, and treason, and there were courts to judge and punish these. There were, however, offenses that were not covered by the list, and there were also officers who had authority over these without the guidelines of the list. Each officer was entrusted to make judgment according to his own ideas. It was assumed that he possessed some kind of themistes and that his authority was accompanied with reasonable justice. As in later England, this involved a dual system of criminal jurisdiction. The system without a list operated on the authority of the officers whose authority ultimately went back to the emperor for whom the officer was a legal agent.[53]

Civil and Religious Courtrooms. Since religion in antiquity was almost always integrated into the government, it is not surprising that people worshiped God in about the same way in which citizens worshiped the judge or the king.[54] Since religion and the courts stem from the same origin, it is normal to expect similarities between the two institutions in program, architecture, procedure, and purpose. For example, the lectern and the pulpit in churches with divided chancels are constructed in the places where witnesses presented their testimonies in behalf of the plaintiff and the defendant. Today, at least, the attorneys face the judge when they argue cases, but witnesses face the audience. Quintilian, a prominent first century teacher of Roman law who trained lawyers for courts, reminded his students over and over again the importance of convincing the audience as well as the judge of the merits of their cases. This may mean that the podiums were placed in antiquity in positions where they could face the audience while they were addressing the judge. The altar is placed in the center where the judge was seated on his bench. Worshipers kneel before the altar in the same way citizens used to prostrate themselves before the king or the judge. In traditional churches worshipers stand while the ministers and the choir members enter and leave just as citizens in court do when judges enter and leave.

In antiquity, as today, there were times when a single judge made a court decision. For instance, David and Solomon were reported to have judged some legal problems without consulting others. There were other times when a judge had a council of advisors, who were assistant judges. A description of the court setting in which a judge functioned with his assistants is preserved in the fifteenth century B.C rules for the Egyptian vizier: "As for everything which this official, the vizier, shall do while holding hearings in the Hall of the Vizier--he shall sit

---

[53]A. N. Sherwin-White, Roman Society and Roman Law in the New Testament (Oxford, 1963), p. 14.

[54]J. H. Tigay, "On Some Aspects of Prayer in the Bible," Association for Jewish Studies Review I (1976):363-72, has shown how closely biblical address to God resembled the attitude shown in the Mediterranean area toward Kings and argued cogently that Israelites and Jews thought of God as a great king and developed a theology based on royal practices.

upon a judgment-chair, with a matting on the floor, a matting over him, a cushion under his back and a cushion under his feet, a [cape] upon him, a scepter at his hand, and the forty leather straps spread out in front of him, the Chiefs of Southern Tens [assistant judges] on two sides of him, the Overseer of the Cabinet [clerk of court] on his right hand, the Supervisor of Clients [bailiff] on his left hand, and the Scribe [court reporter] beside him, one confronting another, with every man opposite him."[55]

Some biblical counsellors or assistant judges were prophets, like Nathan (2 Sam 1:1-13). Sometimes kings, like the Egyptian vizier, consulted a whole group of prophets (1 Kgs 2:5-23). In the same way God was understood to have had a council of advisors, made up of elders or earthly kings. For example, David was later believed to have been a member of the council of God at the same time he was functioning as king over Israel (Acts 13:36). As king of Israel, he was God's apostle who acted in behalf of God in his judgments. When Jesus pictured himself seated on the glorious throne, ruling from Jerusalem, he told the twelve apostles that they would also be seated on twelve thrones, judging the twelve tribes of Israel (Matt 19:8). He may have visualized the thrones of these apostles to have been located within the territories of the various tribes, but another possibility is that he expected them to act as representatives of the twelve tribes as they sat in the judicial council in Jerusalem, chief advisors to the king, and members of the supreme court, the national sanhedrin.[56] If this was the case, they would have anticipated positions in a throne room or chancel that was similar to those of the assistants to the Egyptian vizier in the fifteenth century B.C.

According to the available examples, ancient groups of judges were stationed so that the chief justice was in the center, with assistants at his right and left, as was the case of the Egyptian vizier. This allowed them to face one another and all be visible to the chief justice. The Jewish sanhedrin sat in a semi-circle to accomplish the same purpose (San 4:3; Tanhuma, Shemot 9; ExodR 5.1 [4:9]). The chief justice in this arrangement would have been stationed in the center, with judges at his left and right. When there was a national decision, the chief justice was the king. These seating arrangements were not optional. Rules were made to specify exactly where the vizier should sit in relationship to others, and buildings were constructed and furnished to make this not only architecturally possible, but almost required. In addition to architecture, there were national rules to determine where each person would sit. This further stabilized the tradition. When the king conducted a judicial session, he sat in his throne room which was organized just like that of the Egyptian vizier.

---

[55]J. A. Wilson (tr.), "Egyptian Documents," Pritchard, Ancient, pp. 213-14.

[56]So also J. M. Baumgarten, "The Duodecimal Courts of Qumran, Revelation, and the Sanhedrin," JBL 95 (1976):70-75.

Although the United States Supreme Court justices were normally positioned in a row, all facing the court, recently former Chief Justice Berger changed the position to put them in a slight semi-circle, so that he could see all of the other justices as well as the rest of the court. This shows the practical necessity of the ancient structure. Justices are now seated at the chief justice's right or left, according to seniority. When counsel appears before the Supreme Court justices, counsel faces the chief justice, just as in ancient practice counsel would have faced the king or the dean of the court. Counsel is also positioned at the place where the high priest used to appear, facing the Holy of Holies, where the Lord was present. This is also the position of the minister when presenting an offering or a prayer in behalf of the congregation before the altar in a church with a divided chancel. The similarity was sufficiently striking for ancients to refer to courts as temples of justice. At some time this was found to be a suitable seating arrangement, and at first glance, one is tempted to say these similarities are all coincidence, based on convenience of architecture and tastes of separate countries and cultures, but further investigation shows that these were very well stabilized forms. However they originated, and however various Near Eastern countries shared patterns, once these became ritual and law, there was very little pressure to change the system. Later judges were obligated to dress, sit, and function according to traditional rules. Hamilton-Patterson and Andrews, describing the traditions of Egypt said, "It is partly this conservatism which makes the tangle of Egyptian religion, mythology and ritual so complicated. They tended to hang on to their old beliefs and habits even when these had been overtaken by new ones: they simply incorporated the old system into the new. Over some three thousand years of dynastic history their mass of magic, ritual, spells, customs, beliefs, dogmas, habits and fashions merely went on getting bigger. It is remarkable that anyone in the later dynasties should ever have managed to decide exactly what was the right way of doing anything."[57]

The ancient temples were constructed according to a pattern that was similar to a throne room or a vizier's courtroom. In a Sumerian inscription, Gudea of Lagash told of his vision of the goddess Nine, her brother Ningiran, and her sister Nindub. The first of these commanded him to build a temple; the second pointed out the heavenly temple which Gudea was supposed to copy; and the third gave him a plan of the temple.[58] The exactness with which the temple was to be built was not an unusual feature, either for a court room or a temple. Like this ancient Sumerian temple and the fifteenth-century B.C. Egyptian court rooms, tenth-century B.C. Israelite temples were constructed according to specified measurements (2 Chron 3-4). When Aharoni excavated the Israelite temples at Arad and Lachish he discovered that the measurements fit exactly those described in

---

[57]J. Hamilton-Patterson and C. Andrews, Mummies (New York, c1978), p. 91.

[58]R. G. Hamilton-Kelly, "The Temple and the Origins of Jewish Apocalyptic," VT 20 (1970):7. See also R. E. Clements, God and Temple (Philadelphia, 1965), pp. 65-68, 81-82.

the scripture.[59] Although they are much larger than the Israelite temples, there still exist today the ruins of two fifth-century A.D. churches in the Negev in Israel. Both of these follow the same basic floor plan of a throne room, a judgment hall, or an early Israelite temple. There are no records of divine commandments or national laws telling how these churches were to be built, but there were enough commandments related to other temples and throne rooms to provide a stable pattern to follow.

With such ancient and rigorously applied rules for construction as those for the temple and the Egyptian court room, it is not surprising that the architecture of temples, which in antiquity was similar to the pattern of courts, should continue to be very much the same, year after year. More was involved than imitating earlier structures. Rules were established to determine the right way for doing things. Just as the Egyptian courtroom had specific rules for the way the throne room should be furnished and the way the judge had to be dressed, so there were specific rules governing the content of the tent of meeting and the temple and the dress and ritual of the priests (Exod 6:16-30). Both institutions were kept stable by rules made to maintain tradition. The Lord is reported to have told Moses, "Make me a temple, so that I may dwell among them, according to all that I show you, the pattern of the tent and the pattern of all its furniture. Thus you shall do" (Exod 5:8-9). "Watch and do with their pattern which you saw on the mountain" (Exod 5:40). "You shall set up the tent, according to its regulation which you saw on the mountain" (Exod 6:30).

True to the court parallel, the largest room of a temple was called the "court." At the center, farthest back from the court, was the Holy of Holies, where only the high priest could enter when he made intercession before the Lord on the Day of Atonement. Nearer to the court was the holy place, where other priests could be stationed. This was a wider room, with space both at the left and the right of the Holy of Holies. Between the court and the holy place was a curtain and a few steps. Between the holy place and the Holy of Holies was another series of steps and another curtain (Yoma 5:1). It was believed that the Lord was present in the holy of holies, situated at the place where the king would be seated in a royal court room. As a testimony to the persistence of tradition in religion, in the twentieth century, churches with divided chancels have the choir seated in the location where the priests were stationed in ancient temples and where assistant judges were positioned in the royal court room.[60]

---

[59]Y. Aharoni, "Arad: Its Inscriptions and Temple," BA 31 (1968):18-27. See also R. DeLanghe, "L'Autel d'Or du Temple de Jerusalem," Biblica 40 (1959):476-94, for a thought-provoking study of the function of the altar of incense and its relationship to the altar of gold. For a careful analysis of Near Eastern temples made before Aharoni's excavation of Arad, see W. F. Albright, Archaeology and the Religion of Israel (Baltimore, 1942), pp. 142-55.

[60]Buchanan, To the Hebrews (Garden City, 1972), pp. 140-42, for an examination of the measurements and outline of various temples in antiquity.

Ancient Jews and Christians not only knew of temples on earth, but they thought there was a temple in heaven corresponding to the one at Jerusalem (JBer 4,5.8c). This was thought to look and function exactly like the temples on earth or throne rooms for kings. The Lord was seated on a throne, like a king or judge. The rainbow around the throne probably represented his glory, legal power, and divine manifestation.[61] It was probably staged against the background of a hemispherical wall and ceiling that is typical of throne rooms and holy of holies in temples. The elders were placed in the positions of assistant judges or priests (Rev 4:2-4).

This throne room also doubled as a temple, because it had an altar before God in the Holy of Holies (Rev 9:13). At the same time there was a throne of glory upon which the Most High sat (TLev 3:4-5). This was placed in the center, with angels to the left and right (Asc. Isa 7:14, 4, 9, 33-34). Angels ran errands, sang, blew trumpets, and were clothed in white like subordinate officers in court or Levites in the temple at Jerusalem (Rev 15:5-8). The temple in heaven was filled with smoke as the one from Jerusalem was (Isa 6:4), but when the voice came out from the temple, the angel praised God for his judgments, further blurring distinctions between the temple and the court room or throne room (Rev 15:8-16:7; 19:5). Still today the judge is given thanks for his judgment, even by the attorney whose case is defeated. The Lord from his throne room sat in judgment, opened the books that probably contained the contract involved in this case and the arguments of the plaintiffs and defendants. After examining these he pronounced judgments (Rev 20:11-12).

In the judgment scene in the Kidron Valley, just outside the temple area in Jerusalem, the Lord was pictured as pronouncing judgment against the Gentiles at the same time they were engaged in battle with the Jews there. As the Lord pronounced judgment (Joel 3:2) he roared from Zion, the temple at Jerusalem (Joel 3:16), where the Lord dwells (Joel 3:1). The relationship between the Lord's function as a judge is so closely related to his geographical location in the temple at Jerusalem that it is not certain whether the Lord was understood to have passed this judgment from his heavenly courtroom/temple or from the temple in Jerusalem, but it is clear that ancient Israelites related these two very closely. Furthermore, this was not a unique situation for Israelite thought. The identification of religious and legal offices was confused also on earth. For instance the Egyptian vizier, supreme judge of the land, was also a prophet of Maat, the goddess of justice.[62] Religion and civil law were closely related. Hering correctly observed that law and religion constitute "a pair of twins" which spent their early

---

[61]G. H. Mendenhall, The Tenth Generation (Baltimore, c1973), p. 47.

[62]Wilson (tr.), "The Vizier of Egypt," p. 213.

stages of development supporting and supplementing one another.[63] Therefore it is not surprising that ancient people in the Near East built throne rooms that looked like temples and vice versa, but it is uncertain whether they first had temples and court rooms that were similar and then conceived of a theology that fit the circumstances or vice versa.

CONCLUSIONS

The material shown above makes it clear that there were many points at which the civil court followed the same practices as the church and vice versa. There are similarities in standards of ritual, attitude, dress, and architecture. They originated or became similar centuries ago, and both institutions have made rules, standard forms, doctrines, and procedures that have kept their structures from changing excessively. The attitude of prayer encouraged in church is also considered proper in court. Sometimes a court practice that was decreed in fifteenth-century B.C. Egypt was practiced again in first-century B.C. Rome and again in the twentieth-century United States. Architecture of tenth-century B.C. Israelite temples is very similar to fifteenth-century B.C. courtrooms and also twentieth--century churches and court rooms. This is still a spotty and limited testing ground for the practice of courts and religious institutions over many centuries, but it is thought-provoking and suggestive.

Biblical mythologists visualized heavenly temples to have been patterned after both court rooms and temples that were contemporary to them. They pictured them as if the temple was also a court at the same time. These seem to have come together in this way many centuries ago when kings were also supreme judges, and God was understood to be the highest judge. When the king was believed to be the son of God or the legal agent of God, it seemed appropriate to treat God the way a citizen treated the king. Since the king was legally identical to God it was not hard to make supplication to God the very same way a prayer was offered to the king. These are, of course, conjectures based on the material examined here. Whatever the initial reason, these analogies are close enough to indicate that those who study Jewish and Christian theology and scripture should look carefully into terms and concepts that may have legal connotations.

These similarities are in the form of architecture and liturgical procedure. They also are carried over into traditional ways of thinking. The relationship of God to judges and clergy leaders; apostles and agents; contracts and treaties; legal and theological truth in relationship to actual fact; and the validity of the written word and the word made flesh in the form of an agent are all legal concepts and attitudes toward the written law. Law and the authority of traditional precedents is basic to Jewish and Christian interpretation of scripture, and they are not new. The rest of this book will point out these traditions in greater detail. The next

---

[63]Quoted by C. Phillipson, The International Law and Custom of Ancient Greece and Rome (London, 1911) I, p. 44.

chapter will examine the hearing or the court trial to find still further instances where the court and the church seem to have been closely related.

CHAPTER TWO

TRIALS AND TESTIMONIES

THE EARLY JURY TRIALS

Family Fights. The first trials probably took place within the family with the father of the family making the final decision and determining how punishment was to be administered. Such trials as these may have begun with a complaint by one member of the family against the other with all those members who were involved telling their sides of the story. At the same time the family witnesses also argued the case from their respective sides. Nineteenth century Cheyenne American Indians, a tribe of about three thousand people, managed disputes without an official court system. When a problem arose that could not be settled between the parties involved other members of the community helped to negotiate. If it were still unsettled, the council of chiefs or the military organization helped to determine how justice might be administered.[1]

In Tanzania, Africa, there is a small town composed mostly of relatives, called Ligomba, where the Ndendeuli, a twentieth century Bantu-speaking people, live. They normally settle disputes in an assembly, called a "moot." When a conflict arises, one of the participants has an assembly called. Each side gathers supporters, and the assembly is held at some neutral person's home or out on the lawn in front of a house. In an informal way, all parties argue their complaints and defenses. Some respected leaders of the community act as mediators who listen until all feelings and arguments have been aired. Then this one or these two quietly interpret what they have heard and offer suggested solutions. Then negotiations begin, with people offering their reactions. Leaders remind the group of the importance of settling this dispute fairly so that work and community can continue without friction. The group usually agrees to this and comes to a satisfactory settlement. On occasion, a second meeting is required. The moot is not over until settlements are agreed upon by all parties. This normally constitutes a compromise of some sort.[2] These two societies probably illustrate a second step in the development of a court system, but one system was not automatically eliminated when another began.

Family enforcement of justice is still standard practice in some societies. For example, when an unmarried Muslim woman becomes pregnant, this is considered one of the most disgraceful things that could happen to a family. The shame to the family is too great to be taken to a public trial and prosecuted by a civil court, so members of the family administer the penalty themselves. The

---

[1]K. N. Llewellyn and E.A. Hoebel, The Cheyenne Way (Norman: U. of Oklahoma Press, c1967), passim.

[2]P. H. Gulliver, "Dispute Settlement without Courts: The Ndendeuli of Southern Tanzania," L. Nader (ed.), Law in Culture and Society (Chicago, c1969), pp. 24-59.

woman's father and/or oldest brother are usually the ones obligated to inflict the death penalty on her, without waiting for the justice system of the state to take action.

The sophistication of a dispute settlement program evidently is not determined by the date of the practice but rather by the size and nature of the group and the number of years or centuries it has been in existence. There were court systems in the Fertile Crescent area that were more developed in the second millennium B.C. than those of tribes in Africa today. Other factors, such as the relationship of the group to outside communities and its participation in international commerce were involved in determining the kind of court system required. Mendenhall is probably correct in holding that there were courts before there were laws. Laws were made on the basis of action that had already been taken in court.[3]

Community Court. As a community became larger, and the society more complex, the justice system had to be established to correspond to the needs of the society. It then became the custom for the city, state, or tribal system of justice to relieve the family of this problem. When parents recognized that their son was rebellious, they did not inflict the prescribed death penalty themselves. They took their son to the city gates and told the elders there of their problem. If the elders decided that the son was, in fact, rebellious, then they, rather than the parents, had him stoned to death (Deut 21:18-21). Forsyth believed that jury trials began as functions of town councils. The council met periodically to conduct the normal business of the town, and in the process, also helped settle disputes of the community.[4] By the first century A.D there were both judges and juries deciding cases in Europe and the Near East, and Quintilian trained his law students to present cases for both. There were also court systems where groups of judges made decisions jointly. This was the case of elders at the gates of Jerusalem and Jewish sanhedrin, but there were still earlier instances of the same phenomenon in ancient Mesopotamia and Egypt.[5] There were also councils of judges or assistant judges to assist a chief justice in ancient royal courts.[6] Decisions are still reached

---

[3]G. W. Mendenhall, Law and Covenant in Israel and the Ancient Near East (Pittsburgh, 1955), p. 10. F. C. Fensham, "Courts, Judicial," The International Standard Bible Encyclopedia I (Grand Rapids, c1979), said that in nomadic society legal rules arose from custom.

[4]W. Forsyth, Trial by Jury (New York, 1878), pp. 4-9. Among the nineteenth century American Cheyenne Indians, civil and criminal offenses were normally solved by a committee made up either of chiefs or military officers. The Keresan Pueblo council of New Mexico which made policy also judged cases. So E. A. Hoebel, "Keresan Pueblo Law," Law in Culture, p. 109.

[5]J. A. Wilson (tr.), "Documents from the Practice of Law," Pritchard (ed.), Ancient, pp. 212-23.

[6]Wilson, "Documents," pp. 213-14.

by groups of justices in the United States. There are some courts of appeals, composed of three or five judges, and the Supreme Court consists of nine justices. Neither religion nor law changes all at once nor in certain predestined steps. For example, in twentieth century United States there was a strong Protestant Fundamentalism movement, which was later followed by Liberalism, Neo-Orthodoxy, and Existentialism, but the introduction of Liberalism did not put an end to Fundamentalism; it was just added as a separate movement. This was also true of the other movements. In the same way, early societies solved their disputes in customary manners, applying social pressures and attitudes to enforce discipline. Later some of these customs were replaced by laws and enforced by sanctions, but that did not put an end to customs. There continues to be more regulation of behavior in the United States and Europe today through customs than through law.[7] Although Cheyennes and Crows lived near one another geographically in nineteenth century A.D. North America they observed different customs and different laws at the same time. Although courts of law never operated in a vacuum, free from local customs, this chapter will analyze court systems more than social customs designed to preserve order.

To examine the various aspects that go into a court trial, this study will undertake the topics in the following order: 1) The need for vengeance, 2) court systems, 3) religious conflicts, 4) the argument presented either by the advocate for the plaintiff or the advocate for the defendant, 5) the role of the witness in court.

NEEDS FOR VENGEANCE

Families and Nations. Holmes has argued extensively and convincingly that courts and law were established as alternatives to vengeance. There is a strong desire on the part of an injured party, family, or nation to gain vengeance for damages received. If the desire for vengeance is not satisfied under the terms of the court it will be settled by feuds among families, war among nations, or private retaliation among individuals. Through courts, families can prevent lengthy and destructive conflicts by having the offending family turn over the accused offender to the other family for punishment. If the person were dead, the offended family may be satisfied to receive the corpse to treat in whatever way they might desire. When one nation was preparing to go to war against another, because the other had forced upon it an unfair treaty, the members of the council that designed the treaty might volunteer to turn themselves over to the enemy nation to prevent the war. The threatening nation might then have its need for vengeance satisfied by inflicting pain or death upon the very people who caused their pain without going

---

[7]B. M. Leiser, Custom, Law, and Morality (Garden City, 1969), p. 112.

to war with the entire nation.[8] For example, when Scipio and the Roman soldiers defeated Antiochus III in war, one of the terms of the treaty was that Antiochus turn Hannibal over to the Romans (Polybius 21.17,7; 42,11). The author of Jonah assumed that God had the same needs for vengeance that human beings do, so Jonah was thrown overboard as a hostage in the hope that God would then be satisfied, and the ship with its other passengers might survive (Jonah 1:7-16). The day on which the Lord would hold court and judge the people was called the "day of judgment," but it was also called the "day of vengeance" (Prov 6:34; Isa 34:8; 61:2; 63:4; Jer 46:10). To prevent Israelites from taking the law into their own hands and avenging those who had injured them, the scripture presents the Lord as saying, "To me belongs vengeance and recompense" (Deut 32:35). The Lord was expected to call the offenders into court to judge their actions. The Psalmist pictured the Lord calling the people to court. He was to act as the plaintiff, the witness, and the judge:

> God, the Lord God spoke; he invited the land from the East to the West.
> From Zion, perfectly beautiful, God appeared.
> Our God came, and he did not delay; a consuming fire was before him;
> it surrounded him, burning fiercely.
> He invited the heavens above and the earth to the trial of his people.
> "Gather my saints, [those who] made a contract over sacrifice!"
> Then the heavens declared his righteousness, because God is a judge.
> "Pay attention, my people, and I will speak;
> Israel, I will testify against you.
> I am God, your God" (Ps 50:1-7).

Punitive Compensation. Needs for vengeance were sometimes suppressed by compensation of some kind. For example, anyone who stole a sheep would have to pay for the crime with four sheep; if that person stole a cow, the fine would be five cattle (Exod 22:1-4). If anyone failed to pay a debt he or she would have to work it off at half wages (Deut 15:12-13, 18). Transferring the same vengeful needs to the deity prompted priests and priestly laws to assign various sacrifices as compensation for different kinds of sins against the Lord, hoping in this way to prevent the Lord from fulfilling his need for vengeance (Polybius 31.17, 3), or, if the group was facing a community or national crisis, bring the conflict to a stop. The sins of Israel were considered unpaid debts, and the Lord was expect-

---

[8]When the nineteenth century American Indian tribe of the Crows killed two sons of Red Robe, a Cheyenne, Red Robe mourned their deaths by turning loose all of his horses, saying they belonged to anyone who wanted them. Tribe members caught his horses and held them for him, begging him to take them back, but he said the deity (Maiyun) wanted his sons to die, so he would suffer in mourning. When finally the tribe offered to go to war to avenge the deaths of his sons, he agreed to end his mourning and take back his horses. So Llewellyn and Hoebel, Cheyenne, pp. 3-6.

ed to demand the same terms of debtor slavery for the nation that individual Jews could require by law of debtors who did not pay their debts by the time promised (Jer 25:11-12; 29:10-11; 32:6-15). Sometimes the offense was so great that it would take more compensation than could be provided. Micah held that not even rivers of oil or thousands of sheep would be adequate (Micah 6:7).

Pain as Satisfaction. When compensation is not possible, the person or tribe damaged might be satisfied by inflicting pain on the offender. One of the widely held biblical beliefs was that God inflicted pain upon people to satisfy God's need for vengeance, to change their behavior, or both. Because Jews and Christians believe this, Rabbis said believers should rejoice more over sufferings than over benefits, because if there were no sufferings there would be no pardon. Without pardon and reconciliation the Lord's need for vengeance would still demand satisfaction. Iniquities are pardoned through sufferings. Rabbi Jose ben Judah said, "Beloved are sufferings before God (המקום), because the glory of God rests on those who suffer" (Sifre Deut 6:5; #31, 73b). Sufferings are more beloved than sacrifices, because sin and guilt offerings atone only for special sins, but sufferings atone for all sins (Midrash Psalms 118:18; #16, 243b). Paul is reported to have said that he rejoiced in his sufferings and in so doing was filling up that which was lacking in the sufferings of Christ (Col 1:24).[9]

According to Amos, God inflicted on Israel famine, war, drought, blight, mildew, locusts, and disease, but none of these was effective in turning the Israelites back to God (Amos 4:6-11). Amos assumed that Israel had only two choices. It could continue as it had been and expect still more punishment to satisfy God, or it could submit to God, plead for mercy in the divine court, and hope God would be satisfied with the pain Israel had already received. If not, perhaps the court would mitigate the penalty and assign for Israel a punishment it could endure. Divine courts, early Jews and Christians believed, like human courts, tried to satisfy the need for vengeance in proportion to the offenses committed, so that the retaliation might come to an end. The souls of the martyred saints were stored under God's altar until there were enough hostages supplied to satisfy God's desire for vengeance (Rev 6:9-11). Holmes held that the desire for vengeance has never ceased to be one object of punishment. Law, according to Holmes, not only does but should make the gratification of revenge an object.[10]

---

[9]Buchanan, "The Day of Atonement and Paul's Doctrine of Redemption," Novum Testamentum 32 (1990):236-49.

[10]O. W. Holmes, The Common Law (Boston, 1881), pp. 3-6, 9-10, 40-42. Not all cultures and societies demanded the same kind of vengeance. The Zapotec Indians in Mexico, for example, strive to reach a balance that does not allow either side fully to win or lose a case. The goal is to solve the real problem rather than punish extensively. This sometimes means a fine to the town rather than a payment to the plaintiff. The cases usually end with the judge (presidente) counselling the offenders in ways to act in the future to prevent such problems as those brought

COURT SYSTEMS

Court Variations. As the community acquired more experience in community solutions to community problems, more and more of the disciplinary problems were moved out of the hands of the family into the justice systems of the government. The earliest governmental jury systems were probably not very elaborate, resembling the moot system in Tanzania. The trials probably still admitted all those interested in the case to provide evidence, act as witnesses, or offer arguments in behalf of one of the parties. Quintilian taught his law students with the assumption that there were in the court two groups of people besides the attorneys and the judge. These were placed in different sections of the court so that it was clear which side each person in the court supported.

It was this kind of trial that Rabbi Eliezer ben Jacob had in mind when he described the heavenly court scene where individuals would be judged before the Lord. He said,

> "The one who performs one commandment (מצוה)
> obtains one defense witness [or attorney] (פרקליט);
> the one who commits one transgression (עבירה)
> obtains for himself one accusing witness [or attorney] (קטיגור)" (Aboth 4:11).

In this trial, a whole lifetime of deeds would have lined up on each side of the court room, some ready to testify for, and others against, the individual on trial. Rabbi Jacob was able to imagine a court scene like this in heaven because he knew such court scenes as these took place on earth. Continuations of this practice are evident in many church weddings today, when the family and friends of the groom sit in one side of the church and family and friends of the bride occupy the other side, just as this legal ceremony was practiced thousands of years ago. Quintilian indicated that there were observers in court who sometimes applauded the oratory of the advocate (Quintilian 4.2, 127). Homer also reflected this kind of an atmosphere.

Open Courts. One example of community court was Homer's judgment scene on the shield of Achilles (Iliad 18.497-508). The trial was held in the open air, and mobs of people crowded around to enjoy the show. Different ones cheered

---

to court. Their belief is that a punishment that is excessive might lead to further violence in retribution outside of the court. So L. Nader, "Styles of Court Procedure: To Make the Balance," Law and Culture, pp. 69-91.

The Cheyenne American Indians did not use the death penalty to punish a murderer. Instead they evicted the person from the tribe for a period of time--usually more than five years. The removal of the murderer partially satisfied the need of the family of the murdered person for vengeance. This was followed by a ritual act to cleanse the community of this sin. Cheyennes said the murderer stank. So Llewellyn and Hoebel, Cheyenne, p.158.

different participants the way they might at a horse race or a bull fight. After both litigants had spoken many times, the elders conferred together and, one by one, announced their decisions. Bets were made, and the money laid out beforehand was to be given to the one whose judgment concurred with that of the judge or jury. The same was true for the case of Boaz when he wished to settle a dispute concerning inheritance. He called together the elders of the city who met out of doors at the city gate of Bethlehem (Ruth 4:1-2; Prov 31:23; Deut 16:18). After all of the evidence had been presented, both sides were allowed to state their respective cases. Then a liturgy was effected that acknowledged the decision made and its consequences.

Formal Liturgizing. Sooner or later rules of order were developed which told in what sequence parts of the trial were required to take place. The more sophisticated the trials became the more formal was the discipline and accepted liturgy. All members of the court were given special seats, and positions were provided for the parties to the trial. Oaths were taken to guarantee that those involved in the trial told only the truth. Witnesses were interrogated in an effort to learn the validity of the accusation. Different kinds of evidence were presented to confirm some of the claims that were made. Later armed officers were required to make sure that no violent disruption took place in court.

Professional Advocates. As early as the fifth century B.C. there were specialized advocates trained to argue cases, professionally. They were schooled in rhetoric, observing well-defined and understood rules of debate and logic. Aristotle said rhetoric existed for the sake of judgment (Rhetoric 2:1, 2). Socrates (5th century B.C.) was tried by a community court, a type of city jury. The custom now practiced in the United States of selecting a jury is to pick the jurors from among those who know very little about the case and have no personal interest in its outcome. This, however, was probably not the earliest practice. As with the community of Ligomba, it is more than likely that the people who knew the most would have volunteered to tell that which they knew, and some of the witnessing may have been rather boisterous without severe limitations of function. In fact, Trites and Köhler were probably correct in their claims that judges themselves participated in the act of acquiring information and would sometimes themselves act as witnesses in the case (Ps 50:7, 21).[11]

Corruption in Court. As early as there were official hearings, there was corruption of the trial process. Aristotle knew that judges favored their friends and could be bribed to act in special ways (Rhetoric 1.12,4-9). Quintilian also

---

[11]A. A. Trites, The New Testament Concept of Witness (Cambridge, 1977), p. 27. This book is an important contribution to New Testament studies in relationship to legal concepts. L. Köhler, Hebrew Man, tr. P. A. Ackroyd (London, c1953), p. 96, fn. 1, also held that a witness might also function as a judge.

taught his students the best ways to deal with the prejudices of the judges (Quintilian, 4.1,16-19). The entire concept of a chosen people was the belief that the Lord was also a corrupt judge and would show preference when he judged Israelites (Num 6:24-26). According to the gospel report, Jesus told a parable that involved a judge who neither feared God nor showed deference to human beings (Luke 18:2-5). This probably meant that he was a Gentile judge who would not show preference to Jews. When Moses reportedly appointed subordinate judges, he warned them not to be partial in judgment, showing preference neither to the people of low estate nor to those who were prominent (Deut 1:16-17).

Commandments like this were written into the code, because judges were not always impartial, but laws do not guarantee that there will be no criminals. There continued to be prejudiced judges, and there was also false evidence brought and false witnessing done in early courts just as there are in modern courts.

PARTICIPANTS

For a court trial to take place it is necessary for there to be at least three parties: 1) The plaintiff or prosecuting attorney with his or her client; 2) The defendant with his or her advocate or defense attorney; and 3) a judicial party. This can be one judge, a group of judges, or a jury. The plaintiff is the one who accuses someone else of injuring him or her and is in court to receive reparation (civil) or punishment for the other party (criminal). The defendant is the person accused of the offense by the plaintiff. The judicial party is the person or group authorized to settle the dispute, decide whether or not there really has been an injury or breach of law, and if there is to determine the just penalty or payment necessary to correct the alleged injury.

The Plaintiff. The plaintiff was the accuser or prosecuting attorney. The Greek word for prosecute is the same word that means "persecute" or "pursue." The prosecutor was ὁ διώκων (Herodotus, Hist. 6.82; Xenophon Historia Graeca 7.3, 6; Apologia Socratis 21). Some of the incidents when διώκειν may have been used legally to mean "prosecute" rather than "persecute" in the New Testament are as follow:

> Pray for those who prosecute you (Matt 5:44).
> Bless those who prosecute [you] (Rom 12:14).
> Because of this the Jews were prosecuting Jesus (John 5:15).[12]
> Saul, Saul, why are you prosecuting me (Acts 9:4; 22:7; 26:14)?
> I am Jesus the Nazorean whom you are prosecuting (Acts 22:8; 26:15).
> For you have heard my former way of life at one time in Judaism that I prosecuted the church of God and ravaged it excessively (Gal 1:13).

---

[12]For a defense of this interpretation see A. E. Harvey, Jesus on Trial (Atlanta, c1977), pp. 50-51.

They were only hearing that the one who was prosecuting us at one time now preaches the gospel which he once ravaged (Gal 1:23).

Because Jesus was frequently engaged in situations where his opponents were looking for evidence by which they might try Jesus in court, and Paul was actually trying to get Christians convicted in court of breaking the law, these so-called "persecuting" terms might rather mean "prosecute." At least this should be considered.

Prosecuting was the function of Satan in the heavenly courts. C. L. and E. M. Meyers expressed surprise to find that in Joshua's trial (Zech 3) Satan was stationed in court on the right.[13] They said, "Although the Western reader might expect a hostile power to be on the left side, such is not the case." Why would a Western reader expect the plaintiff to stand on the left? In the United States, at least, the plaintiff always stands on the right in court. That is not only true in the United States, and it is not only true for the twentieth century. When the Psalmist appealed to the Lord for help, he asked that his enemy be brought to trial, with a plaintiff (Satan) at this right hand, and let him receive a guilty verdict (Ps 109:6-7). Satan and God are not stationed dualistically at opposite poles, with God and Satan in positions of equal power, one as the plaintiff and the other as the defendant. God was believed to function as the judge; Satan is the prosecuting attorney in the heavenly court. The defendant was the person or people whom Satan was accusing or opposing. Satan's task was that of cross-examining, confusing, torturing, and misleading the defendant to such an extent that the defendant would lose the trial. In Job's trial, Satan was assigned the task of cross-examining and torturing Job (Job 1-2).

<u>The Defendant</u> The defendant is the person accused of having committed some crime or having injured someone. The Greek word for defendant was ὁ φεύγων (Herodotus, <u>Hist</u>. 6.82). Ὁ φεύγων means the "refugee" or "the fleeing person." This is the one who wants to get away. These legal terms come from non-legal conflict situation. The prosecutor is the one who wants to pursue, persecute, chase down, whereas the defendant wants to get away, to flee, or escape. The way of pursuing an offender was to take him or her to court; the way for a defendant to avoid the persecution of the plaintiff was to defend himself or herself in court. Many of the pious poems of pleading in the Psalms were written by defendants who were pleading to God as the judge to rescue them from the prosecutor.

---

[13]C. L. and E. M. Meyers, <u>Haggai, Zechariah 1-8</u> (Garden City, 1987), p. 186.

RELIGIOUS CONFLICTS

Trites accurately observed that the Bible reports many quarrels.[14] For examples, there were quarrels between Cain and Abel (Gen 24:8-16), Abram's and Lot's herdsmen (Gen 13:5-12); Sarah and Hagar (Gen 21:8-21); Abraham and Abimelech (Gen 21:25-26); Isaac's servants and the men of Gerar (Gen 26:17-22); Samuel and Saul after Saul's battle with the Amalekites (1 Sam 15:10-33). There were many conflicts between the Israelites and Moses in the wilderness, and Jacob and Laban quarreled at Mizpah (Gen 31:36-55). Jesus was frequently involved in conflict with the Pharisees and their legal advisors, the scribes (Matt 9:10-13, 14-15; 15:1-3; Luke 11:37-39; 16:14-15; 18:9-14). Paul had an ongoing conflict with the Judaizers (Gal 2). Since the authors of the Bible lived among people who were frequently involved in disputes, it comes as no surprise that they 1) learned legal techniques for debate, 2) became skilled in rhetoric, and 3) applied these principles to their understanding of theology. Trites has further listed eight instances in Isaiah 40-55 alone which present trial scenes (Isa 41:1-29; 43:8-13; 43:22-28; 44:7-8; 45:20-21; 48:14-16; 50:1; 50:7-9).[15] In order to understand the logic and force of Jewish and Christian arguments it will be necessary to examine the way early Greek and Latin lawyers were trained, because Christianity developed in the Graeco-Roman world where Roman courts were abundant and their rules were widely accepted.

THE ARGUMENT

Rhetoricians. One of the earliest teachers of lawyers whose works have survived was Aristotle, The Art of Rhetoric and Rhetoric to Alexander, who wrote in the fifth century B.C. About five centuries later, the Roman rhetorician Quintilian (first century A.D.) was a prominent law school teacher. Quintilian was well-informed by the works of the Greek and Latin rhetoricians who lived before him, like Aristotle, Demosthenes, and Cicero. He brought together the insights of all of these, added his own experience as a trial lawyer, and prepared an extensive work, Institutio Oratoria, to be used by teachers who trained lawyers. Books 4-6 tell lawyers how to prepare an argument for a trial in court. Some material from both rhetoricians will be used here as a basis on which to compare early Christian literature dealing with legal and court subjects.

The Art of Rhetoric. According to Aristotle, rhetoric is the art of persuasion (Rhetoric 1.2,1), and rhetoricians were trained primarily for their ability to argue in behalf either of the plaintiff or the defendant in a trial. If, for example, the lawyer involved had witnesses and the opposition had none the attorney would

---

[14]Trites, Witness, p. 24.

[15]Ibid., p. 35.

argue on the basis of the importance of witnesses for proving a case, but if the opposition had witnesses and the lawyer involved had none, he should then argue from the importance of giving primary attention to the probabilities of the case and the unreliability of witnesses, since witnesses could testify falsely (Rhetoric 1.2, 17-18). Quintilian concurred with Aristotle, adding that while demolishing the witnesses of the opposition, the advocate should claim that witnesses were unreliable, because they might lie or be bribed. If opponents introduced documentary evidence the advocate should argue that it was untrustworthy, that the contracts were improperly signed, and he should hold that hearsay evidence had no value at all (Quintilian 5.7, 1-6). The authors and personalities of the Bible seemed also trained in some of the same rules of oratory.

Outline of the Argument. Quintilian followed others in dividing causes into four parts: 1) The introduction, 2) statement of facts, 3) verification, and 4) conclusion (Quintilian 4.pr. 7, 6). Each of these was planned with a definite purpose, and the entire argument was designed to persuade the judge or jury of the justness of the cause the advocate represented. The attorney for the plaintiff was assigned the task of showing that the defendant had committed some crime and deserved to be punished or had damaged the plaintiff and should be required to compensate the plaintiff for these injuries. The attorney for the defendant, on the other hand, was required to show either that the accusation was false and that the defendant had committed no crime or damage at all or else to show that the damage or crime was not as serious or as definitive as the accuser had alleged. If that could not be done, then he would try to show that the defendant was an unfortunate but respected person of good character who deserved mercy. The trial involved four parties: 1) the judge, 2) the plaintiff, 3) the defendant, and 4) the attorneys involved in presenting and defending the case. For both sides, the argument began with the introduction (Quintilian 5.13, 6; 4.1, 5-7).

THE INTRODUCTION

The Purpose. The introduction was called a proem by the Greeks; the Latins called it an exordium. The purpose of the introduction was to prepare the judge and the court to be receptive to the rest of the presentation. Of course, this would include tactful praise of the judge, relating the needs of the client to the known character and rank of the judge. The introduction should be prepared in such a way as to attract the mind of the judge and convince him that one pleading the case was himself a man of good character and that his cause was just. In the introduction, the pleader would present the case with moderate emotion and exaggeration, trying to evoke pity from the judge, calling attention to the age, sex, and situation of the client and the meanness, contempt, and hatred of the opponent. These personal matters should not be dealt with in detail, according to Quintilian (Quintilian 4.1, 14-16), because they might alienate the good will of the judge.

The Judge and the Opposition. The attorney should remember that although this quarrel was against the opposing party, and there was a responsive audience in the court room, the argument was presented, not to the opposition or the audience, but to the judge. The lawyer should know as much as possible about the judge, realizing that he would be predisposed to render a verdict in favor of his friends, but that a good pleader might lead him to rule against his own special interests. (Quintilian 4.1, 17-19). If he needed to remove the judge's prejudice, the advocate should subtly present a threat to the judge himself, showing how a verdict in the advocate's favor would be to the judge's advantage. He must present his introduction in such a way as to show that the judge's action against his case would win the displeasure of the Roman people generally. In a Roman court, the advocate for the plaintiff always spoke first.[16]

Quintilian held that there were six kinds of causes: 1) honorable, 2) mean, 3) doubtful or ambiguous, 4) extraordinary, 5) obscure, and 6) scandalous (Quintilian 4.1, 24, 40). The pleader tried in his introduction to define the cause involved to his client's favor. Methodologically, a good advocate would keep his audience informed about the stage in his argument that he was presenting. He would conclude the introduction by telling the judge that he was about to present a statement of facts to substantiate his claim (Quintilian 4.7, 73-79).

THE STATEMENT OF FACTS

Following the introduction, the advocate presents the facts of the case. If the case is simple and turns only on one point of law, this should be brief, according to Quintilian. In fact, it might be omitted altogether if it could be included as part of the introduction or if it was clear that the judge was already moved to rule in the advocate's favor. If, however, the case was complicated, the pleader would be obligated to maintain the judge's attention throughout. The listing of facts should not have the same intensity of emotional appeal as the introduction, but neither should it be a simple listing the facts. The pleader should reintroduce some of the same kind of emotion that he used in the introduction, reminding the audience of the importance of each point, holding their attention by pointing out each movement from step to step, and dramatizing the seriousness of the cause. If not overdone, repetition may occasionally be effective, holding always to the importance of being 1) brief, 2) clear, and 3) credible as possible, but judges of Quintilian's time were not always erudite, so it was necessary for the advocate to educate the judge as much as possible before he made a decision (Quintilian 4.2, 1-45).

---

[16]In Ndendeuli courts (moots), when the offense was well known before the session began, the defendant was allowed to speak first to justify his role. So Gulliver, "Case Studies," p. 33. Jewish courts followed the same procedure as Romans except in capital cases. When there was a possibility that the death penalty might be inflicted the defendant was permitted to say everything he could in his own defense before the plaintiff spoke.

Proofs were very closely related to the statement of facts and partially integrated with them. The general direction of argument, however, was that the facts came first and the proofs or verification followed. Closely related to both of these was a proposition or accusation. This was an attempt to propose the interpretation of the facts and show proofs that the claims were valid (Quintilian 4.4, 8-9). Second Isaiah pictured the Lord issuing a summons to the nations to present their case (ריב) against the Jews in court, bringing whatever strong [proofs, arguments, or defenses] (עצמותיהם) they could muster (Isa 41:21-22).

Oaths were sometimes used in court, but not at the outset of each trial, as they are in courts of the United States today. In ancient Akkadian trials, for example, people were put under oath only when the judges suspected that the person was lying and there was not enough evidence to prove the case without knowing the validity of the testimony. At that point they asked one or more people involved, each, to take an oath. If the person refused out of fear of the divine punishment evoked, the judges assumed the person was lying.[17] Many Christians and Jews were forbidden by their religious laws to take oaths in court. This put them at a disadvantage in court where this religious attitude persuaded the court that they were not telling the truth. Although rabbis allowed fathers or husbands to invalidate oaths taken by women, not all Near Eastern peoples put these limitations upon women. In Egypt, for example, a woman was allowed to present a case against a man before a tribunal of judges. The judges required her to take an oath on the punishment of one hundred blows if she were lying. She took the oath in the name of Amon, without any report of male permission granted.[18]

Quintilian, however, cautioned students about the use of oaths. Forcing the opposition to take an oath with the intention of forcing that person to refuse might not produce the desired effect. Many witnesses had no fear of divine punishment and would commit perjury willingly. If this were done it would establish the credibility of the opposition in the eyes of the judges and relieve the judge of the responsibility of evaluating the evidence, leaving to the gods the task of judging the case (Quintilian, 5.6,1-5).[19] That would be unsatisfactory to the advocate

[17]T. J. Meek (tr.), "Mesopotamian Legal Documents," Ancient, p. 220.

[18]Wilson (tr.), "For the Record of a Lawsuit," p. 216.

[19]Llewellyn and Hoebel, Cheyenne, pp. 151-52, reported an incident when one nineteenth century American Cheyenne Indian, Owl Head, accused two other Cheyenne men, Chief Eagle and Brady, of having been intimate with his wife. His accusation was a ritualistic act: instead of sending them a summons to appear in court, he took the other two men's horses. Chief Eagle did not resist; he gave up his horse. Brady, however, took Owl Head to a Medicine Hat, a sacred object, where the two alleged adulterers took oaths that they had not been intimate with Owl Head's wife. Once this

and his client who wanted the court to decide in their favor that day rather than wait for the gods to punish the oath-taker for his evil and frivolity. Hebrews also were aware of the ease with which some people were willing to commit perjury in court, and they had a commandment against it: "You shall not take the name of the Lord, your God, in vain" (Exod 20:7; Deut 5:11). Because oaths were taken in the name of some deity or religious object, this commandment was made to prevent perjury. The oath normally had the following parts:[20]

1) The name of the deity or religious object that was called upon to enforce the oath;
2) the curses the oath-taker would accept if he spoke falsely or in vain;
3) that which he promised to do or held to be true.

Sometimes the curses were formally omitted but understood. They were omitted for fear of the disastrous consequences God would bring upon his people if the oath were not carried out. A summary of the curses omitted was: "Thus may God do and thus may he add, if . . ." This meant, "May God lay upon you [or me] all of these unmentioned curses, if . . . " For example, Ruth reportedly said to Naomi, "May the Lord [lay upon me many unmentioned curses] if even death separates me from you" (Ruth 1:17; see also 1 Sam 3:17). Some real curses are:

If I have raised my hand against the orphan because I saw my help at the gate, . . . let my shoulder blade fall from my shoulder, my arm break out from its socket (Job 31:21-22).

If my step has turned aside from the way . . .let me sow and another consume; let my produce be rooted out (Job 31:7-8).

The first point of an oath would usually begin, "By the life of the Lord" (Judges 8:19; Ruth 3:13; 1 Sam 14:39, 45; et passim), "By the life of Pharaoh (Gen 42:15, 16),[21] "By the king,"[22] "As Amon endures,"[23] or "By the life of

---

was done, Owl Head had to give Chief Eagle back his horse. The Cheyenne community later judged that these were false oaths, because Brady was wounded in the very next battle with the Crows, and Chief Eagle was killed in the second battle. It was the deity (Maiyun) that brought about the curses accompanied with the oaths. It was this eventuality that Quintilian wanted to avoid. Even though everyone was agreed that these two men were amply punished, Owl Head did not get the horses he deserved for the offenses.

[20]Buchanan, "Some Oath and Vow Formulas in the New Testament," Harvard Theological Review 58 (1965):319-26; M. Pope, "Oaths," Interpreter's Dictionary of the Bible III, p. 576; Trites, Witness, pp. 30-31.

[21]This implies that Pharaoh was accepted as divine or an agent of the deity.

the Lord and by the life of my lord the king" (2 Sam 15:21). Jews also swore by "Heaven [=God]," "the land," "Jerusalem," or "the temple" (Matt 5:34; 23:16; James 5:12)--all of which were held to be sacred. God was also pictured as taking oaths in court (Gen 50:24; Luke 1:73-75; Isa 4:20-24; Heb 6:13; Ezek 33:11). Just as in twentieth century courts, in antiquity people took oaths in court by raising their hand (Gen 14:22; Deut 32:40; Dan 12:7; Ps 144:8; Rev 10:5-6). Because of the severe curses and the dangers of blasphemy many Jews of New Testament times refused to take oaths (Philo, Decal 18.84-95; Josephus, Wars 2.135, 141-44, 152-53; Matt 5:34). When an oath was not volunteered but administered by someone else, the oath-taker responded with "Amen" or "Amen! Amen" (Num 5:19-22). Rabbi Hanina said the word "Amen" always implied an oath was being taken (Sheb 36a). Rabba said that if a person said, "Yes! Yes!" or "No! No!" it was the same as taking an oath (Sheb 36a). According to Matthew (Matt 5:37), Jesus said it was permissible to say, "Yes! Yes!" or "No! No!" so long as the Christian did not actually take an oath. The technical distinction probably was that the person involved did not actually take the name of the Lord or any sacred object and he or she did not call down the curses involved in the oath.[24] The words of Jesus, "Amen! Amen!" are usually rendered into American, "Verily! Verily!" by translators. It would be better translated, "I hereby solemnly swear," calling attention to the legal significance of the expression.

WITNESSES IN COURT

Testimony of Witnesses. Quintilian dealt at length on the way to use witnesses, both those of the opposition and those of the client. There were techniques by which witnesses could be ridiculed or led into traps that made them contradict themselves or even give testimony against the side they represented. However an advocate used witnesses, it is clear that they provided important evidence for winning a case (Quintilian, 5.7,15-36).

World Court. Second Isaiah pictured the Lord acting as the prosecuting attorney for the Jews, satirically sending summonses to all the Gentiles to unite and confront him in court, bringing their witnesses (עדיהם) so that they might either vindicate themselves in court or hear the testimony of the Lord and admit that the Lord and his people were in the right (אמת) (Isa 43:9). For his part, the Lord was confident, because he had the Jews for his witnesses (Isa 43:10, 12; 44:8).

---

[22]Meek (tr.), "Documents," p. 217.

[23]Wilson (tr.), "Lawsuit," p. 216.

[24]RSV has "'Yes' or 'No'" (Matt 5:37). Obviously, the translators did not know the technical significance of saying, "Yes" or "No" twice.

Jewish authors not only pictured the Lord as an advocate and a judge, but at the same time he functioned as a witness (Wisdom 1:6; Rom 1:9; 2 Cor 1:23; 1 Thes 2:5, 10; Phil 1:8; Aboth 4:29).

Role of Witnesses. Among the Dead Sea Scrolls, the monastic Rule of the Community warned the reader not to bring a charge against his neighbor without having adequate witnesses (1QS 6:1). The same warning was given by the Damascus Document (CD 9:2-4). This warning was probably given to avoid abuse of the court system and the corresponding embarrassment this would provide for the sect to which the member belonged. The Damascus Document followed Deuteronomy 19:15 in requiring at least two witnesses, but in the case of the same offense, if different witnesses observed the action at different times, singly, this was considered adequate to establish guilt. The force of two witnesses may have been the reason Mark (6:7) reported that Jesus sent his apostles out in twos. Later Christian leaders also worked together in pairs: 1) Peter and John (Acts 3:1, 11; 4:13, 19; 8:14); 2) Paul and Barnabas (Acts 13:43, 46, 50); 3) Judas and Silas (Acts 15:32); 4) Barnabas and Mark (Acts 15:39); 5) Paul and Silas (Acts 15:40; Acts 16:19, 25); and 6) Silas and Timothy (Acts 17:14-15).The Damascus community did not accept as witnesses anyone who had not been fully initiated into the sect nor anyone who had broken the commandment (CD 9:16-10:3). Rabbis refused to allow slaves or women as witnesses in court (RH 1:8; Yeb 88b, 115a). Philo said only eye witnesses should be accepted, since hearsay was unreliable (Spec. Leg. 4.59-61). One of the commandments is against false witnessing (Exod 20:16; Deut 5:20), and Philo exhorted at length on the wickedness of bearing false witness (Dec. 138-41; Spec. Leg. 4.41-44). When two witnesses could bring adequate evidence to condemn a person to death, it was important that witnesses be trustworthy. To avoid the damage of false witnesses, Quintilian trained his law students to cross examine witnesses carefully. Rabbis also demanded rigorous cross-examination of witnesses (San 5:2).

The author of Matthew, following Deuteronomy 19:15 demanded at least two witnesses before a case could be proved, but the same author accepted scripture as testimony (Matt 18:15-17). The author of Jubilees accepted First Enoch as a "testimony" (Jub 4:16-19). The sect governed by the Sermon on the Mount was more rigorous than the Hebrew Scriptures in its law enforcement. Its members had to be more law observant than the scribes and Pharisees; they were punished if they were even angry with fellow members; and those accused of offenses were encouraged to stay out of the courts. They were to settle with their opponents before the trial (Matt 5:20-26).

Christian Witnessing. Second Isaiah wrote his document as if he believed that the Lord was holding a great court trial in which he was both the prosecuting attorney and the judge. That author knew, however, that witnesses in a trial were very important, so he pictured the Jews as the necessary witnesses for the trial (Isa 43:10, 12; 44:8). The Jews were also the clients whose case the Lord was defending. The opponents in this trial were all the rest of the people of the world, the Gentiles. The concept of Jews being in a cosmic trial in which all of the Gentiles were opponents did not improve community relationships between Jews and Gentiles. Believing, as they did, that God needed their testimony to win the trial strengthened their belief in the doctrine of election and made them more segregated than before. This hostile doctrine prompted hostile responses, and those witnessing Jews acted in such a way as to receive persecution and death (Jub 1:12). This did not reduce the testimony. In Near Eastern hearings where witnesses also argued cases, and judges themselves acted also as witnesses, the role of witnessing assigned to Jews was not simply telling that which they had seen with their own eyes but that which they were defending. The court scene understood was one in which all of the witnesses for the Lord would be lined up on one side of the court, and all the witnesses for the pagan deities were gathered on the other side. Because Jews had been commissioned by the prophecy of Isaiah, which had been accepted as God's word, legally, witnesses (martyrs) were those who vocally argued their positions which were not always popular. Nevertheless among Jews, martyrs were considered heroes, necessary participants in God's legal conflict with the Gentiles. This is the doctrinal and legal background for Christian witnessing.

Just as Isaiah called the Jews God's witnesses, so the author of Acts presented Jesus, after his resurrection, commissioning his apostles as witnesses. They could not know when the Lord would win this great, continuing trial, and the kingdom be restored to Israel, but they were assigned the task of being witnesses to the resurrection of Jesus in Jerusalem, all Judaea, Samaria, and to the end of the earth (Acts 1:6-8). Since there was no visible proof of the resurrection that could stand up in court, witnesses provided the only evidence that could be considered convincing. Luke reported Jesus, in his meeting with the apostles after the walk on the road to Emmaus, reminding his apostles that they were witnesses of the things that had happened and could, therefore, defend this case in court (Luke 14:48). According to Acts the early church began with followers of Jesus witnessing in his behalf (Acts 1:22; 2:32; 3:15; 5:32; Acts 10:39-41; 13:31; 22:15, 20; 26:16). Some of the testimony reported in Acts was given before councils and kings to give the witnessing its full court significance, but the speeches in Acts were both testimony and argument. In this it was consistent with the confusion of these roles in Jewish and other Near Eastern courts. As with earlier Jews, early Christians who were witnesses in behalf of Jesus were segregated, persecuted and killed both for their arguments and their testimony (Rev 2:13; 11:3-10).

<u>Cross-Examining the Witness</u>. After each witness has testified the advocate for the opposition is permitted to cross-examine the witness to clarify points and possibly to find inconsistencies in the testimony. Many of the questions put to Jesus were given by the chief priests and elders or the Pharisees with their scribes

along for legal counsel.[25] The scribes were the lawyers of New Testament times. Although these questions were offered in various extemporaneous situations, the questions asked were the same kind of questions that might have been asked in court, and their purpose was to confuse the witness and force him to say something that would convict of a death sentence (Matt 12:14; 26:59) when he was taken to court. Some of the questions are as follows:

> Why do your disciples transgress the tradition of the elders (Matt 15:1)?
> Is it lawful for a man to divorce his wife for any reason (Matt 19:3)?
> By what authority do you do these things (Matt 21:23)?
> Is it lawful to pay taxes to Caesar or not (Matt 22:17)?

Satan was the prosecuting attorney who was appointed to cross-examine Joshua. He stood at the right hand of the defendant as was customary in ancient courts (Zech 3:1; Ps 109:6). Joshua apparently had an angel as his defense attorney (Zech 3:3-6). Satan functioned as the prosecuting attorney in Job's trial. As in other ancient courts, the prosecuting attorney was not only allowed to cross-examine Job, but he was also given permission to torture him in an attempt to obtain a confession (Job 1:1-2:7).

Evidence. There were rules determining the kind of evidence required to prove a case. For example if someone left one of his animals under the care of his neighbor, and the animal was killed by wild beasts, the neighbor would be obligated to bring to the owner the remnants of the animal to prove that his claim was true (Exod 22:13). If he could do this he would not have to make restitution for the animal. This law was reportedly known by Jacob when he confronted Laban at Mizpah. Justifying his departure, he reviewed for Laban all he had done to earn the flock he took. He claimed that he did more than their agreement called for. He did not even bring to Laban animals torn by wild beasts, but instead he took the loss himself (Gen 31:39). Amos was also evidently familiar with this law, and he used it as an illustration for warning the Samaritans of the danger that awaited them (Amos 3:12). They would be left like victims of a wild beast's attack, and there would be no compensation allowed in court.[26]

Joseph's Robe. This law was also recognized by the brothers of Joseph when they sold him as a slave, but they did not fulfill the legal requirement. Instead of the mangled corpse of Joseph, they took his robe, dipped it into blood from a sheep they had slaughtered, and brought it to their father. They did not say a wild beast

---

[25]Harvey, On Trial has competently shown how Jewish leaders planned ahead for the final trial of Jesus. He concentrated on the Fourth Gospel.

[26]This means they would gain no benefits for their sufferings in the treasury of merits and demerits.

had killed him, but they asked him to act as the judge and decide what had happened to his son, Joseph. The evidence they brought, of course, was false, but it convinced their father that Joseph had been killed (Gen 37:18-36). When King Ahab wanted Naboth's vineyard, and Naboth refused to sell it, Queen Jezebel set up false witnesses to condemn Naboth to death in a trial so that Ahab could confiscate the property (1 Kings 21:1-16).[27]

Biblical Testimony. Joseph's bloody coat was given as evidence for determining what had happened to Joseph, but there was no special word that called this "evidence." Evidence was necessary for judgment, but in Greek and Hebrew writings that which was used in court as evidence was *μαρτυρία* or עדות, "testimony" or "witnessing,"ספר, "book," "scroll," ברית "contract," or עצמות "strong things." When Aristotle spoke of using "evidence" (*μαρτυρία*) in court he meant some ancient proverb or ancient literary source, the use of witnesses, or even torture (Rhetoric 1:15,14-26). Jeremiah said that the Lord had divorced his people as a husband divorces his wife (Deut 24:1), by sending her out of his house and giving her a written document of divorce (Jer 3:8). As a careful legalist, the author of Second Isaiah asked for evidence, but he did not use such an abstract term as that. He asked that those who thought God had divorced his people show him the divorce document (ספר כריתות) which God had written (Isa 50:1). Since no such legal document could be produced, that author claimed that God had never divorced them. He only sent them out of his house.

Scripture and Testimony. Instead of using abstract terms, early Hebrews and Israelites used the term "witnessing" or some specific thing that was to be used for evidence, and this usually referred to Hebrew Scriptures, having as parallels "contracts," "commandments," and "law" (Sirach 45:17). In place of "contracts" (*διαθήκαις*) the Hebrew text has "statute" or "law" (חק); for "testimonies" (*μαρτυρία*), the Hebrew also has "statute" or "law" (חק). The Jews who translated Sirach into Greek thought the best word to render "statute" was testimonies, thinking that testimony from the scripture should stand up in court without question. The chest where the commandments were kept was called the chest of testimony (ארון עדות, Exod 25:22), and the contract or commandments were called the tablets of testimony (לחת העדות, Exod 31:18). Jews and Christians placed a high value on these particular documents and these witnesses. Greek and Latin lawyers were trained to question and challenge written documents, including contracts, and Jewish lawyers did the same with all the documents of the opposition. They tried to get opposition documents thrown out of court, and they challenged contracts in whatever way they could. They questioned the validity of the signatures or the ritual used when writing the contract. They also challenged eye witness testimony of the opposition. They defended only their own documents

[27]For legal details of this action see F. I. Andersen, "The Socio-Juridical Background of the Naboth Incident," JBL 85 (1986):46-57.

and their own witnesses. This is the function of defense attorneys. Other prosecuting lawyers did the same; they disagreed only with their opposition.

Philo called the law a witness (*μάρτυς ὁ νόμος*; Post. 121). This was not true of the Mediterranean world in general. Quintilian said Roman courts were generally suspicious of documentary evidence and would not accept hearsay evidence at all. Jews and Christians, however, did not cross examine the scripture. The accepted rule for Israelites was that no one witness could arise and bring a case to court for any crime or offense that had been committed, but "at the mouth of two or three witnesses the matter would stand" (Deut 19:15). RSV renders this passage "on the evidence of," but the Hebrew "at the mouth of" (על פי) accurately reflects the value of eye witness presence in court. The scripture reflects court concepts much more than laboratory thought-forms. Most Jews and Christians thought the scripture came "at the mouth of" Moses, David, Solomon, or the prophets and was treated as valid witness. The author of the Gospel of Matthew, for example, convinced that the Hebrew Scripture was adequate testimony, "proved" cases by putting together two texts (Matt 15:4, 8-9; 19:4-5, 18-19; 21:5, 13, 42; Matt 22:37-39; 24:15, 21, 30, 31) as witnesses.

Importance of Evidence. One of the important decisions on the part of the judge is that of deciding what can be admitted as evidence. Some evidence is not allowed, because of the way it was obtained, its value in making judgment, its possibility for distorting judgment, or some other reason. Lawyers are quick to move that material which is damaging to their cases be excluded for some reason. If the judge consents, it will be easier for the lawyer who made the motion, but more difficult for the lawyer who needed that evidence to prove his or her case. Because of its importance, Quintilian provided extensive counsel to his students for ways of arguing either to admit or deny certain types of evidence offered to the judge for consideration. Including or excluding evidence or testimony is no new practice. In the second century B.C. it was taken for granted by the author of a mythological court scene. When the Lord of the Spirits approached his bench as judge to conduct a trial, he opened the books that were before him. He decided at the outset to admit as testimony the prayers of the plaintiff as well as the blood of the righteous--implying that the defendant had earlier moved that they not be allowed. Once that decision had been allowed, the case was determined in favor of the plaintiff, the Hasmonean saints (Enoch 47:3-4).

Proof and "signs." Quintilian said there were only four forms of proof: 1) Because one thing is, another is not; 2) because one thing is, another is also; 3) Because one thing is not, another is; and 4) because one thing is not, another is not (Quintilian 5.8,7). Some evidence is irrefutable; some provides suggestive probabilities but is not adequate in itself to prove a case. Probable evidence is called a sign (signum, *σημεῖον*).

It is the task of the advocate to strengthen or weaken the validity of signs, depending on their effect on his client's case. Just because there is a blood stained garment does not prove there was a murder; a woman is not an adulteress just because she was seen associating with men (Quintilian 5.9, 8-15). Quintilian also shows many other instances of ways one might deduce conclusions from available data and the normal assumptions that can be made on the basis of race, nationality, sex, education, occupation, and age (Quintilian 5.10, 17-27). Amos staged a series of "If . . . then" rhetorical questions, applying some of the same logic as the Greek and Latin rhetoricians:

> Do two walk together if they had not made an appointment?
> Does a lion roar in the forest when he has no prey?
> Will the young lion cry from his den if he has taken [nothing]?
> Does a bird fall to the ground in a snare when there is no trap [set]?
> Does a snare spring from the ground when it has taken nothing?
> Is the trumpet blown in the city and the people do not tremble?
> If they blow a trumpet in the city do the people not become afraid?
> If there is trouble in the city has the Lord not done it (Amos 3:3-6).

Amos began this argument on the basis that the questions asked would all receive negative answers. He prefaced his basic argument on seven proofs that he thought were irrefutable. Socrates followed the same kind of logic. He first asked a number of questions to which his opponent could only agree. Then he noted the resemblance between the questions asked and the one his opponent opposed (Quintilian 5.11, 3). Quintilian and Aristotle would have taught their law students to challenge some of these, if they had been presented by the opposition. Two might walk together because they were forced to do so. A lion might roar because it had been hurt, and a bird might fall because it had been shot with an arrow. They might also have said that the seven claims do not necessarily lead to the eighth. Greek and Roman rhetoricans, however, would have argued in the same way Amos did if they had needed to support the same argument Amos did.

Jews and Christians called the deductions they made with reference to future apocalyptic anticipations "signs," and they continued to value these signs even when they were later proved false. They may have given these "signs" the same significance law courts gave to legal probabilities which were also called signs. Because signs were probable and not absolute proof, different Jews evaluated the signs Jesus performed differently.

<u>From the Particular to the General</u>. This argument found something that was true of a particular situation and then applied it to a general condition that was somewhat similar. You might begin with the observation that Socrates was both wise and just and argue that because this was true all wise men were also just. Aristotle said this could be refuted, because wisdom was a probable but not a necessary sign. Not all wise men had to be just by definition. On the other hand there

were things that were true of the particular that were always true of the general. For example, if a particular individual had a fever and was ill, you could argue that all people who had fevers were also ill. The same was true of a woman who had milk and also had a child. You might also argue from the general to the particular. Since all men who were trying to become tyrants asked for body guards, when a particular person asked for body guards he was probably aiming at becoming a tyrant, but he might be asking for a body guard for some other reason (Rhetoric 1.2,14-19). This method of arguing was also employed by the rabbis, who, like Aristotle, argued both from the particular to the general (פרט וכלל) and also from the general to the particular (כלל ופרט).

This is not the same as the argument to the great from the small (maiora ex minoribus), such as, "If it is lawful to kill someone caught stealing at night, it is all the more lawful to kill anyone caught stealing in the daytime." Similar is the argument of the small from the great (minora ex maioribus) "Someone who will commit sacrilege, which is great, will also not hesitate to steal, a lesser crime," or from the opposites, such as "if frugality is good, luxury is bad."

Quintilian classified all of these under the title, "similarities." That argues that if something is true of one thing it is also true of something similar. (Quintilian 5.10, 71-74, 86-92). This logic was also applied to geometry and other fields, such as objects that are similar to the same object are similar to each other. The Jewish and Christian custom of using parables fits under this same category. These arguments have other titles, and they were widely used. Perhaps the argument used by rabbis that was the nearest equivalent Quintilian's "similarities" is one which rabbis called gezerah shawah. If a word or phrase was used in the Torah twice, it was permissible to learn from the detail and context of one to clarify the other. The argument usually began "It says here . . . and it says further on . . ." Just as something is true in the second case, so it would also be true of the first instance, and vice versa.[28]

Light and Heavy. Rabbis called these arguments קל וחומר "light and heavy." They are also called a fortiori "to the stronger" arguments. Examples given by Aristotle are: If not even the gods know everything, then imperfect knowledge is all the more true of human beings. If a man beats his own father, he would all the more beat his neighbor. If a person would lie under oath in a court of justice he would all the more tell lies anywhere else. If a person will commit crimes for which there is assigned punishment he or she will all the more commit crimes for which there is no assigned punishment (Rhetoric 1.14,6-7).

According to the rabbis there are ten a fortiori arguments in the Hebrew Scriptures (Gen 44:4-8; Exod 6:12; Deut 31:27; Num 12:14; Jer 12:5 [2]; 1 Sam 23:3; Prov 12:31; Est 9:12; Ezek 15:5). The first of these texts is the response of Jacob's sons when Joseph's servants accused them of stealing a silver cup be

[28]For details of this argument see M. Chernick, "Internal Restraints on Gezerah Shawah's Application," JQR 80 (1990):253-82.

longing to Joseph. They defended themselves with the following argument:

1. Look! The money which we found in the mouth of our sacks, we returned to you from the land of Canaan,
2. how then should we steal silver or gold from your master's house?"

In their commentary on the manna passage, the rabbis said,

1. If God provided in this way for those who angered him,
2. how much more (על אחת כמה וכמה) will he pay a good reward in the future to the righteous (Mekilta Vayassa 4:432-45; see also TSan 7:11).

In a similar way Jesus used forensic arguments to assure his disciples of God's providence:

1. Consider the lilies of the field, the way they grow. They neither toil nor spin, but I tell you not even Solomon in all his glory was dressed like one of these. If the grass of the field which exists today and tomorrow is thrown into the oven, God thus clothes,
2. will he not much more (*πολλῷ μᾶλλον*) clothe you, [people of] little faith (Matt 6:28-30; see also Matt 7:9-11; 12:11-12; for more examples see Rom 5:8-9, 10, 17, 18, 21; 11:12, 15, 24)?

There are several a fortiori arguments in Hebrews (Heb 2:2-4; 9:13-14; 10:28-29; 12:9; 12:25). The first example is as follows:

1. For if the word which was spoken through angels became steadfast, and every transgression and disobedience received just recompense;
2. how shall we escape, having neglected so great a salvation [as this], which had its beginning when it was spoken through the Lord, was confirmed to us by those who heard, while God supported the testimony with signs, wonders, and various kinds of miracles, and by the distribution of the Holy Spirit according to his will?

Rabbis used thirteen arguments such as those given here--Qal wachomer, gezerah shawah, kelal uferat, and ferat ukelal.

THE CONCLUSION

The conclusion is called a peroration by the Latins and an *ἀνακεφαλαίωσις* by the Greeks. Its function is to repeat and regroup the facts of the case so as to refresh the memory of the judge. This should be as brief as possible. In these last statements the prosecuting attorney has to rouse the feelings of the judge, and the defense attorney has to quiet them. The accusing attorney sometimes makes his audience weep as he evokes pity for the client who has been wronged. In the conclusion, as in the introduction, the pleader brings out emotional details of the case that make it specially in need of correction. The victim is a child, an old man, an honest man, or a benefactor to the state. The emotion sometimes became very high. A chief justice (vizier) in Egypt claimed he tolerated the outbursts of the petitioners.[29] The one who committed the injury, on the other hand, is a worthless, contemptible man who was in a position of excessive power which was abused with malice as he afflicted this damage upon an unfortunate victim. In both the introduction and conclusion, the pleader also offers a prayer of relief for the client whom he represents. This will be shown in the next chapter.

[29]Wilson (tr.), "Documents," p. 213.

CHAPTER THREE

WORSHIP IN THE COURTROOM

INTRODUCTION

Ancient advocates concluded their arguments as strongly as possible and expressed at that point the deepest emotion of their arguments. As part of the conclusion, the pleader offered to the judge or jury his "prayer for relief." This is still done by American lawyers today. The prayer for relief was the request that the judge or jury take this occasion to punish the accused and provide healing and vengeance for the plaintiff who had been injured. The defense attorney, on the other hand, would close his argument with a prayer for defense against the injury proposed by the prosecuting attorney.

In form, purpose, and content the prayers for justice offered before king, to the jury, or judge and the religious prayers offered to the deity in times of crisis are very similar. Christians of every age have been emotionally moved by the pathos of the Psalms without realizing their relationship to prayers offered in court environments. Following the methodology encouraged by Quintilian, the Psalmists charged their prayers with emotion. This is evident from some of the terms used in association with prayer. The worshiper "cried out" (צעק), "called" (קרא), "wept" (בכה), was "embittered" (מרר,מר), "afraid" (ירא), "ashamed" (בוש), or was "jealous" (קנא). Four hundred, fifty occurrences of imperatives are found in the Psalms. These are words like: "save," "redeem," "deliver," "ransom," "help," "bring me out," and other similar verbs.[1] The guilty defendant might also plead in the imperative: "Have mercy" or "blot out my transgressions." The court nature of these Psalms are obvious by the use of such associated terms as: "judge" (Ps 7:9; 26:1; 35:24; 43:1) or "contend" (Ps 35:1; 43:1).[2]

Whether worshipers were defendants or plaintiffs they had no indifferent feelings to express. Prayers in civil court come at the end of the argument, after the case has been presented, and the advocate pleads for the judge to rule in favor of the client he represents. It is the last expression of the advocate before judgment. Many biblical prayers, also, assume that the case had already been presented to the Lord.

The Lord was already acquainted with the justice and injustice of the action. The prayer was offered, not to inform the Lord of the problem, but to review the case and plead for the Lord to act in behalf of the pleader. For example Job was planning his concluding prayer of relief when he said, "I will say to God, '. . . You know that I am not guilty'" (Job 10:2-7). In his prayer for relief the Psalmist said, "You know the afflictions of my soul" (Ps 31:7). While plead-

---

[1]So A. Aejmelaeus, The Traditional Prayer in the Psalms (Berlin, 1986), p. 16.

[2]Aejmelaeus, Traditional Prayer, pp. 21-23.

ing for mercy, another Psalmist said, "God, you know my foolishness" (Ps 69:6). A different poet began his prayer for relief, "Lord, you have searched me, and you know me" (Ps 139:1). Prayers to the Lord, like prayers in court, are feelingful expressions. They are offered in times of crisis, when someone has been injured or unjustly treated. These are not times of casual reflection. The terms listed show the feeling the rhetorical worshiper expressed as he presented his case to the divine judge. There are enough preserved prayers in the scripture to provide a fruitful area of research.[3]

Greenberg counted in the Hebrew Scripture one hundred, forty references to prayers and praying mentioned outside of the Psalms. About ninety-seven of these are prayer texts.[4] Some of the earliest forms of literary expression are prayers. This does not surprise many people, because the human longing for communication with the deity is well known. Individual prayers and community prayers have always been a part of religious expression. This chapter will point out the indigenous relationship between court prayers and prayers found in the Bible and related Jewish and Christian religious literature. For example, in one of the scenes visualized in heaven, there was both an altar and a throne pictured together (Rev 8:3-4).

At the golden altar the prayers of all the saints were mingled with incense. Prayers would be fitting either in a court room or in a temple, because both counsels and worshipers offered prayers in Roman times, just as they do today.

The first step will compare two words related to prayer. One of these is of Latin origin; the other is from Hebrew. The second section will compare the posture of biblical prayers with those taken for granted by authors of court cases in Rome. The third division will compare the outlines found in prayers offered on several different occasions, places, and times. Some of these originated in pre-Jewish paganism and others in Jewish and Christian communities. The fourth unit compares letters to prayers, and the fifth shows how worshipers attempt to obtain favor from the judge.

PRAYERS IN COURT

Prayer Terms. Worshipers who offer prayers today follow the same basic pattern that worshipers used in antiquity. The act of offering prayers to plead a case in court was called orare causam. Orare also means to pray, and the orator was an advocate. The address he made to the judge was his oration, his pleading, or his prayer. A lawyer in Greek was called a rhetorician; in Latin he was called an orator or an advocate.

---

[3]E. S.Gerstenberger, Der Bittende Mensch (Germany, 1980), p. 26, listed these emotional terms.

[4]M. Greenberg, Biblical Prose Prayer (Berkeley, c1983), p. 7.

Prayer and Judgment. The Hebrew word palal (פלל) means to "cut," "decide," "appraise," or "judge." The person who heard cases and judged was a pelil (פליל). The Hebrew verb for praying is hitpallel (התפלל), and a prayer is a tephilah (תפלה). Greenberg say the word for praying is a reflexive which means "to seek a judgment for oneself."[5] The exact interpretation is not certain. It might be judged as a passive "to be judged." That which is certain is that prayer in Hebrew is closely related to judgment, and is an understood court term. This probably means the person who was being judged or whose case was being judged was in a position of prayer. He or she was either asking for a verdict as a plaintiff or waiting for a verdict as a defendant.

Recognizing the close relationship between judgment and prayer, Greenberg rendered Psalm 109:7 as follows:

> בהשפטו יצא רשע
> When he sues, let him be found guilty
>
> ותפלתו תהיה לחטאה
> Let his verdict be--conviction.[6]

The word rendered "verdict" here is , usually rendered "his prayer."

There is no instance in the entire Hebrew Scripture where a priest is shown praying, with the exception of Phineas, and he was made a priest after he had performed the act that used the word involved. Scholars have found that use of wayepallel (ויפלל) very difficult to translate. Revised Standard Version has "and interposed," meaning to interfere, interrupt, or come in between.[7] This ren-

---

[5]Ibid., p. 22.

[6]Ibid., p. 22. Note also that this translation correctly presumes that the word, usually translated "wicked," describes one who had been declared "guilty" in court, and the word, usually rendered "sin" is in parallel. These terms are more closely related to court decisions than has usually been thought.

[7]E. A. Speiser, "The Stem PLL in Hebrew," JBL 82 (1963):301-306, was correct in holding that the basic meaning of this Hebrew term was "assess," "reckon," "calculate," "judge." He did not follow his study through to apply his interpretation to the Phineas passage, but it fits in well here, also. When used metaphorically, mythologically, and theologically, the financial metaphors are often used synonymously with legal metaphors. From a theological standpoint, the day of judgment is the same as the day of reckoning. Metaphorically, sins are both debts and crimes. Debts can be forgiven, financially, and crimes can be pardoned, legally, but metaphorically, forgiveness and pardon produce the same results. For example, the Sermon on the Mount reported Jesus teaching his disciples to pray, "Forgive us our debts, as we forgive our debtors" (Matt 6:12). The reference to debts here obviously does not mean financial obligations but sins in relationship to a recording system. Luke clearly understood this meaning, so he changed the wording to read, "Forgive us our sins," but he continued, "as we forgive those who are in debt to us" (Luke 11:4), mixing the terms "sin" and "debt," probably to avoid redundance by

dering was based on the situation in which Phineas acted to stop the mingling with foreigners that Israelites were doing. Placed in a judgment context, this passage might be rendered:

> Then Phineas stood up and judged [the case] (ויפלל),
> and the plague was stayed,
> and that was reckoned for him as righteousness
> from generation to generation to the age (Ps 106:30-31).

Thus interpreted it would mean that Phineas volunteered to judge the legal case against Zimri and his new wife. He instantly determined that they were guilty of a capital offense, and he administered the death penalty himself. As a result, Phineas himself was tried in the heavenly court for his action. The reckoning was done, not to him but for or because of him (לו), because the plague which had been punishing Israelites was stopped. This means their legal case was judged beneficially because of Phineas. Israel was then judged "righteous" (לצדקה) or free from guilt in that performance. In the first case, Phineas took action, and the verb is active (ויפלל); in the second case, he was the recipient of God's judgment, and the verb is passive (ותחשב לו). His request (which is not reported) would have been that he not be judged guilty of this action and that Israel would be spared further punishment. His request would have been his prayer and would have been the passive form of the same Hebrew verb. This word is closely related to court practice.

Judgment Prayer of the Psalmists. Several of the Psalms would have been suitable for judgment prayers. For example:

> Hear a just cause, O Lord;
> pay attention to my cry!
> Give ear to my prayer (ותפלתי) from lips free from deceit!
>
> Let my law suit (משפטי) appear before you!
> Let your eyes see the right (Ps 17:1-2).

---

employing synonyms.

> Phineas rose up (ויעמד) . . . and it was reckoned (ותחשב, (Ps 106:30-31).

These two Hebrew terms were close enough in metaphorical meaning to put them in parallel. That which Phineas did gained pardon for Israel's debt in the treasury of merits. From either metaphor it works out the same. Phineas either took the case to court or he went to the bank and had the mortgage canceled.

The defendant continued to argue that he was completely innocent, that his accusers were unjust, and that he knew of the judge's integrity. He asked that the just punishment his accusers deserved be visited not only upon them, but also upon their descendants. He concluded with an expression of his willingness to be satisfied with the judge's verdict. As if he had been trained by Quintilian, this Psalmist prepared his introduction with emotion, trying to capture the attention of the judge ("Hear a just cause!"), and win the judge's favor by expressing his confidence in the judge, calling him a savior for those who flee to him (Ps 17:6-7).[8] He set out to attract the judge's pity for himself by affirming his own innocence and the cruel abuse of his enemies in emotional terms. He concluded his introductory prayer with a request for relief by punishing the enemies and delivering the worshiper from his dangerous crisis. He also expressed his willingness to be satisfied with the judge's decision (Ps 17:13-15). This prayer seems to have been composed for use at the very beginning of a trial, following known literary techniques of the rhetoricians. The final verse of Psalm 17 also offers insight into the worshiper's posture in prayer.

POSTURES IN PRAYER

> I will see your face in innocence (בצדק)
> When I stand erect, I will be satisfied
> [to see] your form (Ps 17:15).

Facing the Judge. If the defendant acted pro se, he or she evidently either spoke while standing or from a prostrate, prayerful, position. If the defendant had an attorney, the defendant's counsel probably presented his prayer to the judge, while the defendant himself or herself was worshipfully prostrate on the floor before the judge. If the judge requested, the one on trial could rise, face the judge, and receive the verdict. This could only be done if the judge considered the accused to be innocent (צדק). Evidence for this interpretation comes from Josephus's report of trials related to Herod and his children in the first century B.C.

Herod's Sons on Trial. When Herod's son, Alexander, was on trial before Caesar, since he was well-trained in rhetoric, he offered his own defense. There is no mention of his being prostrate, so he probably spoke from a standing position (War 1.452-54). When another son, Antipater, was on trial before Herod and Varus, jointly, in his introductory prayer for relief, he fell prostrate on the floor before Herod, asking only that he not be condemned before his case was heard.

---

[8]M. Greenberg, "On the Refinement of the Conception of Prayer in Hebrew Scriptures," Association for Jewish Studies Review 1 (1976):72, was not completely correct when he held that the Psalmists did not introduce a prayer by first praising God before presenting the petition, as Tosephta Abodah Zarah 7b-8a recommends. Some Psalms begin with praise, and some do not.

After an interruption, he spoke from his prostrate position, only lifting his head so that he could be heard (War 1.627-39). The judge, Varus, did not invite Antipater to rise, and the verdict was negative. Although this technique was not successful for Antipater, Quintilian said it might produce a good effect if the accused throws himself on the ground and embraces the judge's knees (Quintilian 6.1,34).

After Herod's death, his son, Archelaus, was on trial for the position of Herod's successor. He was challenged by Herod Antipas, whose attorney was a certain Antipater who charged Archelaus with incompetence. Archelaus's lawyer was Nicolas who defended Archelaus's legitimate right to Herod's throne. After this argument, Archelaus came forward, fell on his face at Caesar's knees and remained silent until Caesar raised him up, (so that he could see Caesar's face [Ps 17:15]). Josephus said this act of Caesar was an encouraging one to Archelaus (War 2.37).[9]

Humility in Prayer. Not all details are given in every narrative. Alexander may first have given his oration and then presented himself prostrate before Caesar while he heard the verdict, even though this fact was not reported. There may have been some variation in practice, and since these deductions are made on the basis of traditions in different centuries, conclusions can only be tentative. Humility on the part of the defendant in court, however, was considered proper in many ages and countries. For example, Herod was criticized when he appeared in court in royal garments rather than in sack cloth with his hair allowed to grow long (Ant. 14.173), as was customary for a defendant in court.

Quintilian said it was the custom for the advocate of the defense to bring in the accused wearing shabby clothing that had been poorly cared for (Quintilian 6.1, 30). Defendants were to look like mourners. Quintilian said this was effective in gaining sympathy and in reducing punishment (Quintilian 6.1, 33). A certain Roman Vatinas, who was a defendant in court, was criticized for having a white handkerchief. He was expected to be completely outfitted in black (Quintilian 6.3, 60-61). Prayer to God from a prostrate position was an ancient custom in the Near East, and the same position would have seemed proper in other courts besides the ones Josephus observed. If a defendant fell prostrate before the judge, this would probably have been most frequently done at the intro-

[9]E. R. Goodenough, The Jurisprudence of the Jewish Courts in Egypt. Legal Administration by the Jews under the Early Roman Empire as Described by Philo Judaeus (New Haven, 1929), pp. 10-20, argued that Romans allowed Jews to have the same privileges as the Greeks in Cyrene at about 6 B.C. In cases of Greeks against Greeks, Greeks were allowed to judge their own cases, according to their own rules, wherever possible. When the case was very serious, the Roman ruler of the area either took charge of the trial, personally, or he appointed a panel of judges, some of which could be Greeks. Goodenough's case would have been still stronger if he had known about the trial of Archelaus before Caesar, where Jews were allowed to sit with their panel of judges who advised Caesar (War 1.24-25). Sometimes, as with Herod and Pilate, the Roman judge allowed the local judges to make the initial judgment, under Roman supervision. This may also have been the case with Jesus, whose initial trial was before the high priest.

duction of the case, pleading for attention, just before the concluding prayer, or just after the argument and prayer and before the verdict. It is of this anticipation that the Psalmist expressed, probably in his introduction:

> I will see your face in innocence.
> When I stand erect, I will be satisfied
> [to see] your form (Ps 17:15).

If the Psalmist, like Archelaus, after the prayer for relief, had been raised up so that he or she could face the judge, this would probably indicate a verdict of innocence--an action that would have satisfied the Psalmist. That may also have been the action that Job anticipated when he looked forward to a time when his trial would be over and he would be vindicated by the court:

> I know that my redeemer (גאלי) lives
> and that he will finally stand on the dust.
> Then, when they have cut away this skin of mine,
> from my flesh [alone] will I see God,
> whom I shall see for myself--my own eyes--
> and no one else (Job 19:25-27).

Job's famous trial, which seems to be mythological, pictures Job physically tested and harassed--not because of anything he had done, but because God had a wager with Satan to learn whether or not Job could stand all of the testing upon which God and Satan had agreed. Job's so-called "friends" were all witnesses and advocates for the opposition. They were "friends of the court" (amici curiae), offering suggestions and data that was expected to help determine the outcome of the case, but they were supporting Satan rather than Job.

In this court trial Satan was the prosecuting attorney, and God, the judge, had given him the opportunity to torture Job to get a confession from him. The confession which Satan expected to get under torture was that Job would confess to his guilt and would blaspheme God.[10]

Job knew that God was the highest judge, and that no one could be just in comparison with God (Job 9:1). Job had been put on trial with no opportunity to defend himself. He could not answer his accuser, so even though he was innocent, he had to plead only for mercy (Job 9:14-15). He wished God himself would speak in the midst of this trial of a blameless and innocent man (Job 11:5; 12:4). Even though the judge (God) had allowed the prosecuting attorney (Satan) to put Job under torture, and even though he was actually innocent, if the court

---

[10]The religious word, "confession," like the religious word, "martyr," comes from a court context. When Jewish and Christian martyrs were tortured, like Job, they confessed that they were Jews or Christians. This automatically meant that they were saboteurs to the pagan nation in which they were being tried.

decreed that he was guilty he would have had to endure the punishment associated with the guilt of which he was accused. There was no direct relationship between that which was real innocence and that which was legal innocence. If, instead of torturing Job for a confession, the judge would allow Job to speak before the Almighty and argue his case with him in court (Job 13:3), Job was sure he would win. Even in his frustration, Job somehow was confident of final vindication. It was true that a godless person had no right to appear before God, but Job had a good case prepared (Job 13:16-18); he had committed no crimes, and no one could prove that he had (Job 13:23). In this trial he had to stand alone; no one would put up bail for him, vouch for his integrity, or support him in any way. He had no compurgators, but he still trusted the system. Some unknown redeemer would appear, and Job would get his chance to appear in court. If ever this happened, the outcome was certain. Even though he had been tortured until his skin was all gone, he would stand before God in his raw flesh, all bloody and wounded, and see him face to face the way a person does in court after the judge has heard his case and ruled in his favor.

The torture Job suffered was part of ordinary court practice. When a court trial came to a point where the judge or one of the attorneys doubted the statement of a witness or person being tried, the officials involved could put that person on the rack and torture him or her until the person confessed, died, or the torturers yielded. In this case the person being tried was tortured even if he or she was innocent, as Job claimed was the case in his situation. During the last years of Herod the Great, Herod was suspicious of many members of his family or court, so he frequently practiced torture to exact confessions: Herod's eunuchs (War 1.489); two commanders of his cavalry (War 1.527); Tiro, his son, and a barber (War 1.548); two Arabs (War 1.577); some ladies who had status (War 5.84); some female slaves (War 1.586); a Samaritan agent (War 1.592); and the mother and brother of Antiphilus (War 1.598). In some of these cases, people confessed rather than accept more torture. It is not certain, however, whether they confessed the truth or whether they told lies. In spite of all the friends of the court who came to advise Job to confess his crimes, he would have faced death rather than confess falsely. His whole drama was based on the injustice of a court system that could torture the innocent, but the author of this drama wanted readers to believe that life was like a faulty court system where people were tortured unjustly.

Malachi pictured an important judgment scene when the Lord's legal agent (מלאך) would arrive in court (the temple), take his position at the bench, and begin to entertain the cases Jews wanted brought to trial. Malachi, however, doubted the validity of their case. He asked who would survive such a trial. Who would stand when this judge appeared (Mal 3:2)? Those who survived the trial were the ones vindicated. They would be the ones the judge would ask to stand on their feet before him while he pronounced a favorable verdict. Malachi, however, was asking rhetorical questions. He really meant that no one would stand. All those who requested the trial and wanted the judge to come and conduct a court trial would be found guilty at such a trial as they wanted.

In some cultures torture was used in court trials right up to the twentieth century. In New Mexico, for instance, Pueblos used to hang suspects from the rafters and beat them until they made a confession. One pueblo principale said, "'And they would fasten a man with his neck in a log, his hands bound together so he could not move. Sometimes eight days without food or drink, until nothing was left but skin and bones. Nobody took care of him.'"[11]

In the fifth century B.C., Aristotle (Rhetoric 1.15, 14-26), and as late as the first century A.D., Quintilian recommended to his law students the judicious use of torture (Quintilian 5.pr.4, 1.2-4.2). Following court practice of the Near East, Job's torture may have been understood as part of a court trial in which he was tortured to see if he would break down and tell the "truth." There are other parts of a trial in Job: he spoke of a judge, judgment, witnesses, accusations, crimes, surety, arguments, redeemers, and vindication. In the same context where he claimed he would be vindicated, he also said his torture would sometime come to an end, and he, with his own eyes, would see God. This may have been with the understanding that God was his judge who would acknowledge his innocence by asking him to stand before him the way one of Herod's sons stood before Caesar before he was judged favorably.[12]

OUTLINES IN PRAYER

Before a Court Judge. A thirteenth century B.C. defendant in court prayed to his god, Amon:

> O Amon, give thy ear to one who is alone in the law court, who is poor; he is not rich. The court cheats him of silver and gold for the scribes of the mat and clothing for the attendants. May it be found that Amon assumes his form as the vizier, in order to permit the poor man to get off. May it be found that the poor man is vindicated. May the poor man surpass the rich.[13]

This defendant apparently had failed in lower courts, and was appealing his case to the vizier himself. Like modern clients in court, he had learned that

---

[11]E. A. Hoebel, "Keresan Pueblo Law," L. Nader (ed.), Law in Culture and Society (Chicago, c1969), p. 109.

[12]Previous scholars have argued about whether the redeemer was God or a human being, whether Job stood before God in this life or after death, whether or not this is a witness to the resurrection. See S. R. Driver and G. B. Gray, A Critical and Exegetical Commentary on the Book of Job (in 2 vols; New York, 1921) I, pp. 171-75).

[13]J. R. Wilson (tr.), Pritchard (ed.), Ancient, p. 380.

court costs and the fees of lawyers (scribes) were very expensive, and he thought his attempts at finding justice were lining the pockets of legal officials. In antiquity judges were understood to be legal agents of the deity (see Deut 1:16-17; 2 Chron 19:5-7). In Egypt the vizier was the highest judge in the land. This petitioner, however, did not assume that the vizier automatically spoke the words of his god, Amon, just because of his position. If he were vindicated, he probably would have concluded that the words of the vizier were the words of his god. His prayer, however, was to the god, Amon, and not to the vizier himself.

This worshiper followed many of the rhetorical devices which Quintilian advised his students to include both in the introduction and in the conclusion of the argument: 1) He should gain the favor and good will of the judge by flattering the judge and relating his cause to the known character and status of the judge. The worshiper did this by identifying the vizier with the god Amon and himself as a man in need. 2) He should appeal to the sympathy of the judge by describing his cause in dramatic terms. The worshiper told how needy he was and how unjustly he had been treated by lower courts. 3) He then made his request that would provide justice for him. 4) This would also be beneficial to the judge who would be recognized as the agent of Amon and one who vindicates the poor and needy. Quintilian said that whenever the advocate found a judge leaning away from his wishes, the advocate might subtly threaten the judge by implying some consequences that might not be advantageous to the judge himself if he should rule against the case of the advocate. Here the litigant had already been overruled by a lower court and realized the odds were against him, so, in good rhetorical style, he put a condition on the vizier being a true agent of Amon. This would be contingent upon his judgment of this case.

This prayer would probably have received a high grade if it had been composed by one of Quintilian's law students. This worshiper, however, lived fifteen hundred years before the time of Quintilian and a thousand years before Aristotle. This shows that some of these techniques taught by the rhetoricians were not created by them. They had been employed much earlier. Not only had they been known by this early appellant but they were also reportedly known by Jacob when he offered his prayer while returning to his homeland.

Before a heavenly Judge. A biblical prayer of Jacob had the following points: 1) Address to the deity,[14] 2) attribution to the deity, 3) request of the worshiper, 4) motivation for the deity to fulfill the request.

1) God of my father, Abraham, and God of my father,

---

[14]Greenberg, Prose, p. 10, separated the address to the deity into four sections: 1) Address, 2) description, 3) self-deprecation, and 4) detail. These are all valid parts, but they are sub-units, all of which flatter the judge and prepare the judge to decide this case in the worshiper's favor. These are all normal parts of prayers for relief, either at the first or at the conclusion of a trial, following the rules given by rhetoricians, like Quintilian and Aristotle.

> Isaac, Lord, 2) who told me, "Return to your land, and I will make you prosperous," I am too insignificant for all the faithfulness and all the truth which you have done to your servant, because [when I left the promised land] I crossed this Jordan with [only] my staff. Now I am here [again, returning] with two camps; 3) deliver me, please, from the hand of my brother, from the hand of Esau, because I fear him lest he come and kill me, the mothers, and the children [who are with me]. 4) But you said, "I will surely make you prosperous"--I will make your posterity like the sand on the sea [shore], which cannot be counted because of its large quantity (Gen 32:10-13).

Greenberg correctly observed that formulated prayers followed a simple pattern: 1) address, 2) petition, and 3) motivating sentence. He interpreted this to mean that the outline of prayer was so well known that ordinary, untrained lay people would have known how to compose prayers extemporaneously for any occasion. One of his examples was the beautiful benediction of Abraham's servant (Gen 24:27) when he discovered Rebekah.[15] Greenberg's observation of liturgical structure is correct, but the idea that this literary benediction or the prayer of Jacob was a verbatim, extemporaneous composition of Jacob or Abraham's servant seems unlikely. The entire narrative of the acquisition of Rebekah for Isaac (Gen 24) is a literary masterpiece throughout, and the author of the entire unit probably composed the benediction as well, just as Thucidydes, Josephus, and the author of Acts all composed the speeches the authors thought would have been appropriate to have been made on certain occasions. It was not Jacob and the servant, but the authors who composed these narratives in Genesis, who were well-acquainted with proper literary form for a prayer. These stylistic forms had been developed by still earlier rhetoricians for their use in court rooms.

Collect for Purity. A modern formal Christian prayer, called a "collect," normally has five points: 1) Address to the deity, 2) attributions to the deity, 3) request of the worshiper, 4) motivation for the deity to fulfill the request, and 5) the identity of the worshiper in relationship to the Lord's agent, Jesus. A well-known collect for purity of heart is as follows:

[15]Greenberg, Prose, pp. 17, 30-32. Whereas Greenberg explained the ability of Hebrews to pray the appropriate prayer on the spur of the moment to known outlines that could be filled in spontaneously, J. H. Tigay, "On Some Aspects of Prayer in the Bible," Association for Jewish Studies Review 1 (1976):376-77, said ancients had memorized standard prayers for special occasions. Some of these were even used interchangeably by worshipers of different deities. Both scholars assume that the prayers given were actually prayed in the historical situation as reported and not the work of the person who composed the narratives.

1) Almighty God,
2) unto whom all hearts are open, all desires known, and from whom no secrets are hid,
3) cleanse the thoughts of our hearts by the inspiration of thy Holy Spirit,

4) that we may perfectly love thee and worthily magnify thy holy name,
5) through Christ, our Lord.

This differs only from the three point outline Greenberg accepted by the addition of sub-points two and five, both of which might be included as parts of the three point outline. Two is part of one, and five is part of four. The three basic points are 1) address, 3) request, and 4) motivating sentence.[16]

Prayer to a King. An ancient court prayer of the second millennium B.C. has basically the same structure:

1) To my king
2) with varicolored eyes who wears a lapis lazuli beard, speak;
to the golden statue fashioned on a good day, the . . . raised in a pure sheepfold,
called to the pure womb of Inanna, the lord, hero of Inanna, say: "Thou in thy judgment,
thou art the son of Anu. Thy commands, like the word of a god, cannot be turned back; thy words, like rain pouring down from heavens, are without number."
5) Thus says Urshagga, thy servant: "My king has cared for me, who is a son of Ur.
3) If now my king is [the son of] of Anu, let not my father's house be carried off.
Let not the foundations of my father's house be torn away. Let my king know."[17]

It is not clear exactly what the situation was in which this prayer was made. It is directed to the king, but he was described as someone with a lapis lazuli beard who was himself a golden statue. This may mean the prayer was ad-

---

[16]Motivating sentences in the Psalms are usually given in prepositional phrases, such as, "in your righteousness," "because of your loving kindness," "according to your word," "because of your great mercy," or "for the sake of your name." Another type of motivating clause is the use of the particle, "lest" (פן) The judge is urged to give the kind of verdict the worshipers asks, "lest" something tragic happen (Ps 7:2-3; 13:4-5; 28:1). So Aejmelaeus, Traditional Prayer, pp. 60-63, 67.

[17]S. N. Kramer (tr.), "Petition to a King," Pritchard (ed.), Ancient, p. 382.

dressed to an idol. The prayer may have been left at the base of an idol, where messages could have been left for the king. Later, servants of the king might have picked up all of the messages left there and given them to the king. The worshiper knew that the king had the authority of the god, Anu, when it came to judgment. Like the judges appointed by Moses or Jehoshaphat he functioned as an agent of the deity.

Another possibility is that in ancient Near Eastern antiquity people addressed deity figures in ways like that. The god Anu may have been described as the king with varicolored eyes and a lapis lazuli beard the mythological way the divine figure was described in Daniel. While Daniel was praying he received a message from a character who was clothed in linen. His loins were covered with the gold of Uphaz. His body was like beryl, and his face was like lightning; his eyes were like flaming torches; and his arms and legs were like shining bronze (Dan 10:5-6). There is not enough data to know the answer to this question, but we know more about Urshagga's prayer.

This prayer includes four of the five essential points for a twentieth century liturgical Christian collect: 1) address to the king, 2) attributes of the king which enable him to grant the request, and 3) the petition which the worshiper wanted the king to grant. There is no fourth point--no motivating sentence showing the way these results would be beneficial. Urshagga reminded the king of the king's responsible position and his obligation to Anu to judge fairly. 5) The fifth point of the Christian prayer identified the worshiper as a follower of the Lord's agent, the Messiah. In Urshagga's prayer he accomplished this result by identifying himself as a servant of the king and therefore entitled to certain privileges not granted to foreigners.[18]

The conclusion, "Let my king know," may be a formal liturgical ending, similar to the Christian or Jewish, "Amen." The word, Amen, is also a court term, noting that the worshiper is under oath, just as he or she would be testifying in court (Num 5:11-22; Mekilta Kaspa 2:46-48). Although there are not many ancient court prayers with which to compare this, its similarity to formal Christian collects, biblical prayers, and necessary parts of conclusions to arguments in courts according to Greek and Latin rhetoricians, suggests the possibility that ancient court prayers were something like this. Prayers to gods and prayers to

[18]The idea that every person has the same status in court had developed with democracy. In ancient courts, even though judges were exhorted to show no preferential treatment, this was understood within classes. A slave was not expected to have the same rights as a citizen, Anglo-Saxons had a legal system of ranking participants. People who owned property were appraised as "compurgators," according to the amount of land they owned. The testimony of a compurgator who was evaluated as ten times that of another was rated as equal to ten other compurgators. Compurgators were not used as witnesses in court for or against cases, but they testified to the credibility of the accused or the accuser. Sometimes cases could be settled without trial on the basis of the number and value of the compurgators lined up on each side. See W. Forsyth, Trial by Jury (New York, 1878), pp. 61-63.

judges were probably similar in style and purpose.

Gerstenberger has examined numerous literary requests in the scripture, and he learned that there was a rhetorical structure to prayers which were addressed neither to a court nor to God, but to someone like David (1 Sam 25:24-31), Joseph (Gen 47:18-19), or Sarai (Gen 12:11-13).[19] This further extends the importance of rhetoric in understanding ancient literature. Either the influence of rhetoric in court was so great that it became known by other ancient authors who were not rhetoricians related to the court, such as religious authors, or it was so widely known, generally, that it also found its way into the court.

PRAYER LETTERS

Comparisons. In his examination of Sumerian literature, Prof. Hallo noticed that some of the prayers were very similar to Sumerian letters in structure.[20] They were composed as if the worshiper had written a letter to the deity. Once this has been called to our attention, it is obvious that many prayers are offered as if they were letters. There are respectful salutations and formal complimentary closings in both. Letters usually begin with something like, "Dear Lucy," "Ladies and Gentlemen," "Honorable Sir," "Reverend Madam," or "Highly esteemed Mr. Vielwörter." Prayers begin with salutations like, "Dear Lord and Father of us all," "Almighty God," or "Most merciful God, creator and preserver of all humankind." Letters close with some formality like, "Sincerely yours," "Your loving husband," "With much gratitude," "In friendship," or "Your humble servant." Christian prayers formally close with, "In Jesus' name" or "Through Christ, our Lord."

Special kinds of letters have special inner structures. For example, in a letter of application, there are normally four paragraphs with the following content: 1) The author has heard of a vacancy and would like to be considered an applicant, 2) the author's ability, experience, and training that makes him or her qualified for the position, 3) the names, addresses, and telephone numbers of people who are qualified to speak further about her or his ability and character, and 4) the author's willingness to answer further questions or to be present at the reader's convenience for a personal interview should that be desired. Community prayers also have normal outlines of 1) adoration, 2) confession, 3) thanksgiving, and 4) supplication.

When attorneys in court address the judge, the opening formalities are also similar to read letters: "Mr. Chief Justice" or "Your honor, I realize your deep concern for justice and prompt law enforcement . . ." "Your honor, your record

---

[19]E. S. Gerstenberger, Mensch, pp. 53-59, et passim.

[20]W. W. Hallo, "Individual Prayer in Sumerian: The Continuity of a Tradition," JOAS 88 (1968):77-79.

shows your compassion for the oppressed and your courage in resisting the abuse of the rich and powerful . . ." Kantorowicz offered the following as suitable introductions: "The command of Reason presides in the mind of the judge," "Justice herself examining truth sits on the bench," or "Righteousness of Judgment is seated like a king on his throne."[21] There is not enough data to show how letters came to be structured like court prayers or how court prayers came to follow the same basic structure as letters, but the similarity is thought-provoking. All letters have three basic units: 1) the salutation, 2) the body, and 3) the closing. Prayers have similar units. According to Greenberg prayers were organized according to a simple pattern: 1) address, 2) petition, and 3) motivating sentence.

Salutation. Some Christian and Jewish prayers of judgment presume that the facts are already before the court or soon will be. The prayer, then, is the direct address to the judge for action. The first two points prepared the judge to consider the third point from the worshiper's point of view. Some ancient prayers begin by 1) addressing the Lord and 2) listing his attributions as follows:

Most powerful King, almighty God, who rules all creation with mercy . . ." (3 Macc 6:2).

> Lord almighty, who is in heaven, you, God of our fathers--
> of Abraham, Isaac, Jacob, and their righteous seed--
> you who made heaven, earth, and all their ornamentation,
> who tied up the sea by the word of your command,
> who locked up the deep and sealed it,
> whom all things fear--yes, they tremble at your power;
> for the majesty of your glory cannot be tolerated,
> and the anger of your threats against sinners is unendurable.
> Immeasurable and unfathomable is the mercy of your promise,
>
> for you are a lord who is most high, compassionate, long suffering,
> and very merciful, repenting for the evil acts of men
> (Hermas, Mand. 1-8)

Lord, God of Israel, who brought up your people from the land of Egypt with a mighty hand, with signs, wonders, with great power, and a raised arm, who has earned a name for yourself . . . (Bar 2:11).

Opening sentences of prayer were standard, and liturgical formulas were established very early. For example in an ancient Babylonian prayer, the following salutation was addressed to Marduk,

---

[21]E. H. Kantorowicz, Two Bodies, p. 139.

Marduk, Great Lord, compassionate God, who holds firm the hand of the fallen, who releases those who are tied . . .

The same opening formula was also addressed to Zalbatainu in a different prayer by a different worshiper.[22]

Address to the Judge. Traditional remnants of the ancient court prayers are preserved in the opening demand or the final request, which are considered "the prayer." Judging from the limited data available, ancient courts seem to have had a similar place in the court program for prayers. Prayers like these were offered for the purpose of evoking from the presiding judge a favorable decision, but there are procedural prayers that are usually addressed to the judge at the beginning of the argument. For example, in the United States Supreme Court today, counsels who address the court are advised not to speak until the chief justice invites them. When invited, counsel begins the oration with the words, "Mr. Chief Justice, and may it please the court." In the first century B.C., when Antipater began his defense, he fell prostrate and prayed that he not be condemned in advance but that his case be given a fair hearing (War 1. 621). Quintilian said it was good oratory to ask the attention of the judges at the beginning of the trial, using such expressions as, "I beg you, gentlemen, to give me your attention at this point," or "Listen now to that which follows" (Quintilian 4.1, 73-74).

The formal introduction of the pleading with the words, "May it please the court," is similar to the one often used by the clergy in the twentieth century at the beginning of the sermon in a worship service. In both instances, these humble requests for consideration of the case that is to follow come from ancient traditions. The minister or priest simply quotes a passage from one of the Psalms:

> May the words of my mouth
> and the meditations of my heart
> find favor before you, O Lord,
> my rock and my redeemer (Ps 19:15).

The Body. That which is the body of a letter is comparable to the basic request in a court prayer. This was the heart of the hearing which the advocate wanted the judge or judges to grant as a result of the arguments offered. The chosen people assumed that part of the important data that the Lord should have before him before making judgment was the ad hominem facts of his contractual relationship to them which reflected on him either adversely or positively. Today, prayers are still a part of court proceedings, but they are nowhere nearly as elaborate or flattering as ancient prayers. Today they function as the initial presentation of the complaint and/or the final request to the judge after all witnesses have been exa-

[22]Gerstenberger, Mensch, pp. 94-96.

mined, data presented, and argument completed. These are usually brief and formal. These are called "prayers for relief." For example, in a modern court, after the respectful salutation, a plaintiff prayed:

(1) that the defendant here reconvey and transfer to plaintiff an undivided one-half interest in said personal property and lease, or, in lieu thereof, that the said personal property be sold and plaintiff receive from the proceeds thereof such an amount of money as the court might find from the evidence that the equity of the case should warrant. (2) that the defendant J. L. Smith be restrained by injunction from disposing of * * * said property * * * (3) that the plaintiff have such other and further relief as may be just and equitable, together with her costs and disbursements incurred herein.[23]

Prayer for Relief. In biblical times, some prayers were addressed to the Lord as if they were being conducted in a court room. In desperation, one defendant skipped all of the preliminaries and began his oration to the judge as follows:

> O God [I pray for you] to deliver me;
> O Lord [I pray for you] to help me quickly!
> Let those be ashamed and confused who seek
> my life (Ps 70:1-2).

Asking further for punishment for his accusers and help for himself, the psalmist concluded:

> I am poor and needy--Hurry, Lord (Ps 70:6)!

The following prayer was made by a defendant who evidently needed the judge's mercy more than his objective judgment. Therefore he spent most of the prayer reminding God of God's good and forgiving nature, his ability to deliver, his patience, and his steadfast love. This prayer concentrated on points three, four, and five of a collect: 3) request, 4) motivation (you will have helped me), and 5) the status of the worshiper (I am a pious man).

> Extend your ear, O Lord, and answer me, for I am poor and needy.
> Guard my life, for I am a pious man.
> Save your servant (Ps 86:1-2).

He concluded in the following way:

> Turn to me, and be kind to me!
> Give your strength to your male servant;

---

[23]F. Kerschner v. J. L. Smith, Pacific Reporter 256:196.

deliver the son of your female slave!
Provide me a sign of your goodness,
and let those who hate me be embarrassed,
for you, O Lord, [will] have helped me
and comforted me (Ps 86:16-17).

Another Psalmist reflected a similar feeling:

Deliver me, O Lord, from evil men;
preserve me from men of violence
who plot evil in their hearts.
All day long they stir up war.
Their tongues are sharp like a snake,
and under their tongues is the venom of vipers
(Ps 140:10-12).

In this Psalm the preliminaries were by-passed, and the worshiper began immediately with point three (the request). This theme was repeated many times before the author closed with points two (qualifications of the judge) and four (motivation for giving a positive verdict):

I know that the Lord renders judgment in behalf of the poor,
justice for the needy.
Therefore the righteous will give thanks to your name;
the just ones will sit before you (Ps 140:13-14).

A defendant pleaded his case before the Lord as follows:

O Lord, hear my prayer;
give a receptive ear to my requests.
In your faithfulness, answer me in your justice.
Do not enter into judgment with your servant,
for no one is innocent before you (Ps 143:1-2).

The worshiper concluded with a repetition of his request (point 3), following it with a motivation, arguing for the positive benefits there would be to the Lord if he followed the worshiper's demand (the reflection this action would have on the Lord's reputation) (point 4), and reminding the Lord of the worshiper's identity (your servant) (point 5):

Save my life, Lord, for the sake of your name!
In your righteousness, deliver my life from trouble!
In your loving kindness [to me] cut off my enemies;

destroy all my adversaries,
for I am your servant (Ps 143:11-12).

The Closing. The last part of a letter is the complimentary closing, and the last point of the formal Christian collect is an appeal to the Lord to consider the petitioner's identity, and grant the worshiper special favor because of that. The judge was reminded that the worshiper was a Christian, and considered [Jesus, the] Christ to be his or her Lord. Although Moses warned the judges he anointed to be careful not to show favoritism in judgment (Deut 1:17), the chosen people have a long history of relying heavily on God's special treatment in judgment. This may not have been as improper in those days as it seems today. In antiquity, slaves, foreigners, and non-citizens were not given the same consideration as citizens. Quintilian encouraged law students to elicit the sympathy and good will of the judge by calling attention to important characteristics of the client: he or she was old, infirm, poor, young, inexperienced, highly respected, a person of good character, a citizen, or an officer of good standing with an honorable record. This was to be included in the introduction and/or the conclusion of the argument in court.

The commandment not to show favoritism in judgment may have meant not to judge a citizen or a slave unfairly according to his or her status. Therefore a person on trial reminded the judge of these qualities as a citizen so as not to be confused for a slave or a foreigner. Paul is reported to have received corrected treatment from Roman rulers and officers when they learned that he was also a Roman citizen (Acts 15:37; 23:27). In the court session held after Jerusalem had been destroyed, Titus released only those Jews captured who were also Roman citizens (War 6.383-84). People who thought they were "chosen" by God were no more bashful about claiming their special favoritism with God than they were about claiming their privileges as citizens of the state. This is evident in the priestly benediction. This ancient prayer asks,

> May the Lord look upon you with favor and be kind to you;
> may the Lord show you favoritism [when he judges]
> and give you peace (probably means "declare you innocent")
> (Num 6:25-26).

CONTROLLING THE JUDGE

Trained Oratory. By the time of the closing prayer it is sometimes evident to the counsel for the defense that the case is moving toward the opposition. In that case, both in modern prayers in court and in ancient biblical prayers, the defense attorney included within the prayer part of the argument needed to persuade the judge to change the position that seems to be predominating. Quintilian said this required some of the best skill of the advocate. The following are offered as prose examples of prayers for justice,[24] all of which are examples of an advocate on the defensive, trying to persuade the judge to change his mind:

Crisis in the Wilderness. When Moses stood before the divine Judge after the Israelites started a movement to go back to Egypt and abandon the project led by Moses and Aaron, the Lord threatened to destroy them with a disease and disinherit them (Num 14:1-12). Moses questioned the Lord's judgment. He reminded God that such a plan would damage the Lord's reputation among the Gentiles. It would show that the Lord was not capable of fulfilling his promises or carrying his plans to completion. Moses encouraged the Lord to be as great as he had promised, since it was basic to the Lord's character to be patient, full of steadfast love, and willing to forgive (Num 14:13-19). This is precisely the kind of flattery accompanied with a threat to the judge that Quirinius recommended to his law students. He said they should do this only when it was clear that the judge was prejudiced against the side of the case the advocate was representing. While threatening the Lord with the possible consequences of the Lord's proposed action, Moses did not suggest that the people go unpunished, but that they not be annihilated. His prayer for relief asked for a mitigation of punishment.

Abraham's Rhetoric. When the hypothetical prosecuting attorney presented to the Lord the many sins committed by the people of Sodom and Gomorrah, the Lord was prepared to lay down the law against the entire cities, but Abraham's prayer for mitigation asked the rhetorical question, "Will you really destroy the righteous with the wicked" (Gen 18:23)? Quintilian would have approved this rhetorical question, and he would not have been surprised to learn that Abraham finally persuaded the Judge to reduce the sentence by enough to rescue Lot and his family (Gen 18:23-19:29).

Status of the Judge. When the Israelites made and worshiped a golden calf, the Lord was prepared again to destroy them, but Moses again employed a rhetorical device teachers of oratory would have approved. He entered his prayer for relief, which included a request to the Lord that he think of what this action would do for his reputation. He also reminded the Lord of the promises he had made to Abraham, Isaac, and Jacob. The Lord was persuaded by Moses' argument (Exod 32:1-14).

Mitigating a Sentence. When Joshua lost a battle against the town of Ai, Joshua understood this eventuality as a negative judgment by the Lord. He tore his clothes, prostrated himself on the ground before the chest containing the contract, and entered his prayer for relief. This was in accordance with the rhetoricians' advice for humility on the part of the defendant and mourning attire before the

---

[24]The examples given here were suggested by S. E. Balentine, "Prayers for Justice in the Old Testament: Theodocy and Theology," CBQ 51 (1989):597-616.

judge. Joshua's argument asked the Lord if he had brought the Israelites across the Jordan only to have them destroyed by the Amorites. Then the Lord explained the prosecution's case against the Israelites. The Israelites had broken the contract they made with the Lord (Josh 7:2-11), and their sin would have to be punished before God would judge again in their favor. Then Joshua acted to punish the offenders. The Lord was not persuaded by Joshua's complaint, but mitigated the planned sentence by giving Joshua an opportunity to cure the situation (Josh 7:12-26).

In these cases, the text did not point out that these prayers were structured in court terms or that the one who offered the prayer thought of himself as a defendant before the judge in court, but the nature of the requests and the defendant's posture of prostration in some cases show the understood purpose and situation of the prayers for relief.

CONCLUSIONS

There are more similarities among the various prayers of worshipers, letters, pleadings in court, and prayers for relief than people normally suppose. Prayers in the court room, those offered in behalf of a congregation, and those individual prayers to God are all very similar in structure to letters addressed to friends, business associates, or officials with authority of some kind. The messages of prayers and Psalms are more easily understood when their function is recognized in a court setting.

Individual prayers and prayers of the community offered today in churches and synagogues are similar to modern and ancient prayers for relief. In community prayers sometimes an official clergy leader defends the congregation like an advocate in court offering a prayer for relief. When groups of people join to pray for one cause they resemble friends of the court (amici curiae) or those ancient witnesses and partisans who used to take sides in court trials and stand ready to witness or argue in behalf of the side they supported. The extent of positive comparison between church and court worship provides one more area for understanding relationship between the court and the church. The next chapter will deal with the court setting itself in relationship to two important passages of scripture.

CHAPTER FOUR

LOVE AND CONTRACTUAL THEOLOGY

INTRODUCTION

This chapter will examine the importance and legal significance of the contract. It will study the meaning of secular contracts, biblical contracts, the marriage contracts. Also under consideration will come the parties to the contract, the terms of the contract, the oaths of contracts, the blessing and curses that accompany contracts, and the love that is involved in making contracts.

TYPES OF CONTRACTS

Secular Contracts. A great deal of time is spent in court making decisions in relationship to contracts. Contracts are made when purchases are undertaken, weddings are performed, laborers are employed, treaties are made, divorces are granted, wills are written, leases are signed, and other agreements are concluded. The sixteenth-century English word for contract was "covenant," and this is the word that is still used in modern English Bible translations of the Hebrew and Greek words for "contract." Most Westerners understand something about contracts. They sign contracts frequently in ordinary life and business. An effort is made here to show that the contract is the word used also in the Bible and that "covenant" is only an early English word that has the same meaning. "Covenant" is not a specially theological word of any kind. Like most religious words, it began in a situation where everything was both secular and religious. There was no separation of church and state. When religious activities were separated from secular ones, the word "contract" came up on both sides. In American and English religious circles, however, it was called "covenant." The importance of the treaties or contracts is evident to anyone who examines all of the usages of the terms for contract in the Hebrew Scriptures. Mendenhall was correct when he concluded from his study of treaties and contracts that "[t]heology and jurisprudence have a great deal in common."[1]

Validity of Contracts. Contracts in antiquity were also very common and very important. Greeks required six witnesses for an ordinary contract, usually including an accurate personal description of the witness. Identifying marks such as scars, birthmarks, color of hair, and other such peculiarities, were included.[2] In ancient Mesopotamian documents that have survived, contracts had as few as three wit-

---

[1]G. E. Mendenhall, Law and Covenant in Israel and the Ancient Near East (Pittsburgh, 1955), p. 3.

[2]A. A. Trites, The New Testament Concept of Witness (Cambridge, 1977), p. 10.

nesses and as many as eighteen,[3] but they also sometimes listed in addition to human witnesses natural phenomena, such as heaven, earth, rivers, and mountains, as well as all of the gods of the nations involved.[4] Ancient treaties included the following standard parts: 1) preamble, 2) historical prologue, 3) stipulations, 4) demands for deposit and public reading, 5) witnesses, 6) blessings and curses.[5]

Biblical Contracts. The term berit (ברית) in most English translations of the Bible is usually rendered "covenant," although there are a few cases when berit so clearly involves a treaty, will, or compact that it is translated accordingly (2 Chron 23:1; Neh 9:38; 1 Sam 11:1-2; Gal 3:15). Most scholars have assumed that there is little or no difference between the popular translation "covenant" and the meaning of "contract."[6] Tucker has attempted to show that there was a difference in procedure between private business contracts and international treaties. He called the latter "covenants" and the former "contracts,"[7] but in the scripture the same Hebrew term, berit (ברית) was used for all types of agreements that were formal, whether they were made between God and Israel, kings and people, kings of different nations, or individuals. The term, "covenant," is an English translation decision--not a distinction made in antiquity. Since they were all legal, they were all agreements that today would be understood as "contracts" or "treaties."[8] The following analysis will show this:

Seven times in Hebrew Scriptures this term refers to the agreement made between Noah and God (Gen 6; Exod 24:7), twenty-six times, between God and

---

[3]J. J. Finkelstein (tr.), "Documents from the Practice of Law," J. B. Pritchard (ed.), Ancient Near Eastern Texts (Princeton, 1969), pp. 542-47.

[4]Mendenhall, "Covenant," ID I, p. 715.

[5]Ibid., pp. 714-15.

[6]A. Bentzen, Introduction to the Old Testament (Copenhagen, 1959) I, p. 210; A. Weiser, The Old Testament: Its Formation and Development, tr. D. M. Barton (New York, 1961), p. 55; M. Weber, Ancient Judaism, tr. H. Gerth and D. Martindale (Glencoe, 1952), pp. 78-79; D. J. McCarthy, Treaty and Covenant (Rome, 1963), pp. 4, 47, 149; and G. M. Tucker, "Covenant Forms and Contract Forms," VT 15 (1965):487-503. For more on forms see P. Buis, "Les Formulaires d'Alliance," VT 16 (1966):396-411, and "La Nouvelle Alliance," VT 18 1968):1-15.

[7]Tucker, "Witnesses and 'Dates' in Israelites Contracts," CBQ 28 (1966):42-45, also considered agreements made orally. J. A. Thompson, "Covenant (OT)," International Standard Bible Encyclopedia (Grand Rapids, c1979) I, p. 791, arbitrarily chose to use the term "covenant" to refer to the contract between "God and man," but he made no claim that this contract or treaty was in any way different from other treaties or contracts in antiquity.

[8]O. Lorenz, "Berit-'Band-Bund,'" VT 16 (1966):239-41, has shown satisfactorily, on the basis of both Akkadian and Ugaritic backgrounds, that the word berit comes from a root that means "to bind." It is something held together by a bond, chain, or rope. The binding material, of course, is legal and not material.

Abraham.[9] This was an agreement whereby the descendants of the patriarchs were obligated to keep the commandment of circumcision and God promised to give them the land and posterity.[10] It was called a sworn promise and an everlasting contract. Sometimes the reference was just made to the contract as if everyone knew what it was, but it was not always the same contract that was under discussion. There was the contract made with the fathers, but there was another made at Horeb when the people agreed to observe the ten commandments which were kept in a special chest.[11] Those which were kept in the chest on the altar were sometimes referred to as the "tables of the contract" (Exod 31:18; Deut 9:9, 11, 15). The words of the contract were the ten "words,"[12] the ordinances (Deut 7:12), or the book of the contract (Exod 24:7). The book of the contract that the priests found in the temple was probably the Book of Deuteronomy.[13]

Josiah and the people made a contract with the Lord to keep the words of this book. The Book of Deuteronomy has many of the standard parts of an ancient treaty: 1) It begins with a preamble: "These are the words of . . . " 2) It has a historical prologue; 3) The stipulations of the treaty are given. These are the ten commandments (Deut 5) and the following laws; 4) there are no demands for public reading but requirements for teaching them to the children (Deut 6, 11). 5) No witnesses are given, but 6) there are blessings and curses involved (Deut 27-30).

The word berit was also used with other references. Eighth century B.C. prophets used the term to complain generally about the sad conditions of their times--oaths were taken carelessly, witnesses were despised, and contracts were broken (Isa 33:8; Hosea 10:4). They meant that the law was not taken seriously. Jeremiah wrote of a contract Zedekiah made with the people in Jerusalem which was not kept (Jer 34:8-18). Antiochus Epiphanes made a treaty with the Jews of

---

[9]Gen 15:18; 17:2-21; Exod 2:24; 6:4; Lev 26:42; Deut 4:31; 2 Kings 13:23; 1 Chron 16:16-17; Ps 105:9; Jer 11:10; 34:13; Mal 2:10; Acts 3:25. When Abraham made his contract with God, there was a ritual performed which involved the presence of God, symbolized by the fire and smoke.

[10]Exod 24:8; Zech 9:11; Acts 7:8; Heb 10:29; 13:20.

[11]Exod 34:10, 27; Deut 5:2; 1 Kings 8:9; 2 Chron 5:10; 6:11; Num 10:33; 14:44; Deut 10:8; 31:9, 25-26; Josh 3:3-17; 4:7-18; 6:6; 8:33; Judges 20:27; 1 Sam 4:3-5; 2 Sam 15:24; 1 Kings 3:15; 6:19; 8:1-23; 1 Chron 15:25-29; 16:6, 37; 17:1; 22:19; 28:2; 2 Chron 5:2, 7; Jer 3:16; Heb 9:4. The term "ark" is also an antiquated word. Its use defines its meaning. The same word was used for the chest that held the contract as was employed for the house boat that Noah built. It should probably be translated accordingly. It was normal for international treaties to be placed for security in some temple or sacred area. True to custom, the chest containing the contract was kept on the altar in the temple.

[12]Exod 34:28; Deut 4:13; 10:1-5; 29:1, 9.

[13]2 Kings 23:2, 3, 21; 2 Chron 34:31; Jer 11:2-8.

his day, but later broke it (Dan 9:27; 11:28, 30). Day and night functioned under a contract made with God (Jer 33:20, 25). While being unfaithful to their contract with the Lord, some Israelites made a contract with "death" (Isa 28:15, 18), which was probably a legal way of saying the same thing. Those who were faithful members to the contract were "alive"; those outside the contract community were "dead." A Psalmist complained that his companion broke the contract made between him and his friends (Ps 55:21). David made a contract with Jonathan (1 Sam 18:3; 20:8, 16; 23:18); Abimelek made a contract with Abraham and Isaac (Gen 21:27, 32; 26:28); and Jacob made a contract with Laban (Gen 31:44). Kings made contracts with military leaders, assemblies, or elders of the nation.[14] Suzerainty treaties were those whereby people agreed to obey a new king and accept him as ruler over them.[15] Israel was warned not to conclude treaties with pagan peoples (Exod 23:32; 34:12, 15).

Jewish and Christian sectarians understood themselves to be bound by a contract to the Lord with understood terms by which it could be determined whether either the Lord or the people had broken the conditions demanded. This contract could be read or recited (Ps 50:16). It was written in a book or tablets of stone. Just as normal international treaties contained stipulations about the place where the treaty would be deposited, so the contract with the Lord was deposited in a certain box or chest that was kept in the temple or the tent of meeting, the normal place for treaties to be deposited. On judgment day, the Lord was expected to take out the contract and review it and then judge people on the basis of whether or not they had kept it. On that day the Lord's people expected to be vindicated, and the sinners were to be punished. The vindication of the elect was shown by calling this a "day of contract" (Enoch 60:6). This probably meant that the Lord, on the day of judgment, would fulfill the terms of the contract or renew the contract made at Sinai. The contract by which the chosen people were bound to the Lord was treated as a marriage contract.

MARRIAGE CONTRACT

Husbands and Wives. The contract which Israel had made with the Lord was thought of as a marriage contract, in which the Lord was the husband (Jer 31:32). Apostates were like wives who broke their wedding vows and were unfaithful to their husbands. Because of this they were sometimes called "harlots" or "adulteresses," even though they had committed no improper sexual acts. They, however, had forgotten the contract of their God (Prov 2:17). When the Lord entered into a contract with Israel, he spread his skirt over her, pledged his troth to her, and she became his (Ezek 16:8; see Ruth 3:9). This contract involved the Lord's

---

[14]1 Chron 11:3; 2 Chron 23:3, 16; 2 Kings 11:4; Ezra 10:3.

[15]Mendenhall, Law and Covenant, pp. 29-31. See also H. P. Mueller, Ursprünge und Structuren Alttestamentlicher Eschatologie (Berlin, 1969), pp. 173-218.

acting like a husband, obligated to provide for his spouse, and Israel behaving like a wife and obeying her husband by keeping the terms of the contract.

Ancient Contracts. There are no complete details of biblical marriage contracts to examine, but they probably were something like the marriage contracts of other ancient Near Eastern peoples. One such document has survived, and it contains the following items: 1) time and place where the contract was concluded; 2) agreement on the part of the man to consider himself a husband and the woman as his wife; 3) stipulations of the price paid for this bride; 4) terms by which a divorce might be made if either party chose to initiate it; 5) the kind of treatment required of both parties if a divorce were not to follow and the financial settlement that would follow if the marriage ended in divorce. This document then included the name of the scribe and the witnesses.[16]

These contracts were signed legally by properly authorized officials with witnesses to the deed present. Promises were made, and oaths were taken. In the ancient Near East a marriage contract was a transaction between the prospective groom or his father and the father of the respective bride.

Terms of Contract. In a Hebrew wedding, if the new husband found some "indecency" in the woman he had married, he was permitted to divorce her (Deut

---

[16]H. L. Ginsberg (tr.), "Aramaic Papyri from Elephantine," Pritchard (ed.), Ancient, pp. 548-49. A seventeenth century B.C. marriage contract included the following elements: 1) agreement that the woman will marry the man; 2) financial negotiations 3) understood financial settlement in case either part chose to divorce the other, and 4) witnesses and seals. So T. J. Meek (tr.), "Mesopotamian Legal Documents," Pritchard (ed.), Ancient, p. 219. There were no stipulated conditions of the behavior required of either party to avoid a divorce as there was in the Aramaic contract.

Among the Cheyenne American Indians there were no written marriage contracts as late as the nineteenth century A.D. There was a prescribed liturgy that everyone understood. If a man wanted to marry a girl, he sent a horse loaded with gifts by an emissary to the girl's family. This was understood as a proposal. The girl's oldest brother was the one who made the final decision, usually after a family conference. If the proposal was rejected, the horse and the gifts were returned. If the family accepted the proposal, they kept the gifts, divided them among family members, and sent a different horse back, led by a woman, with the girl mounted on the horse, wearing her best clothing. She also brought with her gifts from her family. This meant the marriage ceremony had been completed. There were no documents signed. If, later, she ran off with another man, her husband understood this as a divorce, and he waited for her new husband to send appropriate gifts to satisfy his injury. Again, no papers were signed, but the acceptance of gifts was understood as the completion of the ritual of a divorce. So K. N. Llewellyn and E. A. Hoebel, The Cheyenne Way (Norman: U. of Oklahoma Press, c1967), pp. 169-211.

This concurs with H. S. Maine, Ancient Law (London, c1901, 17th), pp. 172-73; (U.S.A.: Dorset, c1986). In dealing with the history of contract, he held that ceremony preceded contract in historical development, but that ceremony had a legal validity. "No pledge is enforced if a single form be omitted or misplaced, but, on the other hand, if the forms can be shown to have been accurately proceeded with, it is of no avail to plead that the promise was made under duress or deception (p. 260).

24:1). The scripture does not say of what this "indecency" consisted, and it does not say what the financial arrangement might be. "Indecency" could not have meant adultery. For adultery, the punishment was not divorce but stoning. If the groom married her on the terms that she was a virgin, but the husband claimed that she was not, then she would have been stoned if her father could not produce the tokens of virginity. If he had these to prove that she was a virgin, then the groom could be legally punished for having defamed the character of the family (Deut 22:23-29). This "indecency" may have been something like a woman's inability to produce children, but there are not enough usages of the term in the Hebrew Scriptures to define the term confidently. Even though we do not understand them perfectly, these were laws related to wedding contracts that could be legally enforced.

Parties to the Contract. Possibly because the woman had very little to say about the contract into which she was drawn, theologians have liked to say the difference between a berit and a contract is that with a contract, two or more parties agreed on the terms to which the signatures are attached, whereas with a berit, one party, namely Israel, was an inferior party on whom the deal had been imposed by a superior. The basis for this seems to be the Hittite suzerainty treaties. When a king of a large country made a treaty with a vassal power, he initiated the contract only for the purpose of guaranteeing that the vassal power would be faithful and supporting. He required oaths to that effect, but he took no corresponding oaths. It was the vassal's obligation to trust in the benevolence of the sovereign. This did not mean the sovereign power had no obligations. He was understood to have responsibilities for providing some of the vassal's necessities.[17] Some theologians argue that this is the kind of treaty involved between Israel and the Lord, and they mistakenly argue that it should be called a covenant rather than a treaty or a contract.

W. G. Most has argued strongly that the contract with the Lord was bilateral. Quoting many biblical passages, he showed that believers called on God to keep his side of the contract, which involved hesed (חסד) (loving kindness), sedeqah (צדקה) (justice), and emet (אמת) (fidelity). Moses was reported to have referred to the blood of the contract the Lord had cut with them (עם)--not for them (Exod 24:8). The terms given were that the Israelites were required to keep the Lord's commandments and walk in his ways, and the Lord agreed to make Israelites [recipients of] praise, honor, and glory and set them over all the other nations he had made (Deut 26:17-19). Israelites voluntarily accepted these terms and in so doing, they agreed that the Lord would be their God (Exod 24:3-7; Deut 26:17).[18] This was not the same as the policy of the sovereigns in

---

[17]Mendenhall, Law and Covenant, p. 30.

[18]W. G. Most, "A Biblical Theology of Redemption in a Covenant Framework," CBQ 29 (1967):1-19.

relation to their vassals. In the contract with Israelites, the Lord is reported to have taken an oath himself that he would keep this contract, that he would love Israelites, multiply them, and bless them more than all peoples. He swore to remove their diseases and destroy their enemies. The idea that the Sinai contract was a one-way agreement with the Lord has not taken into account all of the data available.

Contracts and Oaths. Oaths were taken to insure that the parties to a contract were participating seriously. An oath normally included the following parts: 1) The deity or religious object in whose name the oath was taken, 2) the curses the oath taker would accept if he or she did or did not do as stated, and 3) the act stated.[19] For example the following oath was taken in an ancient Egyptian court:

1) "By Amon and by the prince, [3] if I speak falsely, [2] may my nose and my ears be cut off, and may I be transported to Kush."[20]

Regardless of the class under which the Mosaic contract falls, it is true that some agreements were imposed and others were negotiated. Romans had no single, general term for "contract."[21] Hittites and Babylonians, apparently, also had different words for these negotiations. Some were called "oaths and bonds," and others were called "contracts"--or, according to English translations, "covenants." Since the latter term was used in popular English Bible translations for treaties between a sovereign and his vassal, scholars have argued that Israel's contracts with the Lord should be called "covenants." It is true, of course, that Israel is not reported to have composed the terms of the agreement. It only accepted them voluntarily. It is not true, however, that Israelites called the agreement imposed by a superior a berit, and called the other agreement something else.

Breaking Contracts. Like standard international treaties the contract with the Lord had stipulations of conditions that were accepted by both parties. Since treaties were sometimes broken, there were blessings and curses involved in the agreement. Among the curses, Near Eastern treaties called down the anger of the gods to bring upon the one who broke contract destruction, misery, sterility, poverty, disease, famine, and war. Blessings for those who observed the treaty asked that the deity provide protection, health, prosperity, and peace. Israel's contract stipulated that Israel would receive as curses 1) wild beasts, 2) famine, 3) pestilence, and 4) the sword (Lev 26:23-33; Deut 29:20) if Israelites broke the treaty, and

---

[19]Buchanan, "Some Oath and Vow Formulas in the New Testament," HTR 58 (1965):319-26.

[20]J. H. Wigmore, A Panorama of the World's Legal Systems (Washington, D.C., c1928), p. 37.

[21]Mendenhall, Law and Covenant, p. 31.

there were times when the people broke their side of the agreement,[22] even though the Lord remembered and kept his side of the contract.[23] At those times, Israelites were threatened with the curses of the contract. There were many times when a biblical author simply alluded to the contract and may have meant the contract of circumcision, the ten commandments, the Book of Deuteronomy, or the entire Pentateuch.[24]

English Translation. It is still further from the truth to presume that for one the term "covenant" is appropriate, and for the other, the word "contract" applies. This is an arbitrary, dogmatic conclusion that is not based on biblical terminology. Depending on context, the English translation for berit in the twentieth century should be "contract," "treaty,"or "will," but not "covenant." The only objection to the term "covenant" is that it is not an everyday word. It gives the impression that it is more mysterious and technical than familiar words like "contract," "treaty," or "will." An international treaty, whether it was with a vassal state or between powers of negotiating strength, would be called a "treaty" in modern English. A document, dealing with the terms of a marriage is called a "marriage contract," but not a covenant, treaty, or will.

Even from the twentieth century side of the problem there seems to be no problem for using one word to cover different kinds of agreements. In the U.S.A. today the same word is used, on the one hand, for an insurance contract, a contract for a loan, a rental contract, or any other document in which the company, bank, landlord, or any other firm defines the terms and the customer only passively agrees to them, and on the other hand, the kind of document prepared jointly by a building contractor and the employer who hires him or her to construct a building. Both are called "contracts." Neither is distinguished from a "covenant," because it is signed by equals or unequals. Israelites did not make this distinction either. The biblical marriage contract probably involved the groom's promise to love the bride, and the bride's promise to be subject to the groom. These were the terms Paul admonished Christians to observe (Col 3:18-19; Eph 5:25, 28, 33), and these seem to have been the corresponding responsibilities of the marriage contract between the Lord and the children of Israel.

The later Pauline interpreter compared the love a husband had for his wife to the love Christ showed toward the church when he gave himself up for her

---

[22]Lev 26:15-20; Deut 17:2; 29:25; 31:16, 20; Josh 7:11, 15; 23:16; Judges 2:20; 1 Kings 19:10; 2 Kings 17:15; 18:12; Ps 78:10, 37; Isa 24:5; Jer 22:9; Dan 11:32; Hos 6:7; 8:1.

[23]Exod 6:5; Lev 26:44; Deut 7:9; Judges 2:1; 2 Chron 6:14; Neh 1:5; 9:32.

[24]Exod 19:5; 31:16; Lev 24:8, 9, 45; Num 25:12; Deut 4:23; 5:3; 29:12, 14; 33:9; 2 Kings 17:35, 38; 1 Chron 16:15; 2 Chron 15:12; Neh 9:8; Ps 25:10, 14; 44:17; 50:2; 74:20; 103:18; 105:8, 10; 106:45; 111:5, 9; Isa 42:6; 49:8; 54:10; 56:4, 6; 59:21; 61:8; Jer 14:21; 31:33; 32:40; Ezek 16:59-62; 17:13; 34:25; 37:26; Dan 9:4; Hos 2:18; Mal 2:5; Luke 1:72; Rom 11:27; Gal 3:17.

(Eph 5:25). Giving may have been closely allied with loving. In New Testament times Jewish and Christian women had few legal rights and some limitations in owning property. That meant that they were dependent upon men, either their husbands or fathers, to provide their needs. In that social structure, wives were instructed to be subject, and their husbands were commanded to love.

BIBLICAL LOVE

Love and Marriage. Since Paul did not require wives to love, love must have had some meaning that was closely related to the task of providing that was the husband's responsibility and was probably spelled out in the marriage contract. The two commandments seem to have been counterparts: wives be subject; husbands provide. These were also probably the terms under which a citizen was related legally to the king and the believer, to the Lord. If the husbands did not provide adequately for wives who were completely subject, wives would have had to suffer. Therefore, it seems that the requirement commanded was more than feeling; it was a legal obligation written into the marriage contract, if not on the tablets of the mind.

Marriage and Divorce. Since the woman's position was passive, she could be divorced without her consent. The husband simply wrote her a bill of divorce and sent her out of his house (Deut 24:1). This had to be done, of course, under the legislated terms of bride price and dowry. There is a whole tractate in the Mishnah and Babylonian Talmud dealing with the legal decisions related to this law (Gittin). The earliest biblical law said the bill of divorce (ספר כריתות, Deut 24:1; Jer 3:8) had to be placed in the woman's hand. Therefore the question was raised about the use of legal agent or an agent from the court to present her with the bill. Rabbis also argued about the kind of material on which a valid bill of divorce could be written and the kind of offense the court would accept as sufficient to permit the husband to divorce his wife (Gittin 1-9).

National Divorce. Jeremiah assumed that God had divorced North Israel when he sent its citizens away from their temple (called a house) into Assyria as captives (Jer 3:8), just as a wife was divorced after she had been sent away from her husband's house (Deut 24:1). This meant Jeremiah thought the contract the Lord made with North Israel was like a marriage contract. After the Assyrian captivity, it had been dissolved and was no longer valid. Jeremiah also prophesied that God would divorce Judah in the same way and for the same reason.[25] Because the

---

[25]Jeremiah was obviously aware of the law in Deuteronomy 14, and he applied it to his national theology. Like the wife, the nation was sent out of the "house" (temple), he did not follow it consistently. The same rule also said that the husband might never take his wife back and marry her again, after she had married and been divorced from some other man (Deut 24:4). Jeremiah knew about that part of the law (Jer 3:1), but, like Hosea (1:2-2:25), he presumed that the Lord

contract Israel broke was a marriage contract, the Jews or Israelites who broke the contract were considered unfaithful. Being unfaithful in marriage was "playing the harlot" (Ezek 16:8-18). Those who worshiped foreign gods were being unfaithful to their true husband, the Lord. Their worship was classified as "adultery." They had defiled themselves with idols (Ezek 20:7).

To follow the imagery further, Jewish sinners were called "harlots." This is the reason Jesus was accused by the Pharisees to have been mingling with "harlots." The harlots were male Jews who had mingled with Romans. Therefore they were those who had broken the contract with the Lord. These apostles of Jesus were not harlots in the sexual sense of the word. In fact they were probably monks, but since the contract Israel had made with the Lord was a marriage contract, Jesus' male associates were called "harlots."

Second Isaiah, like Jeremiah, understood that there was a marriage contract signed by the Lord in relationship to the people of Israel, but he disagreed with Jeremiah that this constituted a divorce. Because God had obviously sent Israel out of his house, Jeremiah presumed that he also gave Israelites a bill of divorce (Jer 3:8). Second Isaiah asked for evidence for this assumption. It was because the Lord signed a contract that he could be counted on to love Israel. This meant that he would provide for these people and would not abandon them without going through the normal legal procedure of a divorce. A divorce, according to Deuteronomy 24:1 and Second Isaiah involved two things: 1) sending the wife away from the house, and 2) giving her a legal document in her hand saying she was divorced. The second provision could not be taken for granted. God had given the Israelites and Jews a written contract--the Torah. He had sent them away from his "house" (the temple), but he had not given them a legal document of divorce. Therefore the contract was still binding (Isa 50:1).

Divorce and Remarriage. Jeremiah was not as stern as it seems at first. Like Hosea, he offered a solution. Jeremiah promised that after Jews had paid double for all their sins in Babylon that the Lord would propose a new marriage contract with his chosen people (Jer 31:31-34). This would mean the restoration of the people in the diaspora to the promised land, with the promises of the contract fulfilled.The contract in question was one which was given at Sinai when God agreed to accept the Israelites as his people and provide for them. According to the scripture the Israelites agreed to the terms of the contract set down in the commandments. Their affirmation was, "We will perform, and we will obey" (na'seh wanishma'; נעשה ונשמע; Exod 24:7). The two verbs here may have implied, "We will keep [the contract]; we will obey [the commandments]." This was like the marriage relationship Paul advocated: the husband (God) loves and provides; the wife (Israel) is subject and obeys.

---

would marry Israel again and take her back into his "house." Perhaps, as a loophole, Jeremiah reasoned that the Jews who would be taken into captivity, like the Northern Israelites in Assyrian captivity, would never marry another deity in the meantime.

Love and Contracts. The relationship of love to a marriage contract has far-reaching implications. It is not only in relationship to marriage that love was part of a contract, but those called "lovers" were sometimes parties to sectarian contracts, international treaties, and other situations involving contracts.

Jews and Christians were commanded to love and told whom they should love and whom they should hate. This was not novel for the Jewish sects in New Testament times. Such commandments also were made by the ancient Hebrews, but they have puzzled modern scholars.

Quell[26] said that there was an inner paradox of attempting to apply a non-legal word in a legal direction. Hence a statement like, "And you shall love your neighbor as yourself," "although couched in a legal style of the usual demand, and containing the legally very closely circumscribed term (רע) [neighbor], is not really a legal statement [emphasis added], because the attitude denoted by the word is one of natural feeling [emphasis added] which cannot be legally directed." Quell began with an arbitrarily chosen definition of love and then tried to explain biblical usage on the basis of this non-biblical definition. The beginning point should have been a recognition of love as something that can be commanded, as it actually had been in the Bible.[27] The unknown quantity is the effect of the commandment when it was obeyed. Moran held that love could be commanded both in Deuteronomy and in non-canonical texts dealing with contract or treaty relationships.[28] Lohfink concurred with Moran and said the same kind of love was meant in Hosea 9:15.[29]

Joshua urged the Hebrews to love the Lord their God (Josh 23:11). Deuteronomy commanded them to love the Lord their God with all their heart, soul, and might (Deut 6:5), and further instructed them to keep the Lord's charge, his statutes, his ordinances, and his commandments always (Deut 11:1)--which apparently meant the same as loving God (See also Ps 31:24[23]). Israelites were also commanded not to take vengeance against other Israelites, but rather to love the stranger who sojourned in their territory (Lev 19:18), remembering that they themselves once sojourned in Egypt. The Lord commanded Hosea: "Go love a woman . . . " (Hos 3:1). In response Hosea bought the woman for fifteen shekels of silver and a homer and a lethech of barley and made her dwell with him under his jurisdiction (Hos 3:1-2).

---

[26]G. Quell, "Agapao," TWNT 1, p. 24.

[27]Ibid., Lev 19:18. S. R. Driver, ICC Deuteronomy, pp. 91, 94-99, without mentioning the problems directly, emphasized both the inward, intense affection involved and also the duty to render service to the Lord. He dealt with fear and service in much the same way.

[28]W. L. Moran, "The Ancient Near Eastern Background of Love of God in Deuteronomy," CBQ 25 (1963):77-87.

[29]N. Lohfink, "Hate and Love in Osee 9:15," CBQ 25 (1963):417.

There is no indication that affection was a part of the requirement or fulfillment. These commandments in the Hebrew Scripture are too many and too direct to be dismissed as mistakes or faulty communication. Furthermore, in one instance loving had the same meaning as not taking vengeance; in another it meant the proper way to treat a stranger; in a third it meant buying and providing for another person. These did not deal primarily with either the Lord's or the Israelites' feeling but with the way they were expected to behave. To love the Lord with all one's mind meant with all mental skills; with all his soul meant with all his physical existence, being willing to surrender life in the world (among the pagans) for life in the contract community; with all his strength meant with all of his wealth (SDebarim 6:5 #32 [73a]).

Demands of Love. Stauffer correctly said, "The love of God for Israel (Deut 7:13) is not impulse but will; the love of God and for neighbor demanded of the Israelite (Deut 6:5; Lev 19:18) is not passion but act."[30] Believers were to love in deed and truth--not in speech only (1 John 3:18). The commandment to love the neighbor as oneself is a summary of other commandments relating to the neighbor. The corner of the field and part of the fruit crop should be left for him; his property must not be stolen; and he must not be cheated in business or overworked. His wages should be paid day by day. He must not be abused or injured. He must be judged fairly. His neighbor must not hate him, cause him to sin, or bear anger against him. All of this is involved in loving the neighbor (Lev 19:9-18).

The commanded love of the Hebrew Scripture was continued in the New Testament (Matt 19:19; 22:37; Mark 12:31, 33; Luke 10:37; Rom 13:8-10; Gal 5:14),[31] although that will not be demonstrated here.

Parties to Contracts. When Solomon became king, Hiram king of Tyre, sent servants to Solomon, because Hiram had loved King David, which meant that Hiram had supported David in international situations, probably under the terms of a treaty. The supporters of Pashur the prophet (Jer 20:6) and the supporters of Haman (Esther 5:10, 14; 6:13) were called "lovers." Jerusalem's lovers were the countries and political leaders from whom she might have received help before her destruction.[32] Israel's lovers were Egypt and Assyria (Hos 7:11; 8:9-13; Ezek 23:5), with whom Israel had made treaties for mutual military support. The pessimistic wisdom writer noted that the rich man had many who loved him (Prov 14:20), meaning those who stood by to support him because it was to their own advantage.

---

[30]E. Stauffer, "Agapao," [C-F], TWNT 1, p. 38.

[31]Buchnan, The Consequences of the Covenant (Leiden, 1970), pp. 290-305.

[32]Lam 1:2, 19; see also Jer 20:22; 30:14; Ezek 16:33; 23:22.

In these contexts, love was more closely related to international treaties (which involved trade agreements and the terms by which one nation would support another nation in times of national crises) than to any emotional upsurge of feeling. It was also a legal relationship that existed between a slave and his master whereby the slave could expect to have his material needs met by the master who loved him and the master in turn expected work from the slave who loved him. These love relationships had more to do with economic or military advantage than with feelings or affection, although one did not necessarily exclude the other. Such love could be commanded, required, and enforced in court, regardless of the feelings involved. The contract relationship that the Lord had with his people had been taken with an oath as part of a contract, and therefore the people could expect him to fulfill his bargain no matter how angry he became with them. Those who belonged to the community with whom the Lord had made a contract were destined to receive the promises of the contract fulfilled. They were the ones loved by the Lord and therefore they were called beloved.

CONCLUSIONS

The most unifying factor in both the Hebrew Scripture and the New Testament is the belief that God had made a contract with his people, Israel. This contract placed accepted obligations both on God and the people, just as the contract outlined. Jeremiah's prophecy that Judah would fall and the Jews of Judah would be taken into captivity to Babylon, was based on the terms of this contract. Second Isaiah's confidence in the return of the Jews from Babylon to Palestine was based on his interpretation of the terms of the contract. The Christian church is based on the belief that Jesus had instituted the new contract that Jeremiah prophesied that God would make with his people. The faithfulness which God had to his contract was called hesed (חסד), and the fulfillment of the terms of this contract was called love.

Either the written contract was such a basic part of Near Eastern life that early Jews and Israelites assumed that their relationship with God was also one that involved parties to a contract or it was the other way around. Whichever way it was, by the time of Christianity both were in effect. Christians managed their business on the basis of written contracts, and they believed that they were parties to a new contract with God. Maine said that before the church moved into England that written contracts and written wills were virtually unknown. The church was the chief cause for England changing to written contracts and wills.[33]

Love, as examined here, is the action required by contract of the participants involved. Love was the fulfillment of treaties made between nations, and its terms were spelled out in the contract. Love was both commanded and enforced. In the contract between the Lord and his chosen people, the Lord promised to be the people's God, which meant he would love them and provide for

---

[33]Maine, Ancient Law, pp. 172-73 (U.S.A.: Dorset, c1986), p. 143-44.

their needs. The Lord loved Israelites because he took an oath to the patriarchs (Deut 7:8). He was a God who kept contract and steadfast love for those who loved him and kept his commandments (Deut 7:9). They, in turn, promised to keep the commandments taken under oath. This involved the ten "words" and other pentateuchal laws. The various laws in the New Testament and Rabbinic literature were made to guide the human parties to the contract in fulfilling the requirements of the contract. Love was an essential part of a marriage contract, but it did not necessarily involve the feeling that existed between the parties of the contract. It involved the fulfillment that the husband made of the contract signed that he would provide for his new wife adequately.

The legal concept of contract is both basic to the religious theology of Jews and Christians and also necessary for business transactions and legal arrangements. Unfortunately, the idea that God had a special contract with Christians has had some negative results. Secure within the terms of the contract and the trusted legal powers of enforcement, both groups have confidently launched out to acquire for themselves the blessings they thought they were promised. This has manifested itself in religious apartheid and religious warfare that have shown a lack of concern and human kindness for peoples of other races and religions. Coherent with the legal implications of a contract is the belief that there is a court system to enforce the contract, and there will be a time when the terms of the contract will be reexamined. At that time the parties to the contract will be tried. This will be the judgment day, which will be examined in the next chapter.[34]

[34]For a good bibliography, see J. W. McKay, "Man's Love for God in Deuteronomy and the Father/Teacher-Son/Pupil Relationship," VT 22 (1972):426-35. McKay concurs that love from the point of view of a father or teacher demanded disciplining; from the position of the son or pupil it required obedience.

CHAPTER FIVE

THE DAY IN COURT

INTRODUCTION

Many have noticed the juridical quality of the day of judgment that is prominent in the Bible, but they have not spelled out in full detail the court symbolism involved in that special day. This chapter will not be exhaustive, either, but it will deal with three major areas: 1) The court symbolism associated with New Year's Day and the Day of Atonement; 2) The function of garments in court roles in the scripture; and 3) the day of judgment dramatized in Daniel seven with its associated historical significance.

THE HEAVENLY DAY IN COURT

The Judgment. In antiquity, as today, it was believed that an injured person had a right to a day in court when his or her case could be heard and justice determined. Once this had happened the authority of the state was available to enforce the judgment. Judges were expected to hear the cases of all people--rich and poor alike--and they were not to show partiality in judgment (Deut 1:16-18). In actual practice, however, the rich have always had easier access to the courts than the poor. The rich have been able to bribe the right people to get their cases heard, whereas the poor have had to use other methods, such as making nuisances of themselves until the judge found it easier to hear the case than to put up with the annoyance (Luke 18:2-5). The day when the court held session and pronounced judgment was called "the judgment day." Those who anticipated an outcome that would be beneficial to them also called this the "day of vengeance" or the "day of vindication." By changing metaphors from court terms to financial concepts, it was also called a "day of reckoning"--the day the books were audited.

Supposedly, these were terms used in biblical times of earthly days in court, but actually none of the biblical records shows that. These expressions occur in the Bible only in contexts that refer to the Lord holding court, and the entire nation of Israel was staged either as the plaintiff or the defendant. Because God was the judge, the day when the trial was concluded was called both the judgment day and the "day of the Lord." Rabbis called it the heavenly court or the court which is above (בית דין של מעלן, jBer 14c; jBikk 64c; jRH 58b). Amos condemned the people of North Israel for presuming that they had a good case to defend on the "day of the Lord" (Amos 5:18).

While the Lord was conducting a court case in heaven, Israelites were usually[1] engaged in battle on the promised land with all the nations gathered for battle before the temple area in Jerusalem. The battle ground was the Kidron Valley, also called the "valley of decision" (Joel 4:14), and the time was the "day of the Lord" (Joel 4:14). This was the time when the Israelites would have their day in court. The poet described the anticipated battle as if Israel were the plaintiff, and the enemy nations were the defendants. The outcome of the battle would be the decision or verdict of the divine judge.[2] This was also true of Isaiah 40-50 which pictured the Lord engaged in a great ongoing court case for which he was both the judge and the prosecuting attorney. He sent a summons out to all the nations of the world to join together and try to defend their case against him and the Jews in court (Isa 41:1-29; 43:8-13; 43:22-28; 44:7-8; 45:20-21; 48:14-16; 50:1-2; 50:7-9).

Preliminary Material. In Archelaus' trial before Caesar, Josephus said some of his accusers sent letters to Caesar and before the trial prepared a written account of their indictment of Archelaus (War 2.24-25). This is normal practice in courts, today. In extensive trials a huge collection of written interrogatories, depositions, requests for admissions, answers and accusations from both sides, various and sundry kinds of motions, and major arguments are given to the judge before the trial begins. Judging from Josephus' report of trials in the first-century B.C. Roman courts, this is no new custom. In addition to the briefs of the prosecuting

---

[1]There was one notable exception. In the time of Ezra and Nehemiah Jews were returned to the promised land without a battle. Cyrus of Persia conquered Babylon and released Jews from Babylon to return.

[2]G. W. Ahlström, Joel and the Temple Cult of Jerusalem (Leiden, 1971), said, "In Joel 2:1 it [the rams horn, the shofer] is used to announce the coming of the disastrous day of Yahweh. Thus the prophet has used the motif with a different meaning, namely to announce the coming of Yahweh and of one of his holy days, cf. Ps.81:4." Ahlström, Joel, p. 67, said further that the day of the Lord meant war against enemies, chaos, Leviathan, etc. (Zeph 1:14-18). Therefore this day occurs in another context as a day of God's anger (Lam 2:22; cf. Ps 110:5, Zeph 2:2 f., Isa 1:5, 13:13). He observed that the Kidron was a place where ritual destruction of other deities took place. This makes it easier to see the Kidron Valley as a valley of judgment (p. 80).

J. Morgenstern, "The Cultic Setting of the 'Enthronement Psalms,'" HUCA 35 (1964):15-42, argued that the Mount of Olives was called the Destroyer Mountain and was the home of the deity, Tammuz. Here the New Year was introduced and the king installed into his office. Here the old Tammuz died and the new Tammuz was raised. This fits in well with Joel's prophecy of a great battle in the Kidron Valley and the Day of the Lord.

H. M. Segal, The Pentateuch. Its Composition and its Authorship and other Biblical Studies (1967), p. 160, has shown that three main themes of the pre-exilic psalmody occur in the liturgy of the Synagogue for the New Year's festival as well and that this is no matter of chance (p. 159). The three themes involved are: the creation of the world on the New Year, the manifestation of God's kingship over the world on the New Year, and the judgment of the world by God on the New Year (p. 158).

and defense attorneys the judge might also have had the contract by which to judge whether or not it had been broken. In the midrash on Daniel,[3] found in Enoch (Enoch 45:1-48:10), the "books" are classified as the "books of the living ones," which seems to have been understood as the list of those who had already been judged favorably. That may also be the meaning intended by the "books" in Daniel 7:10, but there are problems with that conclusion. The "books" mentioned in Daniel appeared in the trial before judgment was made. The materials judges read before the trial are the kind of books lawyers prepare for the judge to read. These were opened and examined by the judge before the judge heard the oral arguments (Dan 7:10-11) or pronounced a verdict. If they had been "books of living ones," they would have appeared at the conclusion of the trial.

After reviewing all of the written briefs presented in advance, the judge would be prepared to try the case. In the case before the Lord of Spirits, the opposition had already moved that the prayers of the plaintiff and the blood of the righteous not be admitted as evidence. The judge declined the motion (Enoch 47:3-4). In a later mythological, heavenly court scene the blood of the saints who were killed for the word of God and the witness which they bore was also offered to the divine judge. It was accepted as important testimony for the hearing, but not yet enough to bring the case to trial in behalf of the saints (Rev 6:9-11).

Biblical Courts. Two examples in the Bible of heavenly judgment days will be given here as illustrations. 1) One of these was an interpretation of the restoration of the land in the time of Ezra and Nehemiah in the sixth century B.C., and 2) the other was associated with the restoration of the land through the leadership of the Hasmoneans in the second century B.C. These were both mythological or theological interpretations of historical events. When the land was restored to the Jews, Jews believed that this was the judgment of the Lord God Almighty, who issued a verdict against their enemies and in their behalf. This was a heavenly judgment, when the Jews had their day in court and were vindicated.

JOSHUA'S DEFENSE

The first biblical court scene was also a mythical drama depicting the way Jews interpreted God's activity at the time they were released from Babylon to return to the promised land after the Persians conquered Babylon. Jews believed God punished and rewarded them in terms of court justice. They also believed firmly that God held court sessions during which he judged charges against the nations, vindicating some and condemning others. When Jews were taken into exile to Babylon, they believed, of course, that there had been a judgment day,

---

[3]For a demonstration of the midrashic character of Enoch in relationship to Daniel, see G. K. Beale, The Use of Daniel in Jewish Apocalyptic Literature and in the Revelation of St. John (Lanham, c1984), pp. 67-68.

and their punishment was the result of God's adverse judgment against them. Their time spent in Babylon was a prison sentence, sometimes called a captivity, which God decreed on the judgment day when the temple was burned in 586 B.C. After ten weeks of years, when it seemed that the Jews were freed to return and reestablish the nation, Zechariah described this conviction in terms of a divine court scene.

The high priest, Joshua, was the one on trial, and he was stationed before the Lord's angel, who apparently was acting either as Joshua's defense attorney or as the court bailiff. At Joshua's right hand was Satan, the prosecuting attorney assigned to cross-examine Joshua. The Lord rebuked Satan and vindicated Joshua. At the time Joshua was wearing filthy garments, which symbolized the sins both of Joshua and the entire Jewish nation, because, as high priest, he was the authorized agent of the people (Ber 4:4-5; RH 4:9; Yoma 5:1). Shabby clothing or mourning garments were also standard dress for the defense in court. Those worn by Joshua were more than shabby; they were filthy. The term used could also apply to excrement or a drunkard's vomit.[4] The filth was intended to indicate thoroughness of the guilt it represented. The language is vivid, similar to the expression used by Second Isaiah when he compared Israel's "righteousness" to cloths stained by the blood of a bride on her marriage night to prove her virginity. (Isa 64:5). All such people are not righteous, but defiled. Quintilian counselled his law students to bring their defense clients to court wearing clothing that was worn and torn to elicit the sympathy of the judge. The Lord did not pronounce Joshua, or the people he represented, innocent, but he announced to all the people standing in court that he had passed over the iniquities involved, so that Joshua was pardoned (Zech 3:1-10).

The angel was assigned the task of removing Joshua's filthy garments and dressing him in clean, respectable clothes, appropriate for a high priest. Then, in his address to the accused, the Judge told Joshua that if he kept the assignment given to him, God would give Joshua charge over God's temple and courts. God said he would bring the Messiah to rule with Joshua, and God would remove the guilt of the entire promised land in one day. Then each man could sit under his own vine and his own fig tree. That one day would be the day of judgment, the day of vengeance, or the day of vindication for which Jews longed. It was also either New Year's Day or the Day of Atonement, which occurred ten days after New Year's Day, or a combination of the two, when Israel's sins could be obliterated in one day. Although the judgment day was held on New Year's Day, the sins were obliterated on the Day of Atonement, when the judgment could be made functional.

The historical situation that was mythicized here took place after Persia had conquered Babylon, and Cyrus had agreed to let the Jews return and reestablish the promised land. He had no intention, however, of their reestablishing the

---

[4]So also J. C. Vanderkam, "Joshua the High Priest and the Interpretation of Zechariah 3, " CBQ 53 (1991):555.

kingdom as an independent territory, separated from the Persian empire. He planned for them to have a high priest, but no king. Jews accepted these terms as a way to get started, but they did not privately accept its limitations. Once they got their "foot in the door" they planned to push all the way in. They intended to restore the Davidic kingdom, and they wanted their own messiah, Zerubbabel, a descendant of David, to become their new king. This myth was composed before that became a fact. They understood the new historical opportunity to be proof that their sins had been forgiven and that Joshua had been accepted as the new high priest. The promise that had to go unexpressed publicly was that, if Joshua (and by implication, the Jews under his dominion) performed their responsibilities faithfully, then God would later send the Messiah to complete their dreams and reestablish the Davidic kingdom. Once that happened, each Jew would sit under his own vine and his own fig tree.

One of the important symbols of that myth was the change of garments, which accompanied the judgment and symbolized the change of status of the defendant from that of a prisoner and defendant to that of a high priest in the promised land, free from guilt. This symbol seems to have had its origins in court rooms but to have expanded into many other areas.

Garments and Courts

Garment Symbols. The relationship of changing garments to forgiveness of sins, baptism, and church membership has been recognized for many years.[5] It has not been previously observed, however, that there was a judgment quality involved in this action. The myth of Zechariah's court verdict prompts a reanalysis of the garment symbol from a legal point of view. This symbol was used by Zechariah in this drama, because it was well-known and widely practiced. It was probably related in some way to the beliefs that motivated people to tear their clothes when they were lamenting or horrified and dressing in sack cloth when they wanted to win the Lord's favorable decision. The following judgment situations related to change of garments will show how widely garments were related to court practice.

Abraham. The court session in Zechariah 3 was the basis for a chapter in the Apocalypse of Abraham. While Abraham was leaving his Father's house under the counsel of the angel Yaoel, he was confronted by Azazel who directed him toward the earth. Then Yaoel warned Abraham against Azazel, referred to Azazel as "counselor," and made a judgment against Azazel and for Abraham. This involved removing Abraham's clothing and giving them to Azazel and removing Azazel's clothing and giving them to Abraham. That meant the heavenly garment that had once been Azazel's allowed Abraham to ascend to the heavenly spheres,

---

[5]Buchanan, The Consequences of the Covenant (Leiden, 1970), pp. 194-210.

as one free from guilt, and his own former clothing of corruption destined Azazel to live with corruption as a defendant (Apoc. Abr. 13:1-14).

Eliakim. When Isaiah prophesied that Eliakim would become king of Judah, he described the event in terms of garments. God would call Eliakim, dress him with a royal robe, place a belt around his waist that identified him as king, and place a royal staff in his hand to show his authority. He would also place on his shoulder the key of the house of David. This would not have been the kind of key a person uses to unlock a door and would carry in his pocket. It was a legal key to be "carried" on his shoulder. The key was his responsibility of rulership. It gave him authority to open and no one would shut, and he could shut and no one else could open. Then he would be placed on the throne where David once sat (Isa 22:20-23). Dressing Eliakim in royal garments was a dramatic way of saying that he would become the anointed king of Judah.

Son of Man. Enoch's report of the mythological court scene showed that the Jews (elect ones) won the case and were given back the promised land. This happened under the leadership of Judas, the Son of man. The elect ones were saved on that judgment day, and the author's wishful thinking motivated him to believe that God's elect ones would never see the faces of their oppressors and sinners again; they would continue under the leadership of the Son of man; and they would wear garments of glory. These were also called the "garments of life" bestowed upon them by the Lord of Spirits who had been the acting judge (Enoch 62:13-16).[6]

Jehoiachin. After he had been conquered by the king of Babylon, Jehoiachin, former king of Judah, was thrown into prison in Babylon. Later Evil-Merodach, king of Babylon, pardoned Jehoiachin. He took him out of prison, made a contract with him, and removed his prison clothing (2 Kgs 25:27-30). The scripture does not say that he was dressed in different clothing that was suitable for his new status, but that is implied. This was a court case in which Evil-Merodach was the acting judge who had the authority to pardon. When he pardoned Jehoiachin, he had his garments changed.

Herod. When Herod had been ordered to appear before the Sanhedrin, he came with a bodyguard, and one of the judges observed that everyone else who came before this judicial body came humbly, wearing black clothes, with his or her hair allowed to grow long, and appearing fearful, humble, and as one who was hoping to receive mercy. Quintilian encouraged his law students to prepare their defendants by dressing them in mourning garments with hair allowed to grow long and be uncombed. Quintilian said this was effective in evoking pity from the judge. Herod, however, came royally garbed in purple, with his hair carefully arranged,

[6]Note also that Elijah took off his own coat and put it on Elisha when he wanted to appoint Elisha as his legal successor (1 Kings 19:19). The garment evidently has an understood legal symbolism.

seeming to threaten the entire court with his demeanor and force (Ant. 14.172-73). This was an insult to the legal process, but it symbolized that which Herod intended--he was not accepting the role of a defendant in the situation.

Joshua. According to Pseudo Philo 20:2-3, God told Joshua to take Moses' clothing of wisdom put it on himself, and become another man. The expression "clothing" here was used metaphorically. He would put on Moses' clothing by studying and increasing his knowledge. It was his mind that would become transformed, but quite apart from his increase in wisdom he was legally transformed as soon as he took over the office Moses had held before his death. The change of clothing was the legal ritual by which this transformation was made legally valid. The metaphorical transformation was based on the understood imagery of changing clothes.

Jesus. When Jesus appeared before Herod Antipas for judgment, Herod insisted that he could find him guilty of no crime, but he and his soldiers mocked Jesus. Then Herod had him dressed in splendid garments and sent him to Pilate (Luke 23:8-11). The new clothes, like those new garments put on the high priest, Joshua, after he had been pardoned by the judge, apparently symbolized innocence. When Pilate saw him in fine clothes, he seems to have understood their meaning at once, because he began to argue with Jesus' accusers that Jesus was guilty of none of the things of which he had been accused (Luke 23:13-17). It was customary for Romans to allow peoples within the Roman empire to judge people of their own race or tribe. That meant Greeks could judge Greeks; Jews could judge Jews; Persians could judge Persians; and Egyptians could judge Egyptians. If the Jewish court had made a decision, Pilate was trained to accept it if no further violence was involved. One problem with this interpretation is that an innocent verdict from Herod should not have been accompanied by mockery. The shining garments were probably excessive to indicate that Herod was ridiculing Jesus' so-called innocence. In either case the clothes were understood to signify innocence.

Other Instances. It was Joseph's robe that made his brothers jealous of him. There was status and legal significance to the kind of garment he wore. It meant he had preferred status in the family (Gen 37:3-4, 23, 30-33). The garments Aaron was given to wear were specified in great detail (Exod 28-29). With the clothing of Aaron came the anointing and the authority. Directions were also given to dress the sons of Aaron with the same kinds of coats and anoint them at the same time (Exod 40:14; Lev 8:1-10). The sign, "Holy to the Lord," was placed on Aaron's turban and on his crown. With this sign he could take upon himself the guilt of the people when he offered the sacrifice necessary for their atonement (Exod 28:38). The Ancient of Days appeared at the judgment scene wearing a robe that was white as snow to symbolize his holiness (Dan 7:9).

David's daughter, Tamar, wore a special dress showing that she was a virgin. After Ammon raped her, she tore her dress and put ashes on her head to show that she was no longer a virgin (2 Sam 13:18-19). Nearly three thousand years later and thousands of miles away, among the American Cheyenne Indians unmarried girls wore chastity belts. Associated with the wearing of these belts was a strong social pressure to keep unblemished.[7]

When Ezekiel prophesied the downfall of the leaders of Tyre he said they would remove their embroidered clothing and dress themselves with trembling (Ezek 26:16). When the Psalmist wanted to say that the Lord was king he said he was dressed in majesty, girded with strength (Ps 93:1). There was obviously status and authority significance to the garments people wore. This symbolism was applied to court situations where status and authority of people were changed by the judgment. Garments were changed accordingly.

Legal Implications. These reports of court scenes indicate that it was considered proper etiquette for an accused person to appear before the judge, humbly, wearing sack cloth. Quintilian also said Roman courts considered this to be proper clothing for a defendant. Joshua was like the scriptural defendants who came confessing that they were poor and needy (Ps 70:6; 86:1-2). This is in keeping with the ancient Oriental courtesy practice of showing deference to those in authority. For example, at a banquet, the approved etiquette was for a guest to take the lowest seat and wait for the host to invite him to take a higher seat (Luke 14:8-11). The defendant in court, likewise, hoped that the judge would acknowledge this humility and grant him or her either mercy or justice. Therefore, on the day of the Lord, people were called to weep and mourn, wearing sack cloth (Isa 22:12). Whether the court decides to vindicate or pardon the defendant, the change of status might be symbolized with a change of garments to acknowledge that the defendant was then freed from his or her former accusation and stood before the world as an innocent person. The change of clothes was so often related to a court situation that it seems likely that the practice of changing garments in relationship to pardon or forgiveness implied that a verdict of "not guilty" had been understood.

In the parable of the prodigal son, the father expressed his forgiveness by offering the son a change of garments. The custom of changing clothes with baptism was widely practiced. Initiates "put off the old" and "put on the new" (2 Cor 5:17; Col 2:11; 3:9-14; Eph 4:22-24) when they were forgiven and baptized into Christianity. Baptism itself came to be called "the wedding garment" which the initiate had to have before he or she could participate in the holy meal.[8] The

---

[7]K. N. Llewellyn and E. A. Hoebel, The Cheyenne Way (Norman, c1941), p. 261.

[8]Buchanan, "Worship, Feasts, and Ceremonies in the Early Jewish-Christian Church," NTS 26 (1980):285.

change of clothes is related by context to the reminder that "we must all appear before the judgment seat of Christ" (2 Cor 5:11). More study may find still further theological significance to this metaphor, but this is all the attention that will be given to it here. The next point in this chapter will deal with the famous court scene in Daniel seven.

THE HASMONEAN JUDGMENT DAY

Antiochus on Trial. One judgment day that was portrayed with only a small amount of detail describes, theologically or mythologically, the eviction of the Greeks from the temple by Judas the Maccabee and the establishment of the first Hanukkah, when the temple was cleansed and controlled by the Jews. This happened about 164 B.C., when Antiochus Epiphanes was ruler of the Syrian Greeks, and Judas was the leader of the Jewish rebels. The historical events that happened then were told as if this military victory were really a divine judgment scene. This will become clear when the parts of a court trial are identified in Daniel seven.

In a normal court trial in the United States, the following would be the program of events: Judging from the trials reported by Josephus, Roman courts followed a similar order in New Testament times.

1) Announcement of the judge approaching the bench, and a request for those present to stand.
2) People stand and observe a respectful silence.
3) The judge reviews the briefs already in his possession.
4) The plaintiff makes the accusation.
5) The defendant argues in opposition.
6) Both parties conclude with prayers to the judge.
7) The judge either announces the decision or notes that it will be made at some later time.
8) The people are asked to rise as the judge leaves the bench.

The myth of Daniel 7 was written only to dramatize a conviction of the author. This conviction was that God had ordained the events that had happened to Israel. The Hasmonean victory over the Greeks and the restoration of the Davidic kingdom to the Jews was part of God's design. His myth was the dramatic way he had of expressing this religious belief. No attempt was made to report every detail of this court case, but enough details were given to show that this is the imagery intended by the myth.

The Announcement. No description was given in Daniel of the way the Judge's presence was announced to those who were in the court room, but it has long been a custom in courts to announce the arrival of the judge. Today in the United States Supreme Court, for instance, before the judges enter the court room, at precisely the right moment, the marshall taps his gavel, the marshall calls all those present to give their attention to the hearings that are about to follow. He then taps his gavel again and tells the people to be seated and come to order. This happens only after the judges are seated in their respective places.[9] Today, in lower courts, the clerk or bailiff announces the arrival of the judge in a court room and tells all the people present to rise and come to order. The early description of the vizier's court room does not tell how a court session was conducted, but provision was made for officers to take care of administrative details, such as these.

Since the Lord was understood as the highest judge, the following call to worship in a temple is probably like the kind of calls for attention that were made in ancient court rooms:

> The Lord is in his holy temple!
> Hush, before him, all the land (Hab 2:20).

The Session. The scene in Daniel began as chairs were set up in preparation for the arrival of the heavenly judge. The judge (the Ancient of Days or God) approached the bench and took his seat. He was described as wearing a white robe, like priests to indicate his holiness and purity, and his chair was surrounded by flames of fire, another symbol of the deity.

Although Daniel did not say that the marshall, clerk, or bailiff announced the Lord's arrival at the bench, and no call for attention like that given in Habakkuk was quoted, asking people in the courtroom either to stand or be silent, Daniel told of the response of the court room: "A hundred million stood up before him" (Dan 7:10). This suggests that the author of the myth was acquainted with court procedure that included the announcement that the judge was approaching the bench, and the people present were told to rise, as they were pictured as having done. It also implies that the original readers knew enough about court cases that the author did not have to slow down the movement of the narrative to include all the details that took place.

The thrones were set up, apparently, for the supreme judge and his assistant judges. Rabbis anticipated a time when this scene would be repeated. Then the angels would give the thrones to the proper people. One would be for God, the president of the court of justice, and the others would be for the great ones

---

[9]The marshall begins his call for attention with the words, "O yea! O yea! O yea!" No one seems to know the origin of these terms nor their exact meaning. It is generally supposed that this is a mispronunciation of the town crier's expression, "Hear ye! Hear ye! Hear ye!" in ancient England. There were other English expressions that have similarly been mispronounced, so this is possible. Some are: hoc est corpus became "hocus pocus"; ad me mea, beati Maratini became "that's all my eye, and Betty Martin"; and "by our Lady," became "bloody." The word "patter" probably came from Pater noster. The very words used to open a session of the Supreme Court may owe their origin to England, but the call to attention probably has an earlier origin.

of Israel. Jointly they would function as a sanhedrin, judging the peoples of the world (Buber, Tanchuma Lev 36b).

The Books. After the judge and all of the people had been seated (Dan 7:10), the next part of the agenda would have been for the judge to review the briefs of the contenders in court. This action was reported by the statement, "The books were opened" (Dan 7:10). These were opened before the trial, so they seem to have been lawyers' briefs rather than "books of the living ones," which would have come at the end of the trial as part of the verdict. Among these books may also have been the contract between the Lord and his people. This would have been a standard reference used to see whether the contract had been broken or not.

The Participants. Then it was that the conflicting parties had their day in court. Quintilian said there were four parties to every court hearing: 1) the judge or judges, 2) the plaintiff, 3) the defendant, and 4) the attorneys. In Daniel, the Ancient of Days was the judge; the Son of man was the plaintiff; the horn and the beasts were the defendants; the advocates were not mentioned. In normal Roman procedure, the plaintiff would have presented his accusation after the court was seated, and the books had been read, but this procedure was not practiced everywhere. In twentieth century Southern Tanzania, for instance, in Ndendeuli hearings, whenever the accusation is well known by everyone present, the defendant is allowed to begin the rebuttal at once.[10] Rabbis said Jewish courts followed Roman procedure except in capital cases. In those situations, the defendant was allowed to tell everything he or she knew for his or her own defense before the prosecuting attorney began the attack (San 3:4). Daniel seems to have been staged on that basis, because the defendant, the horn, was given the first chance to speak and was later given a capital sentence. He spoke "many words" (Dan 7:11), evidently in his own defense. Daniel did not say what these words were, but they probably followed the same outline Quintilian recommended and the same outline that was followed by other arguments in the ancient Near East: 1) Introduction with opening prayer to the judge; 2) statement of facts; 3) verification; and 4) conclusion, including the final prayer for relief.

The defendants included the "four beasts"--the mythical representation of the Gentile kings who ruled Israel after the fall of the temple in 586 B.C. They were insultingly called "beasts" to describe the way the Jews felt about them. Animals were frequently used in antiquity to characterize the aspects of certain people. Aesop's Fables provide ample evidence of this. Anyone who reads these fables understands that a cow and a dog at a manger holding a conversation about allowing the cow to eat the hay were really speaking about people. The myth about cows and sheep reported in Enoch is really a mythicized historical report about the chosen people, the Lord's flock.

---

[10]P. H. Gulliver, "Dispute Settlement without Courts; The Ndendeuli of Southern Tanzania," L. Nader (ed.), Law and Culture in Society (Chicago, c1969), p. 33.

The main contestant from this group of beasts in Daniel seven was the "horn," which was a code name for Antiochus Epiphanes, the ruler of the Syrian Greeks at the beginning of the Hasmonean rebellion. He was the principal defendant in the case, and he spoke "many words," which probably means he offered an extensive or exaggerated argument in his own behalf. This does not necessarily mean that he was understood to have represented himself pro se. He may have been represented by adequate legal counsel in the narrator's imagination, as Herod and Archelaus were in actual trials nearly two hundred years later. At least since the time of Aristotle Greeks had trained rhetoricians for this function, and their rhetorics were similar to court methods employed in the Fertile Crescent a thousand years earlier. In antiquity, historians often credited kings with winning battles fought by the national army and navy when the kings were not even present. Since the "horn" was a mythical name for a king, he may have been credited with the defense offered in his behalf. Since this was a mythical trial, these details are important only to show that there are enough to make it clear that this was understood as a trial scene.

The Verdict. The judge in this court case decreed that the dominion would be taken away from the four beasts, but that they would escape with their lives, at least for the time being (Dan 7:12). The horn received special treatment. The judge's decision meant, mythologically, that the horn would receive the death penalty, and his body would be burned (Dan 7:11). This explains why he was allowed to speak first.

The Defendant's Death Sentence. Burning a person's bones was a specially despicable punishment (Lev 20:14; 21:9; Josh 7:25). Historically, all that this meant was that it was God who hardened the heart of Antiochus Epiphanes so that he would leave the Palestinian scene to make war in the eastern colonies, hoping to plunder the temple of Artemis in Elymais so as to gain enough spoils to pay for the military costs of his battle against Judas the Maccabee. His campaign was unsuccessful; he lost the battle; he became ill and died in the eastern colonies (Ant. 12:354-59; Polybius 31.9). According to the author of Daniel, Antiochus died because of the prior heavenly court trial in which God pronounced a verdict of a death sentence for Antiochus.

Ancient peoples often attributed excessive torture to the deaths of the people they hated. They assumed that God must hate them, too, and at their deaths would have taken them to the heavenly court, put them through many tortures to force confessions from them before punishing them for the many sins they had committed during their lifetimes. The torture they suffered at death would have satisfied the enemies of the dying person that after death he or she would endure still further punishments after the verdict had been given. For example, Herod the Great is reported to have died with a raging fever, itching of the skin, pains in the intestines, tumors of the feet, inflammation of the abdomen, and gangrene of the genitals, creating worms. He had asthma and convulsions.

Jews believed this treatment was God's judgment on Herod, because of the cruelty he had shown the rabbis whose students tried to chop down the Roman eagle over the gates of Jerusalem (War 1.656). Josephus also said Antiochus died after a severe illness, confessing that these tortures came as divine punishment for his sacrilege in defiling the temple at Jerusalem. Other historians reported differently. Polybius of Megalopolis said Antiochus died because he tried to plunder the temple of Artemis in Persia (Ant. 12.357-58). These were contradictory opinions of the same divine judgment. Part of the basis for this deduction was the action of civil courts that often tortured witnesses or defendants to discover the truth, force confessions, or punish defendants for their offenses. They assumed that God's court ruled in the same way.

Court Drama. The mythologist was following ordinary Jewish court practices when he presented the defendant first, but this also had the more dramatic effect of saving the best for the last. When the judgment had been made, and the horn was condemned to death, then the plaintiff entered and took his place on the stage together with the clouds of heaven.[11] The text does not say that the Son of man was a plaintiff, but he clearly functioned as a plaintiff and received the verdict as a plaintiff would. Furthermore, since Antiochus was the defendant, and Judas was the one who opposed him in actual warfare, it seems most likely that the mythologist understood Judas the Maccabee to have been the one in the divine court who accused Antiochus Epiphanes before the Lord. Furthermore it was normally expected that the judgment day took place in heaven at the same time that a crucial battle was being fought on the promised land. The death of Antiochus Epiphanes and the victory of Judas the Maccabee all took place during the Hasmonean rebellion, promptly after the famous battle of Beth-horon. The events of history prompted the author to compose the myth of the judgment day.

The judge decreed in favor of the Son of man, announcing that he would receive "the dominion, glory, and a kingdom" that was under contest in the Hasmonean rebellion (Dan 7:14). At the same time the judgment was for the saints of the Most High, namely the Jews contemporary with Judas (Dan 7:22), who were to receive the kingdom at the very time Judas was to receive it--they as cit-

---

[11]Buchanan, To the Hebrews (Garden City, c1972), pp. 38-51. It is ridiculous to presume, as W. S. Towner, Daniel (Atlanta, c1984), pp. 108-15, does that Daniel seven is mythologized history right up to the point where the Son of man and the saints receive the kingdom, and then suddenly, without warning, ceases to be mythology and is to be taken literally. This provides Towner many obstacles, as he admitted. It meant he had to acknowledge that this "prophecy" was false, which he was reluctant to do. Still more difficult is the interpretation of authors like S. B. Ferguson, Daniel (Waco, c1979), pp. 145-66, who still thinks Daniel actually prophesied the whole book from Babylon. He ignored the Greek period of history with Antiochus Epiphanes, and identified the fourth beast with the Romans. He expects the end of the age still to come.

izens, and Judas as the ruler.[12] This refutes Casey's position that the Son of man is only a symbol of the saints of the Most High, without any essence of its own.[13]

---

[12]M. Casey, Son of Man: the Interpretation and Influence of Daniel 7 (London, 1979), p. 34, tried to dismiss this possibility of Judas being the historical equivalent of the mythical Son of man by saying, 1) "The fact that the author never mentions Judas Maccabaeus is a fatal objection to this view." 2) He admitted, however, that the suggestion ". . . fits so beautifully into the Syrian tradition of interpretation, which saw the Maccabaean victory under Judas as the meaning of the triumph of the Saints of the Most High, and could easily have seen Judas Maccabaeus as a type of Christ." Casey's second objection was that he thought this was too neat to be true. If Judas had really been the intended Son of man, he argued, the church would have perpetuated the tradition. That might have been so if Christians and Jews had been in defensive positions in the Roman empire after the two revolts of the Jews against Rome (A.D. 66-70 and 132-35), but they were not. After the Bar Cochba defeat, Romans inspected Jewish and Christian materials to learn if they contained any subversive material. This is evident from an early rabbinic report.

> Once the [Roman] government sent two officials and said to them, "Go and become [false Jewish] proselytes, and examine the Torah of the Jews, what its nature is." They went to Rabban Gamaliel at Usha, and they read the Hebrew Scripture; they studied the Mishnah, midrash, halachot, and haggadoth. When they left they said to them [the rabbis], "All of your teachings are good and admirable, except for one item. Stealing from a pagan is permitted, but from a Jew it is forbidden, but we shall not disclose this matter to the government" (Sifre Deut 33.3, Piska 344.143b).

In order to survive, Jews and Christians had to censor their literature to conform to Roman demands. They quickly learned the importance of their success in proving to the Romans that they had no aggressive or subversive ideals such as the Hasmoneans and the later rebellious Jewish nationalists had. This meant that it would not have been wise to picture Jesus as an antitype of the leader of the Maccabean revolt. Casey's first objection has no validity. Not only did Daniel not once mention Judas the Maccabee, by name, but he also did not mention Antiochus Epiphanes, specifically. He was describing this history mythically and symbolically, as Casey has argued in many places.

Casey, himself (pp. 51-70), observed that Syrian fathers identified the saints of the Most High with Hasmonean Jews, contemporaries with Judas, without mentioning the Son of man. Casey took this to mean they believed the Son of man was merely a symbol for the saints and had no reality. He overlooked the fact that, following the Bar Cochba war (A.D. 135), it was not wise to mention such nationalistic figures as Judas the Maccabee. Believers could safely mention the saints who were contemporary with Judas, who participated in the war and the victory, and pious Jews or Christians would know all the rest that was implied. This is the way people communicate as a fifth column.

[13]Casey, Son of Man, "Moreover he is a pure symbol, that is to say, he is not a real being who exists outside Daniel's dream; he is only a symbolic being within the dream" (p. 25). "There are no previous examples of purely symbolic beings coming with the clouds in the OT because there

The Revised Version. Enoch was probably describing in a still more exaggerated fashion the same court scene that was detailed in Daniel seven. The Son of man appeared before the judge (the Head of days). The judge gave the Son of man a name and authority needed to rule the land. This means God appointed Judas to be the ruler of Palestine. The Son of man became a hope to the holy and elect ones, as Judas surely did, a light to the Gentiles, and a cause for misery to the kings and mighty ones who were delivered to the hands of the elect ones, according to the author. This meant that the Gentile powers who had ruled the promised land were overthrown by the Jews under the leadership of Judas the Maccabee (Enoch 48:1-10; 62:7-12).

There were many Syrian leaders who fell during the Hasmonean Revolt, some in battle with the Jews and others by intrigue and civil war, and the author of Enoch was willing to give Judas the credit for all of this, but it was really giving Judas and the Jews more credit than they deserved. The Roman power, wealth, arms, guidance, and empirical designs were behind the whole movement. The Romans were using the Hasmoneans to weaken the power of the Syrian Greeks with the ultimate goal of taking over their kingdom completely. The Romans finally succeeded in doing exactly that, ruling all of the territory from Great Britain at one end to Persia at the other, including all of Europe and North Africa. At a crucial point in history, the Hasmoneans were instrumental in weakening the Greeks enough so that Rome could later push still farther. The Syrian Greeks never recovered from this blow. During the seventh decade B.C., when Pompey took over Jerusalem, marking the beginning of the end of Jewish freedom, Romans also put an end to the Seleucid rule.[14] The hyperbole of the Jewish description was normal for an author with a doctrinally subjective point of view, but it is not an objective report of the facts.

Divine Symbols. Daniel said that the Son of man came before the Ancient of Days with the clouds of heaven (Dan 7:13). The text does not say that the Son of man was "coming down" [emphasis added], as Casey rendered the text.[15] Since the Ancient of Days was God, what would be higher than God that could come down from a more exalted sphere to God? The text does not say he came down. It just says that he came to the Ancient of Days. He was not an angel coming to earth, but, more than likely, a man, mythically coming up to God in heaven to be judged and found innocent. After this he was installed as the divinely

---

are no previous examples of purely symbolic beings coming at all" (p. 28).

[14]For forty years Mithridates of Pontus had conducted a war against Rome on various levels. Pompey learned of Mithridates' death on his way to Jerusalem. Romans celebrated his death with a public festival for ten days. After forty years of trying to fence him in Rome was finally successful. In the process Romans also conquered all of Asia Minor and Syria as well and toppled the Seleucids at the same time. So Peters, The Harvest of Hellenism, p. 320-22.

[15]Casey, Son of Man, p. 28.

appointed leader of the Jews. There are still scholars who hold that the Son of man was an angel,[16] because they understand the clouds literally.

This requires them to ignore the fact that they are dealing with a myth. This myth is a complete unit, beginning with the judge approaching the bench and concluding with a verdict that gave the kingdom to the saints of the Most High (the Jews) and the Son of man (Judas) while giving the death penalty to the horn (Antiochus).[17] Historically, Antiochus died either just before or just after the first Hanukkah, so that it was reasonable for a mythologist to include both events as part of the same divine judgment. Mosca compared the mythical character of Baal in Ugaritic studies to the mythical character of the Son of man in Daniel 7.[18] He thought the hyperbolic way Baal was divinized was also the way David was referred to as the "most high" and "firstborn son" of God in Ps 89.

Jesus and Judas. Wenham correctly claimed that the Book of Daniel provides the primary background for the gospel teaching about the Kingdom of God and Jesus's identification with the Son of man. The two concepts, Kingdom of God and Son of man belong together and are related to the restoration of Israel and the

---

[16]Like J. J. Collins, The Apocalyptic Imagination (New York, c1984), pp. 82-83; Daniel (Grand Rapids, c1984), p. 82; Daniel, First Maccabees, Second Maccabees (Wilmington, Delaware, c1981), pp. 78-79. Others who thought the saints were angels are C. L. J. Proudman, "Remarks on the 'Son of Man,'" CJT 12 (1966):128-31; Towner, Porteous, M. Noth, "Zur Komposition des Buches Daniel," TSK 98/99 (1926):143-63, etc. In opposition to these, A. Lacocque, The Book of Daniel, tr. D. Pellauer (London and Atlanta, 1979), said, "Let us add that in Dan. 7 the dominion and the royalty are given to the Saints while we nowhere find any mention of an angelic kingdom" (p. 127). Lacocque, however, had in mind a "wholly spiritual sanctuary" (p. 126). Porteous, Daniel, p. 15, said the saints of the Most High were not all Jews in general but only the non-collaborators, those who resisted Antiochus Epiphanes. Porteous did not notice that the greatest of these resisters were the Hasmonaeans and their following. For a list of scholars who hold that the Son of man was an angel, see L. F. Hartman and A. A. Di Lella, The Book of Daniel (Garden City, 1978), pp. 89-90, fns. 212-213. They have also competently shown the ridiculousness of such an idea as this (pp. 90-95).

[17]R. Hanhart, "Die Heiligen des Höchsten," VT Suppl. 16 (1967):90-101, after analyzing the views of other scholars, the use of the expression, קודשים, in the Hebrew Scripture, apocryphal literature, and the Dead Sea Scrolls, concluded that there were a few passages that might be translated either as human beings who were pious or angels, but in the majority of cases, the Hebrew and Greek expressions could make sense only as "saints," and should not be interpreted as heavenly angels.

[18]P. G. Mosca, "Ugarit and Daniel 7: A Missing Link," Biblica 67 (1986):496-517.

people of God.[19] Hanhart said further, "The heavenly kingdom is the earthly Israel."[20]

Once scholars allow themselves to entertain this close relationship between the Kingdom of God or of Heaven and the Son of man, both in Daniel and in the New Testament, and the identity of the Kingdom of Heaven to Israel, the parallels become obvious. Jesus, as the antitype of the Danielic Son of man, was seen as a new Judas the Maccabee. Like Judas he was called the Son of man; like Judas he set out to lead his people into possession of the kingdom; like Judas he was "like a lamb that is led to the slaughter" (Isa 53:7) and was killed by the enemy for his people, giving his life as a ransom for the many. Since Jesus was the new Judas, he was expected to perform as Judas had, and the later church was able to explain his death in terms of type-antitype. Since Judas was made to suffer and die, it was to be expected that the new Son of man must also suffer and die (Matt 16:21; 17:22-23; 20:18-19; 20:28).

Coppens and Dequeker held that Jews had been expecting a savior who would establish a new kingdom, the Kingdom of Heaven. This kingdom would be established by God at the time when the Son of man came. They correctly argued that the author of Daniel (whom they believed was a redactor of an earlier text) was a Maccabean who clearly reinterpreted this expectation nationalistically. For him "The promised Kingdom of God would be no more in the first place the Kingdom of Heaven or the domination of angels, but instead the earthly rule of the Jewish people, after the victory which it had already won over Antiochus Epiphanes, thanks to the decisive intervention of the Lord in favor of his elect."[21]

They were correct in noting that Daniel, as it now is preserved, was understood to apply to the Maccabean victory, and the establishment of the Jewish kingdom which followed. They were also correct in thinking that this conclusion was reached and this literature written after the victory of the battle of Beth-horon and the death of Antiochus Epiphanes.[22]

---

[19]D. Wenham, "The Kingdom of God and Daniel," Expository Times 98 (1987):132-34.

[20]Hanhart, "Heiligen," p. 100.

[21]J. Coppens and L. Dequeker, Le Fils d l'Homme et les Saints du Trés-Haut en Daniel, VII, dans les Apocryphes et dans le Nouveau Testament (Bruges-Paris, 1961), p. 54.

[22]They were incorrect, however, in concluding from all of this that the Son of man was an angelic figure, and the saints of the Most High were also angels.

Clouds and Sun Disks. There is no good reason to be distracted by the clouds into shifting from myth to history, as many scholars have been. Clouds were frequently used, mythically, to depict the presence of God in a theophany (Exod 24:15-18). Mendenhall has shown that the "clouds" imagery is related to the ancient symbol of the winged sun disk which indicated the manifestations, glory, power, and dignity of gods like Re, Horus, Zeus, Ahura Mazda, and Baal Shamem. In some ancient art, the winged sun disk provides a frame for the king himself, with his bow and arrow drawn against the enemy. This winged disk was held to precede the kings into battle to terrorize and destroy the enemy. Victory scenes showed the king coming back with booty with the flying sun disk nearby. This flying disk was the manifestation of the deity's power and was frequently related to victorious kings. It was also reflected in the famous Israelite victory poem, after Jael had pounded a tent stake through Sisera's temples: "So may all your enemies perish, O Lord, but your friends like the sun [disk] rising in its power" (Judges 5:31). When the Assyrians lost their power over Israel, the anan (ענן) of the Assyrian king came and rested on the Judaic king, Josiah.[23]

The Divine Leader. The Hebrew anan, which is usually rendered "clouds," played the same role for Hebrews that the flying disk did for other Near Eastern political powers. It was this anan which went before and behind the children of Israel when they crossed the sea at the border of Egypt. It had as its religious equivalent, the Hebrew mal'ak (מלאך), which is a messenger, angel, or agent. According to scriptural report, the Lord promised Moses that he would drive out the inhabitants of Canaan for the Israelites under the leadership of the Lord's messenger, the mal'ak (Exod 23:23-30). Like the mal'ak, the anan was present when the Israelites crossed the sea (Exod 14:19-20), and it was with Moses on Mount Sinai (Exod 24:15-18). Both Targum Neophyte and the Jerusalem talmud on Exod 12:42 pictured Moses and the Messiah, like the Son of man, both leading on top of a cloud. Moses would come from the desert and the Messiah would come from Rome. The cloud clearly had the same symbolism for the Son of man, Moses, and the Messiah--none of which was an angel.

The anan was transferred from Sinai to the tent of meeting to Solomon's temple. It was associated with Moses and Solomon. Near the end of the Seleucid rule of Palestine, Hasmoneans expected the kind of divine help that was normally associated with the sun disk, cloud, or angels. Judas and his followers entered into battle, "with the Lord going before them" (2 Macc 10:1), just as he had when the Hebrews crossed the Sea (Exod 14:19). In one of their battles the enemy of the Jews saw five magnificent creatures from heaven on horses with golden bridles supporting the Jews in battle (4QM 12:8). In the myth of Daniel seven the cloud accompanied Judas in his victory at Beth-horon and was reestablished at the

---

[23]E. Mendenhall, The Tenth Generation, pp. 32-66, 210-11.

dedication of the temple about three-and-a-half years after the temple had been defiled.

The Clouds and the Son of Man. The Son of man came before the Ancient of Days in or with the clouds of heaven just after Judas the Maccabee had won the famous battle of Beth-horon. The mythologist believed that the Lord's anan was present with Judas in that battle, so he symbolized it by showing Judas, as one like a Son of man, coming with the anan of heaven, just as Egyptian, Assyrian, and other ancient Near Eastern kings came home from battle with the flying sun disk in the sky just above them. This symbolized the divine presence and authority with the victorious leader--here Judas. Just as other ancient artists presented kings with a drawn bow inside the sun disk, so the mythological artist of Daniel seven presented Judas arriving at the judgment scene with the anan or in the anan. In this court session the one like a Son of man became the Son of God and God's agent, who the Ancient of Days decreed would receive the kingdom, power, and glory. Jews believed that it was God who gave Judas his victories, and they went into war confident that God's presence would go before him, striking down his enemies, no matter how many there were. Therefore the presence of Judas before the Ancient of Days in a cloud was fitting symbolism.

Writings of the Contestants. The mythologists deliberately described the rule of the foreign power that governed the Jews from the fall of Jerusalem in 586 B.C. to 164 B.C. as leaders under the control of demonic powers that came up from the great deep and the new kingdom Judas was establishing as having come from heaven with the power and authority coming from the Ancient of Days and accompanied with the Lord's anan. This anan is often accompanied by fire, lightning, and thunder. Here the anan might be part of the atmosphere associated with the flames of fire that surrounded the seat of the Ancient of Days. When Moses went up Mount[24] Sinai to receive the commandments, the mountain was wrapped in smoke, and the Lord descended in the fire (Exod 19:18-20). The Lord was present in the pillar of cloud and fire at the tent of meeting (Exod 33:7-11). On the Mount of Transfiguration, the Lord announced through the cloud that Jesus was his Son (Luke 9:34-35). An angel who descended from heaven was dressed in a cloud (Rev 10:1). The two witnesses who were taken up to heaven, ascended in a cloud (Rev 11:12). In Daniel's judgment scene the fire and clouds were prob-

[24]J. Vander Kam, "The Theophany of Enoch 1.3b-7, 9, " VT 23 (1973):129-50; F. Schnutenhaus, "Das Kommen und Erscheinin Gottes im Alten Testament," ZAW 76 (1964):3; P. D. Miller, Jr., "Fire in the Mythology of Canaan and Israel," CBQ 27 (1965):256-61. F. Cumont said that in Mazdean faith legitimate kings rule by the will of the supreme god, and they are given a special divine grace, called Hvareno. This did not make the king a god, but it provided him a unique destiny and supernatural power. Cf. F. Cumont, "Mithra," Dict. des antiquites grecques et romaines, ed. Daremberg and Saglio; Les religions orientales dans le repandit dans paganisme romain (Paris, 1929), pp. 131 ff.; and Les mysteres de Mithra, pp. 91-96. M. Rissi, The Future of the World (Naperville, n.d.), p. 19, said the white cloud was a sign of the parousia.

ably added to let the reader know that God was present in this entire judgment, and his influence surrounded, not only the throne, but also the one for whom the verdict was pronounced, Judas, as one like a Son of man.

History and the Court. It is clear that Daniel seven and the judgment scenes in Enoch constitute a glorified mythicization of the history of the Jews from the destruction of the Jerusalem temple in 586 B.C. to the restoration of the temple in 164 B.C. and the death of Antiochus Epiphanes sometime shortly before or shortly after that time. This narrative was told in terms of a court scene in which the kings of the four countries that ruled Palestine after 586 B.C. (Babylonia, Media, Persia, and Syria) were characterized as four "beasts." They were also pictured as all being present at one time, even though Nebuchadnezzar of Babylon ruled long before Darius of Persia or Antiochus Epiphanes of Syria. In a heavenly scene, however, played out as myth, these details are no problem. Mythically, they were all part of the same heavenly judgment scene, and Judas emerged as the victorious Son of man.

The role of the Plaintiff. Real beasts do not often appear as contestants in court, but these kings were being insulted posthumously as if they were monstrous characters who all lived at the same time, came out of the same place together, and appeared altogether later in court, when, in reality, one king ruled at a time. The second king (= beast) did not begin to rule until the reign of the first one was over, but this provided no problem to the author of the myth any more than the passage of time provides an obstacle to a play writer. Scenes change, time is passed with a few stage changes, and the play goes on. Judas, portrayed as one like a Son of man, was the plaintiff, and God, as supreme judge, was the Ancient of Days. The Son of man received power and authority in this mythical judgment scene. He and the saints were not judges here. Later, after the authority had been in force, they could function as judges--the Son of man as the supreme judge, and the saints as subordinate judges. Scholars often confuse the function of the participants in this court trial.

Theology and Myth. By mythicizing this important period of history, Jews were expressing their belief that God had decreed the Hasmonean victory over the Greeks. The Battle of Beth-horon was their day in court, just as there had been a judgment day in 586 B.C. at which the verdict had been pronounced against the Jews. The rule of the "beasts" was of demonic origin; the rule of the one like a "Son of man" was of divine origin. It was accompanied by God's anan. This vision mythicized historical events shortly after Judas won a decisive victory over the Greeks at Beth-horon. At the mythical court session, Jews were vindicated (Ant 12.285-312).

CONCLUSIONS TO DANIEL SEVEN

The mythical nature of Daniel seven is clear because Daniel was mythicizing history that can easily be demythologized. Since the history is well known and the dates all synchronize, there is not much question about the figures involved. By recognizing the mythical nature of this entire chapter it is also necessary to acknowledge that Daniel was written after the rededication of the temple and the death of Antiochus Epiphanes. This also makes its pro-Hasmonean tendenz obvious, refuting many other scholars who have tried to claim that the myth turns to history at the point where the Son of man comes with the clouds before the Ancient of Days. Then it turns back again to myth at the beginning of chapter eight. This is certainly not the logical way to read Daniel seven, but scholars have been led to this interpretation, partly for dogmatic reasons and partly because of the textual problems involved in Daniel eleven.

Problems. One of the reasons scholars have been distracted from the normal conclusions expected from decoding Daniel is that the long mythicized historical report of Daniel eleven follows logically up to Dan 11:39, with Antiochus Epiphanes as the chief enemy character. Then the paragraph from Dan 11:40-45 is not a historically accurate report of the events that happened to Antiochus Epiphanes after he had defiled the temple at Jerusalem.[25] It does, however, provide a reasonably accurate account of some of the last ventures of Antiochus the Great, Antiochus Epiphanes' father.

Confusion of Kings. The history that Daniel mythicized in relationship to Antiochus the Great is reported without myth by Josephus, Polybius, and Livy. About 198 B.C. Ptolemy V made military moves to extend his boundaries to the north. He sent General Scopus north with the hope that he would conquer also Coele-Syria (Palestine), but he was stopped by Antiochus the Great at Panias. Antiochus then advanced farther south, with many troops and elephants, taking all of Palestine--Judah, Samaria, and Phoenicia, leaving Edom, Moab, and part of the Ammonites (Dan 11:41). He found little Jewish resistance, because Jews were eager to have the Egyptian yoke removed (Ant. 12.131-54). The news of the north and east that alarmed him (Dan 11:44) prompted him to leave Egypt and move north, pitching his tents on the Palestinian coast (11:44) on his way to strengthen his

---

[25] Lacocque, Daniel, p. 8: "He alludes to the revolt of the Maccabees and the first victories of Judas (166). But he is unaware of the death of Antiochus autumn 164; (see Dan 11:40 ff.) and the purification of the Temple by Judas on 14 December 164. We can at least situate the second part of the Book of Daniel (chapters 7-12), therefore with a very comfortable certainty, in 164 BCE." Porteous, Daniel, p. 169: "At v. 40 the writer passes from pseudo-prophecy to genuine prediction as is shown by the fact that he is speaking of the eschatological event or at least of events immediately preceding it." These are representative of the interpretation that is most widely held today.

borders against the Romans in Asia Minor, but he was not successful. He was defeated at Magnesia on the Meander River in Lydia (Livy 37.39-45).

THE ROUTE OF ANTIOCHUS III

It was only after Antiochus III had failed in Asia Minor that he turned east to pillage a temple at Elam to pay his huge war debt, but he was killed there by the local Elamites. The mythical account of this is found in two parts of Daniel eleven. The data contained in both five-verse passages (Dan 11:14-19 and 11:40-45) is similar, as the following outlines will show:

A. Daniel 11:14-19	B. Daniel 11:40-45
	1. Egyptian army attacked Judaea and Coele-Syria
1. Many arose against Egyptians	2. Antiochus raised many troops
2. Antiochus had the support of Jewish rebels.	
3. Antiochus surrounded Panias	3. Antiochus took Panias
4. Egyptians forced to retreat	
5. Antiochus entered Palestine (glorious land)	4. Antiochus entered Palestine (glorious land)
6. Antiochus made a treaty involving the marriage of his daughter to the Egyptian king	5. Antiochus continued into Egypt and gained support of Libya and Ethiopia
7. Antiochus then turned to the coast lands of Palestine	6. Bad news prompted Antiochus to turn along the coast lands of Palestine
8. There he was confronted by Scipio and the Roman troops	
9. Returned toward his own land. Fell and was not found.	7. Came to his end with none to help him.

When this myth is applied to Antiochus the Great, rather than Antiochus Epiphanes, its meaning makes good sense. The two accounts vary in details. Account A (11:14-19) does not tell of the Egyptian attack of the North before being resisted by a Syrian force, as account B (11:40-49) does, but it tells of Jewish cooperation in the Seleucid resistance to Egypt. It also tells of the treaty between Egypt and Syria, which B omits, but does not report the extent of Antiochus' campaign, including support from Libya and Ethiopia, as B does. That, however, seems likely to have happened before the treaty was signed. Neither does account A tell of the bad news which prompted Antiochus to turn north. Both accounts tell of his reaching the coast lands of Palestine, probably the Gaza strip. According to Account A, he met the Roman commander there and was forced to give up the gains he had secured from his victorious campaign against Egypt. Account B simply said he met his end there with none to help him.

In this context "his end" (11:45) is not his death, as scholars have assumed; it only means he was stopped in his tracks by the Romans, frustrated and embarrassed, and his expansion plans ended, as account A specifies. Account A omitted the rest of the story of Antiochus the Great before beginning the account of Antiochus Epiphanes. Account B was not discarded as an unnecessary duplicate by the editor who chose to put account A in its chronological position. B was added to the end of the Seleucid account as sort of an appendix, which scholars now consider a prophecy. The authors of both accounts omitted many events that occurred during that period of history. Failure to report the death either of Antiochus the Great or Antiochus Epiphanes does not mean they had not yet died, but that accounts of their deaths were not necessary to these narratives. All authors choose what they will include and what they will omit, irrespective of their knowledge.

Once B (Dan 11:40-45) is recognized as an alternative version of A (Dan 11:14-19), account B does not have to be used as a prophecy which was never fulfilled. The entire Book of Daniel, then, was written after the fact as a mythicization of a very important period of history celebrated by Hanukkah. The Seleucid narrative ends with Daniel 11:39, and the account of Antiochus' defilement of the temple. It is hard to overemphasize the importance these six verses (11:40-45) have had in confusing the function of the Book of Daniel in later Christianity and Judaism. Without these verses, which were evidently added as an alternate reading for Daniel 11:14-19, there would have been almost no basis for not reading Daniel 7 as a unit and as a myth throughout. Sahlin, Casey, Porteous, Coppens and Dequeker were all impressed with the logic of following the chronology of the beasts and the Son of man as being in the same sequence as the Gentile kingdoms and Judas the Maccabee. It all fits perfectly, but only Sahlin concluded that this was actually the case. The rest were distracted by the confusion that followed Daniel 11:40.

The narrative continues (Dan 12:1-13) with the assurance that the end of these wonders would come in three and a half years--the time required for the temple to be cleansed and the first Hanukkah to be celebrated. The author evidently knew when he wrote what the end amounted to and how long it was after the defilement of the temple. The time between 586 B.C. and 164 B.C. is 422 years rather than 490. If the author had been anticipating future history, completely committed to a sabbatical doctrine, he might have simply waited another sixty-seven years for his ten Jubilees actually to have taken place. He knew, however, before he began to write when the last half week was over. He was mythicizing past history, so he designed his myth accordingly, forcing numbers to fit facts the best way he could.

CONCLUSIONS

Biblical mythologists visualized heavenly temples to have been patterned after both court rooms and temples that were contemporary to them. They pictured them as if the temple was also a court at the same time. These seem to have come together in this way many centuries ago when kings were also supreme judges, and God was understood to be the highest judge. When the king was believed to be the son of God or legal agent of God, it seemed appropriate to treat God the way a citizen treated the king.

This examination of two Hebrew Scripture passages that deal with mythological court cases shows that the authors of these documents were acquainted with normal court procedure. Furthermore, they believed that the Lord acted in judgment the way human judges acted in human courts. The Lord conducted court in about the same basic order as civil courts, made authoritative judgments in relationship to the cases involved, and his orders were followed out historically.

The consequence of one judgment scene was that the high priest, Joshua, had been cleansed of all his sins. Since the high priest was a legal agent for the people, his cleansing was symbolic of the forgiveness that took place for all Israel. Since the Israelites were removed from their land and put into exile in Babylonia as a punishment for their sin, forgiveness meant that they would be released from their captivity and returned to the promised land with their own high priest and later their own messianic king, Zerubbabel.

The second mythical court scene was reported in Daniel seven. This is the central section of the Book of Daniel, and it was structured according to Jewish court practices, with the defendant of a capital case appearing before the plaintiff. This mythical court case was made to parallel the battle of the Hasmoneans against the Syrian Greeks. The defeat or death of Antiochus Epiphanes was mythicized as a defendant in court who had been given a death sentence. On the other hand, Judas the Maccabee overthrew the Greeks at the famous battle of Beth-horon and cleansed and rededicated the temple, celebrating the first Hanukkah. This historical event was mythicized as a plaintiff who won his case in court. To him, the Son of man, was given the glory, dominion, and power of national leadership with the support of the saints of the Most High. A knowledge of Jewish court practices makes it possible to untangle this myth in a clear and simple way.

This insight should clarify much confusion in the Christian church today. When Daniel seven is understood as myth of completed history, it will no longer be necessary for Christians to anticipate a future reenacting of Daniel seven in the world. Correctly demythologized Daniel will also help with the identification of the "Son of man" title that was applied to Jesus. The historical role of Jesus will become clearer in the next chapter when Jesus is compared to the legal officer called an "agent."

CHAPTER SIX

CHRISTOLOGY AND CANON

INTRODUCTION

One of the legal concepts that has been very influential in the formation of Christian theology is the doctrine of legal agency. Without this legal doctrine it would be very difficult to make sense out of 1) the idea that the Bible is the word of God and 2) that Jesus is both divine and human. This chapter will 1) first introduce the concept of "legal agent" in comparison with the religious term, "apostle." 2) The second step will be to study the basis for believing that the Bible is the word of God, "The Authority of the Bible." This will be examined under three headings: 1) The Agent Moses, 2) Prophets as Agents, and 3) Kings as Agents. The third division will examine the legal basis for Christology, "The Authority of the Messiah." This section will analyze the historical Jesus as 1) an apostle, 2) a legal agent, 3) a king, and 4) a sent one. The fourth major division of this chapter will consider the implications of legal agency for the later church.

AGENCY AND APOSTLESHIP

Modern Law

Legal Agents. One of the legal concepts that is necessary for survival in today's business world is "legal agency." This means a person who cannot be at two places at the same time can employ someone else to act in his or her behalf at one place or the other. The person employed, if given the proper legal authority, is called an "agent."

According to Sell, the agency relation is basically a fiduciary relationship in which the agent agrees to act primarily for the benefit of the principal in relationship to the items he or she is assigned to transact or the services he or she is employed to perform. The agent is different from most other fiduciaries such as executors, trustees, etc., because he or she remains under the continuous control of the principal so far as matters relating to the object of his or her agency are concerned, and this condition continues throughout the entire period of the agency. The agent is obligated, at all times, to obey additional directions of his or her principal, even though the principal may have said at the outset that he or she would not make any such additional instructions. Unless, however, the agent is a particular kind of agent called a servant, he or she is not subject to the control of the principal so far as his or her actual physical activities are concerned while performing for the principal. As a fiduciary, the agent must account to the principal for any profits arising out of the transaction he or she is to conduct, and she or he must not act adversely to the principal's interests, either to benefit himself, herself, or anyone else.[1]

Agency applies in many non-commercial areas, but in our day, most of the world's work is done by agents. In business, a person increases productivity if he or she can procure others to work with or for him or her. In such arrangements, "he [sic.] who obtains the services of others is the principal; he [sic.] who gives the services is the agent."[2]

If the principal authorizes an agent to perform certain tasks, the agent does them in the name of the principal, for the principal, and at the responsibility of the principal. In fact the action of the agent is understood to be the action of the principal. The agent is only the means through which the principal speaks or acts. If, however, a person claims authority of a principal, but the principal has not acknowledged the principal-agent relationship, then the agent is personally responsible for problems that arise as a result of that action.[3] In general it is understood that an agent cannot bind the principal to a contract entered into by the agent in excess or in derogation of the authority given.[4] The agent would be personally responsible for damages done in excess of his or her authority.[5]

Even if an agent acted contrary to instructions, but within the apparent scope of his or her authority, the principal would be bound by the actions, unless the third party knew the agent was exceeding his or her authority. For example, if a real estate agent misrepresented the condition of a building or the expenses of running a hotel he or she had sold on behalf of the former owners, the vendors would be responsible for the agent's misrepresentation, even if it was done without the approval of the principal, because the purchasers had good reason to think the agent was representing the vendors according to instruction.[6] This is because an agent's authority is generally accepted with the same validity as that of the principal.

Many English and American scholars have held that the term "agency" is a comparably new concept. For example, Hunter said, "It must be remembered that the absence of Agency characterizes every department of ancient law."[7] As

---

[1]W.E. Sell, Agency (Mineola: The Foundation Press, Inc., 1975), p. 2.

[2]H. G. Reuschlein and W. A. Gregory, Handbook on the Law of Agency and Partnership (St. Paul: West Publishing Co., 1979), p. 3.

[3]W. A. Seavey, Handbook of the Law of Agency (St. Paul: West Publishing Co., 1964), p. 3.

[4]Meyer and Klensch 175 N.E. 2d, p. 870.

[5]Miller v. Hartford Fire Ins. Co., 102 N. W. 2d, p. 368.

[6]Aresto v. National-Ben Franklin Fire Ins. Co., 133A, 2d, p. 304.

[7]Hunter, Roman Law (4th edition), p. 609.

Levinthal has observed, those who make such sweeping statements as these have overlooked Jewish and church law.[8] Simmons demonstrated years ago that the rabbinic laws regarding legal agency were very similar to the ones observed by Rome at the same time and that later English law resembled both.[9] Modern American courts of law follow most of the same assumptions as were made in antiquity. Church and rabbinic law of nearly two millennia ago reflect a familiarity with the function and capacity of legal agents, and messengers in the ancient Near East were sent with official legal responsibilities as early as 3,000 B.C. Speaking of all kinds of messengers, including agents, Greene said, "[F]or an extended period of time messenger, as understood by the inhabitants of the A[ncient] N[ear] E[ast], was constant; as a concept it did not change from year to year, decade to decade, century to century, or even millennium to millennium."[10]

Messengers and Agents. Considering the importance of messengers, Greene also said, "If one can imagine living in a country which has no radio, television, computers, postmen [sic.], newspapers, or libraries, and where people are forbidden to congregate to gossip and exchange bits of news and information, then one can imagine what cultural isolation is like; it is a dark age as long as these conditions exist and prevail. Such an age prevailed at times in the A[ncient] N[ear] E[ast] whenever messengers for one reason or another were hampered from their missions."[11] In normal times, messengers and letters were indispensable for the Ancient Near East. Messengers and letters were carried by caravans and ships that moved commerce from place to place. Letters were transported this way to keep the organization of the early Christian church together, and distant Jewish leaders kept Jews all over Europe and the Near East informed of the orthodox beliefs of Jews, offering theological, practical, and ethical counsel in particular times during the Middle Ages. The same situation made the legal agent indispensable.

Greene's thorough analysis of the function of messengers in the ancient Near East is very informative. He has given examples of messengers in action, performing many kinds of service--all of which involve something done at a distance from the location of the sender. Messengers were sent to demand or pay tribute, bring reports of news, propose marriage, negotiate business, lead wars, complain about situations, kill people, give orders to a third person, submit to the enemy, propose treaties, argue cases, spy out situations, declare war, deliver merchandise, defend someone in court, et al. Some of these were apparently sent as

---

[8]I. H. Levinthal, The Jewish Law of Agency (New York, 1923), pp. 18-19.

[9]L. M. Simmons, "The Talmudical Law of Agency," JQR 8 (1896):614-31.

[10]J. T. Greene, The Role of the Messenger and Message in the Ancient Near East (Atlanta, c1989), p. 41.

[11]Greene, Role, p. 43.

agents, although Greene nowhere made any distinction between a legal agent and any other messenger.

Some of the important laws of business, commerce, and government deal with the terms of principal and agent. In government, the principal is the one in charge--the king, governor, general, or other leader who has subordinate officials working under his or her direction.[12] In business, this is the person or firm that sells products or service.[13] In antiquity, when kings wanted to negotiate treaties with other countries, they did not always travel to these countries in person. They often sent ambassadors or other authorized officials with authority to act in their behalf. Even though the laws involved may not have been precisely like modern laws, ancient Near Easterners, nevertheless, had a concept of agency in practice. There were officials who had discretionary authority to act in behalf of some others. These were legal agents.

Christianity and Judaism

Theology. Since Jews and early Christians were well acquainted with legal concepts, it is not surprising to learn that they understood theology in terms of legal agency. After all, an agent was an intermediary between two negotiating parties. The Lord was the judge with whom they wanted to negotiate. Because they had no direct access to the Lord himself, they needed authorized intermediaries, just as kings needed ambassadors (see Num 16:48; Deut 5:5).

The Deity, Agent, and People. The one who stood before the ark to offer prayers in behalf of the congregation was called a shaliach hatzibur (שליח יציבור) (agent of the congregation). Since the congregation, in this instance, was the principal who was responsible for the agent's actions, it was a bad omen for the congregation if the agent fell into error while saying the prayers (Ber 5:4-5). The members of the congregation were bound by the agent, both in good and bad performances. When the agent of the congregation recited the tefillah (prayer) he fulfilled the obligation that rested on the congregation to recite the tefillah (RH 4:9). The high priest acted as an agent for the congregation. When he entered the holy of holies, he offered a short prayer, but he did not pray long so as not to put the congregation in terror (Yoma 5:1; see also Luke 1:8-25). They would have feared

---

[12]"Principal to third Person," American Jurisprudence Pleading and Practice Forms vol. 1, p. 864.

[13]Some modern jurists distinguish between the relationship of a slave and a master and that of a principal and an agent, holding that the principal could give authority of discretion to an agent, but a master could not do that to a slave. The Greek and Hebrew terms for slave (δοῦλος and עבד), however, were not limited to the use of those who had no freedom. Any subordinate official might have been called a servant of a king, although he had discretion to direct the nation's military forces. Abraham, for example, called the agent he sent to find and propose marriage to a woman who would become the wife of his son, Isaac, a "servant" or "slave" (עבד), even though he was in charge of all of Abraham's possessions (Gen 24:1-10).

that the Lord might have killed their agent the way he once did with the sons of Aaron when they made a mistake in their performance of the liturgy (Num 3:4). Part of the fear of being at the mercy of an agent is that if the agent of the congregation or the high priest sinned in his functions, the whole congregation or all Israel was considered sinful. If a community sins the guilt is much greater than the sum of the offenses committed by the individual members.[14] Scripture ordered that the whole congregation of Israel should slaughter the Passover lamb (Exod 12:6). Simmons noted that rabbis assumed that the priest who was offering sacrifice for the congregation of Israel functioned as an agent. The only way the whole congregation could slaughter the required Paschal lamb was to have it done in their behalf.[15]

The high priest was anointed to function as the agent of the people. The king was anointed to function as the legal agent of God in negotiating with the people. There were periods when the offices of high priest and king were united in one person as in the case of the Hasmoneans, but Israel's traditional expectation was that there would be two messiahs, one of David and one of Aaron. When Rome ruled Palestine, Rome was willing to allow a high priest to function under its control, but not a royal messiah. There were obvious reasons for that--the king was an agent for God, so the people felt obligated to obey his commandments; the high priest, however, was only the agent of the people.

Apostleship[16]

Apostleship in the Bible. There are many legal technicalities and expressions which may be recent in origin, but the concept of agency is very old. In Greek, (ἀπόστολος) Hebrew (שליח), and Latin (nuntius) the term "the sent one" frequently signified a legal agent.[17] By the third century A.D. rabbis claimed that "a man's agent is like the man himself" (Ber 6:5), and the concept of apostleship was well-known in the first century. The apostle Paul knew the legal terms of his office when he said he was not sufficient of himself, but his sufficiency was from God who had made him sufficient by appointing him a minister of the new contract (2 Cor 3:4-6).

---

[14]H. S. Maine, Ancient Law (U.S.A.: Dorset Press, c1986), p. 105.

[15]Simmons, "Agency," p. 617. So also Levinthal, Agency, p. 29. Although some rabbis argued that the priest was a mediator for God rather than the congregation (Simmons, "Agency," p. 620).

[16]This section of the study is a slightly updated version of an article: Buchanan, GWB, "The Function of Agency in the Formation of Canon," Explorations 8 (1990):63-79.

[17]In Hebrew the principal was called a meshalleach (משליח) and the concept, agency, was called shelichut (שליחות). The word for authorization or power of attorney as harsha'ah (הרשאה).

Jesus, reportedly, also understood these terms when he told his disciples, as he sent them out with apostolic authority, "It is not you who are speaking, but the spirit of your Father speaks through you" (Matt 10:20). This is reminiscent of Moses' charge to his subordinate judges when he reminded them that their decisions were not theirs but the judgments of the Lord (Deut 1:16-17). According to the Fourth Gospel, Jesus said he and the Father were one (John 10:27-30), but he obviously did not mean that they were one person, which would have been masculine (εἷς). The term he used for one, however, was ἕν, neuter. That which he meant was that they were legally one unit or entity, one as the principal and the other as the agent.

Affirmations and Explanations. Biblical scholars have analyzed the scriptures, knowing that they have held a position of authority for Jews and Christians. They have discussed authority of the Bible in relationship to canon, inspiration, and the authority of the church. Some have said it was infallible but not without error. The Bible has been called both the word of God and the word of the inspired writers.[18] Some have even admitted that it was difficult to show in what way it was really authoritative.[19] This has been explained so far as its users are concerned in terms of psychology, but scholars have not shown how anyone ever got the idea that this body of literature was considered to be God's word when other literature was not. They have noted that some prophets have said that they spoke God's words, but prophets whose works were rejected by the canon also said they were speaking God's words.

Some have said that prophets who deny any responsibility for their messages or who speak against their own will are evidently speaking God's word and have authority,[20] but many have spoken against their own will who have not spoken God's words. None of these explanations is very satisfactory. Somehow the authority of the Bible as the word of God is related to the authority of media through which the text was conveyed. This involves the authority of 1)Moses, 2) kings like David and Solomon, 3) prophets, and 4) Jesus the Messiah. The authority of all of these is related to apostolic authority.

The Necessity of Agents. In antiquity, when there were none of the modern means of communication from a distance, messengers were indispensable. Messengers were the means by which all types of communication took place. Some of these tasks were rather elementary, but others were professional and required

---

[18]R. Gnuse, The Authority of the Bible (New York, c1985), p. 6-33.

[19]B. O. Long, "Prophetic Authority as Social Reality," G. W. Coats and B. O. Long (eds.), Canon and Authority (Philadelphia, c1977), p. 3.

[20]Ibid., pp. 6-7.

skill and confidence. A messenger who simply delivers goods is not an agent. An agent is a messenger who has authority to act, speak, and negotiate.

An agent was and is someone with the power of attorney through which someone else may act or speak. The person who acts is the principal; the person through whom the principal acts is an agent. The agent performs actions in the name of the principal, at the responsibility of the principal, and for the principal. Legally the agent is the principal, although personally the agent is different from the principal. Normally the agent is employed to perform some duty for the principal at a location different from that of the principal. As Rengstorf has shown, the Greek name for a legal agent was an "apostle."[21]

The Agent Moses

Traditional Claims. Jews claimed that Moses was the "apostle between Israel and their heavenly Father" (Sifra, behuqqotai, perek 8:12; Lev 26:46). As the great apostle (magnus nuntius), Moses prayed "every hour, both day and night . . . to him who rules all the world" (Test Mos 11:17). Samaritans called Moses a good apostle, a righteous apostle, an apostle of God, and the apostle of the True One whom God specially chose for apostleship. As apostle, he was also called "Son of the house of God," God's "man," "savior," "prophet," "faithful one," "crown of the righteous of the world," and "light of prophethood." As an apostle, Moses was entrusted with the mysteries and honored in the things revealed. To Moses was revealed that which preceded creation and also that which follows the day of vengeance. To him was opened the gateway of the unseen. He had drawn near to the holy deep darkness where the Divine One was and had seen the wonders of the unseen (Memar Marqah 2 #12; 3 #6; 4 #5; 5 #3; 6 #3, 11). In his commentary on Deuteronomy, when the text said, The word our God spoke to me at Horeb, saying (Deut 1:6), the author added, "Moses said to them, 'I am not speaking to you on my own authority, but from the mouth of the holy One blessed be He, I am speaking to you'" (Sifre Deuteronomy #5, 66b, et passim). In New Testament times Jews were confident that God had spoken to Moses (John 9:29). Therefore Moses was authorized to speak God's words. Furthermore, the Lord not only spoke through Moses, but he acted through Moses. When the children of Israel passed through the sea at the border of Egypt it was the Lord who led them, but he led them "by the hand of Moses" (Ps 77:20). This means Moses was the legal agent who functioned in behalf of the Lord.

Pentateuchal Assumptions. Not only did later Jews and Samaritans presume that Moses was a legal agent of the Lord, but the Torah itself reflects this assumption. When Moses appointed subordinate judges he reminded them that their decisions were not theirs but the judgments of the Lord (Deut 1:16-17). This means that the judges were legal agents of the Lord with authority to speak his word. It also

---

[21] K. H. Rengstorf, "Apostleship," Theological Wordbook of the New Testament 1, p. 66.

shows that Moses himself was held to be an apostle of the Lord with authority to appoint subordinate agents with the Lord's authority. Pentateuchal authors dramatized Moses' authority as a legal agent by picturing God teaching Moses what he should say (Exod 4:12) and Moses claiming that Yahowah had sent him to do that which he did, and that he did not do them on his own authority (Num 16:28). God had put his own words in Moses' mouth, according to Deuteronomy 18:18.

This status for judges is consistent with other biblical attitudes toward judges. It was probably on the basis of legal identity that the Deuteronomist spoke of appearing before the priests and judges as if this was the way they could appear before the Lord: "If there is a legal conflict between two men, and [the two men] stand before the Lord, before the priests and the judges which will be in those days, the judges will interpret well" (Deut 19:17-18). Appearing before the Lord meant appearing before the judges who were God's legal agents.

In a Psalm dealing with judgment, the poet said, "I said, 'You are gods (אלהים), sons of the Most High'; nevertheless, you will die like [other] human beings" (Ps 82:6-7). The author probably thought that those who would die like [other] human beings were only legally gods. Divine status was given to them because of their official positions as judges. The council of gods into which God took his place may have been a group of judges among whom God was legally present, by having judges for his legal agents (Ps 82:1). Since a judge was an agent of the deity, anyone who looked for justice from a pagan court was in effect paying tribute to a pagan deity. That is one of the reasons Paul was as upset as he was with the Corinthians who went to Roman courts to achieve justice from one another. This was an act of idolatry, and Paul reminded them that no idolater would inherit the Kingdom of God (1 Cor 6:9).[22]

According to Deuteronomy, Moses himself was chief judge, agent of the Lord, and authorized to speak for God, in the name of God, and at the responsibility of God. Therefore, anything Moses wrote was legally God's word, and any contract Moses proposed between God and his people was a valid contract. This provides the authority for claiming that Exodus, Leviticus, Numbers, and Deuteronomy constituted the legal word of God. Moses, however, could not have written Genesis or Joshua, because Genesis belonged to the period before Moses, and Joshua reported Moses' death.

Prophets as Agents

Genesis, Joshua and the "Earlier Prophets". Genesis and Joshua were also accepted as the word of God but on a different basis, and there is a basic unity to the Hexateuch that adds these two books to the other three. Abraham entered the land at Shechem, and Joshua concludes with a contract made at Shechem. These books hold a prophecy-fulfillment relationship. The logic for accepting Genesis and

---

[22]For a careful analysis of 1 Corinthians 6 see J. D. M. Derrett, "Judgement and 1 Corinthians 6," NTS 37 (1991):22-36.

Joshua seems to be this: In the word of God according to Deuteronomy, one of Moses' books, God, through his agent Moses, said that prophets would arise and claim to speak the word of the Lord, but Israelites should not accept their claim uncritically. They should wait to see if that which had been prophesied actually came to pass. If it did, they should accept the prophecies as true and the prophets as valid prophets (Deut 18:21-22). Genesis was the book that contained the promise given to Abraham, but since this was not the word of Moses it could not be accepted until the promise was fulfilled.

Abraham was promised the land in Genesis. This promise was partially fulfilled in Joshua. Therefore Joshua proves that the promise or prophecy in Genesis was fulfilled, and therefore Genesis was the word of God. Since Joshua was necessary to prove the validity of Genesis, that probably also justified the inclusion of Joshua in the "canon." Joshua, however, could not be admitted on the basis of God's word given through Moses. It had to be called "prophecy" and classified together with Judges, First and Second Samuel, and First and Second Kings. These are called "the earlier prophets," even though none of them is really a prophecy at all; they are all books of history. They are called prophets, probably, because they report the fulfillment of the prophecies made in Genesis, bringing the history all the way to the establishment of a monarchy, a temple, and kings to rule the country.

James Sanders believes that the Torah is mainly story, and he asked where it begins and ends.[23] He observed that the story continues on into Joshua and the early prophets. Sanders is descriptively correct in holding that there is a strong element of story in the Torah, but from the Hebrew's point of view, the Pentateuch was not primarily story. It was primarily the word of God mediated through his agent Moses.

The Later Prophets. On the basis of the same passage in Deuteronomy the eighth century prophets were included, because they prophesied the downfall of Samaria, and it happened. In a similar way, books like Jeremiah and Ezekiel were valid, because they prophesied the captivity of the Jews into Babylon. Other books were justified in similar ways, but books were also omitted on the same basis. There were prophets who disagreed with Jeremiah, for example, that were judged to be false prophets--not because they were evil or insincere people, but--because their prophecies did not come true.[24]

Prophets as Messengers. The major point of Greene's informative book is to show that the prophets were not messengers as many scholars have thought, even

---

[23] J. A. Sanders, Torah and Canon (Philadelphia, 1972), pp. 9-13. For an analysis of canon in Jewish and Christian history see R. Beckwith, The Old Testament Canon of the New Testament Church (Grand Rapids, c1985), pp. 1-13, 254-56.

[24] On the character of false prophets see Sanders, Torah, pp. 87-105.

though he acknowledged that Haggai had been called a messenger in the scripture. Greene dismissed that fact in the following way:

> I emphasize, however, that with the exception of Haggai, no historical prophet, especially Haggai's contemporary, Zechariah, was ever called or referred to himself, as a messenger in the Hebrew Scriptures [emphasis his].

He could say this, even though he acknowledged that the book of Malachi "is pregnant with references to messengers," and that the title of the book is "My Messenger" in Hebrew. He followed Martin Buss, however, in arguing that Malachi was not a historical prophet, but that the name was only added by someone else later.[25] Greene, therefore, concluded:

> It becomes apparent, then, that there is no evidence available to demonstrate or maintain steadfastly on form-critical or any other grounds that the speech of a prophet was the speech of a messenger, or that the prophet was a messenger, and that both he and his audience understood him to have been such [emphasis his].[26]

This was so, Greene held, because messengers in the ancient Near East always traveled some geographical distance to deliver the message, and that was not done by the biblical prophets.[27] Greene overlooked three important points in making his conclusion. 1) The prophet claimed to be speaking the words of God to the people. He was not a great distance from the people to whom he delivered the message. Messengers seldom are, but God was in heaven, and God was the principal or the sender from whom the message was sent. The prophets did not have to go to heaven to get their messages from God; they had only to receive them and deliver them to the people.

They were messengers, nevertheless, because they were bringing a message from God to the people. Furthermore they had the authority of agents, and they were judged agents after the fact. 2) Greene did not deal at all with the legal function of an agent who was one kind of a messenger. The legal agent functioned legally as the principal who sent him or her. Therefore, even though the agent might have phrased things in his or her own words, the words were legally those of the principal. 3) The prophets delivered the words of the Lord. This was tested in two ways. Either the prophet quoted words from previously written scripture or his words were proved by later history to have been true. This method had also been allowed by scripture itself (Deut 18:21-22). Jeremiah pro-

---

[25]Greene, Messengers, p. 257.

[26]Ibid., p. 148.

[27]Ibid., p. 256.

vides only one of many examples in the Hebrew Scripture where the prophet proved that his message was the word of God by quoting from Hebrew Scripture. Here are a few examples: The Book of Deuteronomy was accepted as "canon law" in Judah as well as in North Israel. This, for Jeremiah was, "the word of the Lord," and he quoted it often:

DEUTERONOMY	JEREMIAH
And your dead body will be for food for all the birds of heaven, and for the beasts of the earth; no one will frighten them away (Deut 28:26).	Therefore, Look! the days are coming, says Yahowah, and the dead bodies of this people will be for food for the birds of heaven, and for the beasts of the earth; and no one will frighten them away (Jer 7:32-33).

That which Yahowah said, according to Jeremiah, seems to have come from the Book of Deuteronomy. The same is true of the following sample passages.

DEUTERONOMY	JEREMIAH
You shall totally destroy all the places where the Gentiles worshipped their gods, [places] which you captured, upon the high mountains and hills and under every green tree (Deut 12:2).	You will say, "I will not worship," for upon every hill and under every green tree, you bow, a harlot (Jer 2:20) . . . says the Lord, Yahowah (Jer 2:22).
The Lord will bring a nation against you from afar, from the end of the earth, swift as the eagle flies, a nation whose language you do not understand, a nation of stern countenance, who will not regard the older person or show favor to the young, and will eat the offspring of your cattle and the fruit of your ground, until you are destroyed; who also will not leave your grain, wine or oil, the increase of your flock (Deut 28:49-51).	Look! I am bringing against you a nation from afar, O house of Israel, says Yahowah. It is an enduring nation, it is an ancient nation, a nation whose language you do not know, nor can you understand, what they say. Their quiver is like an open tomb. They are all mighty men. They will eat up your sons and your daughters; and will eat your flocks and your herds. They will eat your vines and your fig trees; your fortified cities in which you trust they will destroy with the sword (Jer 5:15-17).

Yahowah

will scatter you among the peoples, from one end of the earth to the other; and there you will serve other

gods of wood and stone, which neither you nor your fathers have known (Deut 28:26).

Cursed be he who does not uphold the words of this Torah by doing them. Then all the people will say, "Amen" (27:26). But the Lord has

taken you, brought you out of the iron furnace, out of Egypt

to be his people, his inheritance, as this day
(Deut 4:20).

It will be because you will pay attention to these ordinances, guard them, and perform them, Yahowah, your God will guard the contract and steadfast love which I swore to your fathers (Deut 7:12).

Has any god ever attempted to go and take a nation for himself from the midst of another nation by trials, signs, wonders, and war--by a mighty hand and an outstretched arm and by great terrors, according to all that the Lord your God did in Egypt before your eyes (Deut 4:34)?

Therefore, thus said Yahowah of armies, the God of Israel,

I will scatter them among the nations

which
neither you nor your fathers have known (Jer 9:16).

Thus said Yahowah, the God of Israel, "Cursed be the man who does not pay attention to the words of this contract which I commanded your fathers when I

brought you out of the Land of Egypt, out of the iron furnace, saying, 'Pay attention to my voice, and to all that I will command you,

and you will be my people, and I will be your God,

so that I might uphold the oath
which I swore to your fathers" (Jer 11:3-5).

Thus said Yahowah, God of Israel (Jer 21:4) . . . "I will make
war against you with
an outstretched hand and a strong arm, in anger, fury, and great wrath" (Jer 21:5).

To this people you shall say, "Thus said Yahowah, 'Look!

I have given before you this day, life and good, death and evil (Deut 30:15).

I have given before you the way of life and the way of death'" (Jer 21:8).

But there you will look for Yahowah your God, and you will find him, because you will look for him with all your heart and with all your soul (Deut 4:29).

"You will look for me, and you will find me, because you will look for me with all your heart, and I will be found for you, said Yahowah.

When all these things happen to you, the blessing and the curse which I have put before you and call them to mind among all the nations where Yahowah, your God, has driven you . . . then Yahowah, your God, will restore your fortunes and have compassion upon you, and he will gather you again from all the peoples where Yahowah, your God, had driven you (Deut 30:1, 3).

"I will restore your fortunes, and I will gather you from all the places where I have driven you, says the Lord, "and I will bring you back to the place from which I sent you into exile" (Jer 29:13-14).

If your brother, a Hebrew male or a Hebrew female has been sold to you, he shall serve you six years, and in the seventh year you shall let him go free from you (Deut 15:12).

Thus said Yahowah, God of Israel, (34:13), . . . "At the end of six years each of you must set free his brother, the Hebrew who has been sold to you and has served you six years" (Jer 34:14).

Greene, therefore, has rendered an important service to scholarship by bringing his examples of ancient Near Eastern messages together, but he has not proved his case that prophets were not messengers and that their prophecies were not messages. The function of a prophet was to act and speak as an agent of the Lord. If his predictions came true, he was judged a true agent of the Lord, and his words were included in the canon. The basis for this judgment was documented from Deuteronomy, a book that had already been accepted as God's word, given through his agent Moses. Jeremiah understood his own prophetic office as a fulfillment of God's promise to raise up another prophet like Moses into whose mouth God would put his words (Deut 18:18). Like Moses, Jeremiah resisted his calling, objecting that he was not rhetorically qualified (Exod 4:10; Jer 1:7-8). Like Moses, Jeremiah had to write his prophecies twice (Exod 34:1; Jer 36:28).[28]

Most scholars have overlooked the possibility that prophets read the word of God before they proclaimed that word, but the illustration of Jeremiah's use of Deuteronomy is only one of the examples that demonstrates this. Lindblom, however, overlooked this possibility. He said, "The word 'vision' suggests something that is literally shown and seen, whereas the content of a revelation may be apprehended by hearing, or may consist simply in thoughts and ideas which come into the mind of the inspired persons."[29] "Yahweh has spoken, the prophet preaches what he has heard from Yahweh, Yahweh has revealed something in the ears of the prophet."[30] Sanders said, "The 'word of the Lord' is a phrase used most frequently in the OT to describe the medium of revelation. God speaks, and his prophet hears."[31] Von Rad noted that the expression "word of Yahowah," occurs 241 times in the Hebrew Scripture. Ninety-three per cent of these relate to prophetic oracle. Therefore, he was convinced that there could be "no doubt but that this collocation was used as a technical term for an oral prophetic revelation."[32]

The prophet was a legal agent whose authority had to be proven by the events that followed (Deut 13:1-5; 18:15-22; Matt 7:14-15). Not everyone acknowledged his authority by virtue of his office. The Teacher of Righteousness, reported in the Dead Sea Scrolls, for example, was probably considered a prophet by members of the community, but the unbelievers did not listen to his words to recognize that they were from the mouth of God (מפי אל) (1QHab 2:2-3). His followers claimed that he had been taught by God all the mysteries of the words of his servants the prophets (1QHab 7:4-5). This does not mean God whispered in his ear, but that the Teacher of Righteousness had studied the scripture and learned its special meaning from them the words of God.

It is clear now that many of these words of the Lord came to prophets--not orally in ways that the prophet could hear with his ears--but visually while he was reading the Hebrew Scripture that had been accepted as God's word before he

---

[28]M. -E. Boismard, Moïse ou Jésus (Leuven, 1988), passim, has shown how the author of the Fourth Gospel also pictured Jesus as a prophet like Moses who fulfilled the prophecy of Deuteronomy 18:18.

[29]J. Lindblom, Prophecy in Ancient Israel (Oxford, 1963), p. 108.

[30]Ibid., p. 135.

[31]J. N. Sanders, "Word, The," Interpreter's Dictionary of the Bible 4, p. 868.

[32]G. Von Rad, Old Testament Theology 2, tr. D. M. G. Stalker (Edinburgh, 1965), p. 87.

began to preach. At least some of the prophet's visions came while he was looking into the scripture. On the basis of legal agency it is possible to understand how early sages judged the Hexateuch, the earlier prophets, and the latter prophets as God's word. But how about Psalms and Wisdom literature? These also can be approved on the same basis.

Kings as Agents

King Jehoshaphat and Subordinate Judges. When King Jeshoshaphat appointed new judges, he said, "You judge not for man but for the Lord. He is with you in giving judgment" (2 Chron 19:6).[33] For this image to be consistent this claim meant that Jehoshaphat, like Moses before him, was authorized to appoint judges as legal agents of the Lord. Therefore, their words were not theirs but God's, and the judges they appointed were also agents, whose judgments became the judgments of God. This presumes that King Jehoshaphat, like other kings, was the chief justice of the land. As such he was God's legal agent with the authority to appoint other legal agents. Like other agents of the Lord, kings also had the authority to speak God's words.

Psalms and the Wisdom Literature. Jews attributed the Psalms to the Lord's agent, David, and the wisdom writings to the Lord's agent, Solomon. This was not done frivolously. There was a legal basis for this judgment. David was reported in the scripture to have been a musician who had entertained Saul. Therefore, he probably also wrote music and poetry (1 Sam 16:18-23). Solomon was also known for his wisdom; therefore he must have written all of the wisdom literature (1 Kings 10:1-10).[34] Since both David and Solomon were kings they were by definition agents of God, and their words were also God's words. A Hebrew poet placed on David's lips the claim he thought was just for anyone in David's position: "The Spirit of the Lord speaks through me; his word is on my tongue" (2 Sam 23:2). In other words David was God's authorized legal agent through whom he spoke. When Israel had no king ruling from Jerusalem Jews anticipated a messiah who would function as king. One messianic expectation was that a certain Melchizedek would "raise up vengeance of the judgments of God" (11QMelch 13). Since he was fulfilling God's activity, performing God's vengeance, Melchizedek seems to have been understood as God's agent or future king. There are places in the text that are missing, so it is not certain, but the

---

[33]It does not matter whether King Jehoshaphat actually said this or not. The important thing is that the author of the text knew the basis of authority by which kings appointed judges.

[34]B. F. Westcott, The Gospel according to St. John (London, 1908), p. 70; M. -J. Lagrange, Evangile selon Saint Jean (Paris, 1948), p. 290; R. H. Lightfoot, St. John's Gospel (Oxford, 1956), p. 209. J. A. Fitzmeyer, "Further Light on Melchizedek from Qumran Cave 11," JBL 86 (1967):25-41.

claim may have been that Melchizedek would sit as chairman of the council of God (11QMelch 10) just as Acts claimed that David sat in the council of God when he functioned as king of Israel (Acts 13:36).

The Clay Feet of the Agents. When David was king he was also believed to have been serving the council of God. This was because of his official position as God's legal agent (Acts 13:36). Saul's son, Mephibosheth, told David that David was like a messenger (מלאך) of God with authority to do whatever he wanted to do (2 Sam 19:28). The woman of Tekoa who came to David, ostensibly asking for his judgment on a criminal case, said David's wisdom was like the wisdom of a messenger (מלאך) of God to know all of the things in the land (2 Sam 14:20). The judges who functioned as God's legal agents were neglecting the poor and needy and showing favoritism to the wicked (Ps 82:2-4). They were not good agents, because they had not represented God fairly. Even though this was true, the consequence was that God, as the principal, was to blame for having neglected the poor and needy (Ps 82:2-4). Although they were called gods, these judges were not very intelligent, and the power they abused made the foundations of the earth tremble (Ps 82:5). They had misused their fiduciary offices. The deaths of the agents would remind them of their limitations. As agents of God judges were legally God, but the Psalmist reminded them that they were not the principal.

Others have argued that the אלהים of Psalm 82 should be taken to mean "judges" on the basis of some rabbinic interpretation and also on the basis of one of the Dead Sea Scrolls (Ber 6a; Mid. Ps. 82; 11Q Melch).

Neyrey has shown convincingly that other rabbis interpreted Psalm 82 to refer to the reception of the word of God at Sinai and the worship of the golden calf (Aboda Zara 5a; Sifre, Piska 320; NumR 16:24). Rabbis argued that the clause, "You are gods," referred to Israel after the Israelites had received the word at Sinai; the clause, "You will die like human beings," came to the Israelites after they had worshiped the golden calf. He also showed that rabbis related these two clauses to the creation and fall of Adam and Eve. Neyrey has made a good case for holding that John 10:34-36 is also a midrash on Psalm 82 and that the author of this midrash was familiar with some of these traditional interpretations, but Neyrey erred in concluding that the Gospel of John had moved from a "low" to a "high Christology."[35] Had Neyrey been acquainted with the status and role of legal agency he would have known that the Gospel of John, like other early Christian witnesses, thought of Jesus as a legal agent, and apostle of God, who was physically and personally a human being ("low"), but

---

[35]J. H. Neyrey, S.J., "I said 'You are Gods": Psalm 82:6 and John 10," JBL 108 (1989):647-63. Neyrey also overlooked some recent studies when he suggested that John 10 "might be the earliest example" of Jewish midrash." Midrash can be traced back in the Hebrew Scripture to the eighth century B.C. In this study alone it is clear that Jeremiah was acquainted with the midrashic method and wrote part of his prophecy on the basis of earlier texts.

legally he was equal to God ("high"). These either/or judgments about christology as being either "low" or "high" do not apply to a legal agent of God. The fact that some rabbis made a good midrash on the interpretation of Psalm 82 relating the passage to Israelites in relationship to Sinai and the golden calf does not argue against the function of agency in the use of Psalm 82. John 10, consistent with other parts of John, interpreted Jesus' role as that of an agent, so that, on the one hand, anyone who saw Jesus saw the Father (legally) (John 14:9), and Jesus held a status that was legally equal to God (John 10:33), but, on the other hand, the Father (as the principal) was greater (John 14:28) than the Son, who was the agent.

When, through a messenger, David commissioned Joab to arrange for Uriah's death, the prophet Nathan accused David of striking Uriah with the sword ואתה הרגת בחרב בני אמון, which meant he had Uriah killed "by the sword of the Ammonites" (2 Sam 12:9). As the principal, however, David himself was guilty.

Jewish and Samaritan Agents and Canons. Since the prophets included in the Jewish canon were either from Judah or were Judaized, it is reasonable for the Samaritans to reject them. The same is true of the works attributed to David and Solomon. Samaritans did not believe either David or Solomon was a true agent of God. Therefore words attributed to them could not be considered God's word. For the Samaritans and the Sadducees, only the Torah of Moses was acceptable. By whatever other logic Jews and Samaritans accepted books of the Bible to be the word of God, it all hinged on their acceptance of the agents involved. Samaritans accepted Moses and the books associated with him; Jews also accepted books ascribed to other Jewish leaders who had been accepted as agents, such as the prophets and kings.

Even the eighth century prophet, Hosea, who has often been mistakenly thought of as a northern prophet, was pro-Judaic, urging the northerners to return to the Lord their God and David their king, which meant to return to submission under Judah (Hos 3:5). Hosea also complained that if Northern Israelites kept on in their idolatrous behavior, they would have a bad influence upon Judah (Hos 4:15; 5:5)--his primary concern. These are not the kind of statements one might expect from a pro-northern prophet. The message was for the Northern Kingdom, but by a prophet from the Southern Kingdom. This is one of the reasons it was considered the word of God by Judah and not Samaria.

In Judah the Pentateuch, Psalms, and Proverbs were considered God's words because they were delivered by the legal agents of the Lord, namely Moses, David, and Solomon. The prophets whose words were fulfilled were also considered agents of the Lord. God's legal presence in his word became very important when the believers were taken away from their country, and their temple was destroyed. When there was no temple where God could be present in their midst, their next resort was to deal with the legal presence of God in his written word. Through his written word, God could be "with them" to "the end of the

[Babylonian] age" (Matt 28:20). This enabled them to survive, but they never ceased to long for a new legal agent of the Lord--the Messiah, their own king, ruling over the promised land. The written word could not replace the word made flesh.

Royal Agency. Earlier and later kings were held to be agents of the deity. Pharaoh, for example, was claimed to be the son of two gods at the same time, a physical impossibility. The divine right of kings has a long history.[36] For example, when Rothair was king of the Lombards, beginning in A.D. 636, he organized into one code many well-known laws of the kingdom. According to these laws of Lombard, if anyone killed someone else by the king's order, he or she was entirely without blame. Neither the person who performed the deed nor any of that person's heirs was allowed to suffer any punishment or trouble of any kind, because "we believe that the heart of the king is in the hand of God, it is inconceivable that anyone whose death the king has ordered could be entirely free of guilt."[37] It was presumed that the king was God's legal agent and therefore free from blame. If anyone was to blame it would have been the principal and not the agent through whom the king acted. Since the king was an agent of the deity, his guilt was also transferred, leaving him legally innocent. The legal action by which a citizen was crowned as king and became God's agent was an action of the spirit.

The Word and the Spirit. The word that was mediated through Moses, David, Solomon, the prophets, Jesus, and the apostles was considered legally the word of God, and it was also held to be inspired or "in spirited." There are some interesting relationships between legal authority and being filled with the spirit. Second Isaiah said the spirit of the Lord was upon him (Isa 61:1). The targum on the same text said the spirit of the prophecy of the Lord was upon him. The targumist knew that it was through the prophets that the spirit of the Lord rested upon people. Prophets were legal agents, and God's spirit worked through them.

An anonymous Norman said that at the moment of the king's consecration, the spirit "leaped" into the terrestrial king and made him "another man" (alius vir),[38] just as the spirit of the Lord took possession of Gideon (Judges 6:22), Jephthah (Judges 11:29), and Samson (Judges 14:19; 15:14) and they became

---

[36]29 Neither Engnell nor Frankfort spoke of the king as God's apostle or agent, but the data they give provide that implication. Engnell, for example, said that in ancient Egypt the king was described as god on earth (I. Engnell, Studies in the Divine Kingship in the Ancient Near East [Oxford, 1967]), p. 12). Frankfort said the king of Egypt was the god Horus incarnate, although the deity was not exhausted by his incarnation. This implies that the god Horus was the principal, and the king was the agent. the relationship seems to have been legal (H. Frankfort, Kingship and the Gods [Chicago, c1948], p. 36).

[37]K. F. Drew (tr.), The Lombard Laws (Philadelphia, 1973), pp. 17, 53.

[38]E. H. Kantorowicz, The King's Two Bodies (Princeton, 1957), p. 47.

leaders. The spirit came upon Saul after he had been anointed king of Israel (1 Sam 10:1-10). When these people became judges or kings they were transformed, but this was not a physical change. When a citizen became a king he went through a legal transformation. He was no longer a citizen but a king.

Royal Authority and the Spirit. The legal authority that comes to kings when they are enthroned comes to them at the same time they receive the spirit. This is the significance of the references in the gospels to Jesus' reception of the spirit. At his baptism the spirit of God came upon Jesus and he was acknowledged as God's Son (Matt 3:16-17; Mark 1:10; Luke 3:21-22; John 1:32-34). After Jesus' baptism, he was addressed as one who was "full of the Holy Spirit," which meant he had the authority of God's legal agent (Luke 3:38-4:1). According to Luke Jesus claimed that the words of Isaiah 61:1-2, saying, "The spirit of the Lord is upon me," were fulfilled in him (Luke 4:18-21). This meant he claimed that he was the Messiah upon whom the Lord had set his spirit. Those who heard his message observed that he spoke with authority and power (Luke 4:36). Paul said Jesus was God's son, even though he was from the seed of David, according to the flesh. He had been established son of God in power and according to the spirit of holiness (Rom 1:3-4).

Matthew claimed that the prophecy of Isaiah 42:1-4 was fulfilled in Jesus, meaning that God had put his spirit on Jesus, just as he had put his spirit on the servant of Isaiah. This gave him divine authority to perform miracles. When the Pharisees challenged his authority and claimed that Jesus was acting as an agent of Beelzeboul, Jesus responded with several arguments, claiming that it was through the spirit of God that he cast out demons and that the Pharisees had committed the unpardonable sin of blasphemy by depreciating the Holy Spirit which worked through him (Matt 12:15-32; Mark 3:29-30; Luke 12:10). Even when challenging Jesus' authority and identity, the Pharisees acknowledged that they knew the rules of legal agency and its relationship to spirit.

When David was king he spoke with divine authority. That is why the words attributed to him are also considered the word of God. Jesus said David spoke through the spirit when he said the words attributed to him in the Psalms (Matt 22:43-44; Mark 12:35-36). The Holy Spirit spoke through the mouth [agency] of David when the Psalms were written and were recognized as God's words (Acts 1:16). The angel who spoke to Mary before Jesus' birth told her that God would give her son the throne of David, and he would rule over the house of Jacob. The Holy Spirit would come upon Mary, and her son would be called God's Son (Luke 1:30-35). These concepts are related; one who ruled over the house of Israel would also be king and the Son of God. It was the Holy Spirit that brought about this condition whereby Jesus would have the authority of God and would function as a king. Before commissioning his apostles as his legal agents,

Jesus was reported to have assured them that he had authority to do this: "All [legal] authority has been given me in heaven and on earth" (Matt 28:18).[39]

THE AUTHORITY OF THE MESSIAH

Jesus the Apostle. That which was true of Moses, Jehoshaphat, and their subordinate judges was also true of Jesus and his apostles. The apostles received their authority from Jesus, and Jesus received his authority from God.[40] This is the significance of Jesus' statement that the one who received his apostles whom he had sent received Jesus himself, and not only Jesus, but the one who had sent him (Matt 10:40-42; John 13:20; see also GenR 22:26, #78; B.K. 113b). It is true because legally Jesus was God, and Jesus' apostles were legally Jesus himself. The words that they spoke, then, had apostolic authority as the word of God. This authority was theirs "until the end of the [Gentile or Roman] age" (Matt 28:20). That may be the reason why the early church was very careful to include in its collection as canon of the word of God only those texts which they believed had been written by apostles. Gospel writers recognized Jesus as God's apostle and said that Jesus cast out demons by the spirit or finger of God (Matt 12:28; Luke 11:20). He spoke as one who had authority (Matt 7:29; 21:24; Mark 1:27; Luke 4:30), meaning the authority of God which would be spoken by God's legal agent, the Messiah. All authority had been given him in heaven and on earth (Matt 28:19). Whenever Paul quoted words of Jesus, he called them the words of the Lord (1 Cor 7:10, 12, 25; 9:14; 11:213-26; 14:37; 1 Thes 4:15-17), indicating that they were God's words and had the same authority as scripture. They were not just the independent words of Jesus. He obviously accepted the apostolic authority of the Messiah.

The legal agent was the one through whom the principal acted. God acted through the legal agent, Jesus. Jesus acted through the apostles. Many of the early church fathers knew the significance of this, and said that the apostles acquired

---

[39]R. T. Beckwith, "A Modern Theory of the Old Testament Canon," VT 41 (1991):385-95, opposed J. Barton, Oracles of God: Perceptions of ancient Prophecy in Israel after the Exile (London, 1986). Barton thought there were originally two divisions to the Hebrew Scripture; Beckwith thought there were three. Neither raised the question of basis for canon. M. Turner, "The Spirit of Prophecy and the Power of Authoritative Preaching in Luke-Acts: A Question of Origins," NTS 38 (1992):66-88, related the authority of the Spirit primarily as the spirit of prophecy. In this he agreed with many of the rabbis and authors of targumim. Many times the rabbis interpreted the word "Spirit," as "the Spirit of prophecy," even though the ones who received the Spirit frequently were not prophets. For example, "Joshua." Some of those who received the Spirit prophesied, but some became kings or functioned as agents for some principal in other ways, like kings. The Spirit provided the agent the authority to speak or act in the name of the principal. In the scripture the authorizing principal was God.

[40]Buchanan, To the Hebrews (Garden City, 1972). On Jesus as an agent, see also C. A. Wanamaker, "Christ as Divine Agent in Paul," SJT 39 (1986):517-28. See also A. E. Harvey, Jesus on Trial (Atlanta, c1976), pp. 116-19.

perfect knowledge through our Lord Jesus Christ (1 Clement 45:1-2). Justin said God's voice spoke through the apostles (Apology 1.36). Athenagoras said the Holy Spirit functioned through the scriptural authors the way a flute player blows through a flute (Leg. pro Christ 9; so also Hippolytus De Antichristo 2; and John of Chrysostom, Hom. in John 1.1). Theophilus said the human author was an instrument or organ of the Holy Spirit (Ad Autol. 2.9, 10). Jerome said the Holy Spirit was the real author of the scripture. The human scribe was only a tool with which the Holy Spirit acted (Comm. Isa. 29:9; Ep. 70.7; 65.7; 82.7; De Ps 88). These fathers trusted the scripture as being the true and valid word of God because they believed the agents through which the word came were true legal agents.

Tertullian showed his familiarity with these legal concepts in his argument with Marcion. Marcion denied that the Hebrew Scriptures were the word of God. Therefore he could not show that his Christ had been commissioned and authorized by God, whereas Tertullian could show that the prophets had foretold the coming of a future agent, the Messiah. He held this on the basis of understood rules for agency. If the sender (principal) had not acknowledged the sent one (agent) before the act, the agent would not have the proper authority. The Christ whom Marcion invented, said Tertullian, was not properly authorized and acknowledged to be God's agent and Son (Contra Marcion 3.2-4). The requirements Tertullian demanded of an agent are still required by twentieth century law courts. The Odes of Solomon (42:6) pictured the risen Jesus saying that he would continue to speak "by the mouth" of those who love him. This means his immediate followers were his legal agents who continued his work and message.

There are many indications that Jesus and the early church knew the rules of agency, understood them in relationship to God and the Davidic Messiah, and believed that Jesus, himself, functioned as God's agent. If Raymond Brown had realized all of this he probably would not have called it "the unsophisticated christological terminology of the 1st century."[41]

Jesus the King. An apostle was identical to the one who sent him or her--not physically but legally (LamR 1:18-19 #53; Song of SongsR 1:2, #3). An apostle had the "power of attorney" to act for, in the name of, and at the responsibility of the one who did the sending and was legally identical to him or her. The New Testament apostles were agents of Jesus, and Jesus was an agent of God. This is not just a logical deduction; it is the claim of the New Testament. The author of Hebrews called Jesus "the apostle and high priest of our confession" (Heb 3:1). Since the high priest was an apostle of the people, and since Hebrews describes Jesus as a high priest who offered the perfect sacrifice, the author may have meant that as high priest, Jesus was the apostle of the people, as other high priests were. The other possibility is that in saying that he was both high priest and apostle, he meant that he was both high priest and king. That is the way

[41]R. Brown, The Gospel according to John (Garden City, c1966), vol. 1, p. 13.

Clement understood it. He said that the Lord was "an apostle of the Almighty" (HE 6.14, 4), which is another way of saying he was the Messiah or king and not just an apostle of the people the way the high priest was. In claiming that Jesus was both apostle and high priest, he was fitting Jesus into a Hasmonean mold.[42]

Jesus as Agent. Furthermore, Hebrews held that Jesus, as God's Son, bore the very stamp of God's nature (Heb 1:3). The legal agent was one who was authorized to bear and use the stamp or seal for giving written proof of the principal's approval. In the second century A.D. Tertullian argued against Marcion that Jesus was the true Son of God and the "sent one." Tertullian made a point of saying that Jesus was not just a Son; he was the sent one or agent. By this Tertullian meant that Jesus was God's apostle or legal agent. Tertullian said no one would believe in a sent one if the sender (Mandator) had not commissioned him. No one recognizes first the sent one (agent) and after that the sender (principal). The sender comes first and after that the sent one. This is a legal relationship between the sender and the sent one. In this case the Father was also the sender and the Son was also the sent one (Contra Marcion 3.2).

Tertullian was still using legal terminology when he said the Creator could represent himself with any form that he chose, but once he had chosen human flesh he made that flesh worthy of himself (Contra Marcion 3.10). This is true because the agent is legally the principal, and legally worthy of the principal.

When Jesus said, "He who has seen me has seen the Father" (John 14:9), he probably said this to establish his legal, rather than his physical identity, with God, because in the same chapter, he said, "The Father is greater than I" (John 14:28). At least legally, the Father was greater, because the principal, in the context of a principal-agent relationship, is always greater than the agent who acts in his name. It was legally, and not physically, that God was in Jesus, Jesus was in God, God and Jesus were both in the apostles, and the apostles were in both the Father and the Son (John 17:20-26).

Paul probably understood these legalities when he said Christians saw the glory of the Lord as in a mirror and were being (legally) transformed into his image (2 Cor 3:18). It was because Jesus, as the messianic king, was understood to be legally identical to God that he was considered the human image of the invisible God. By the same token Paul said we had such confidence as this "through the Christ to God" (2 Cor 3:4). The principal acted through the agent, and the third party also acted through the agent to the principal. The author of the Fourth Gospel made the same claim when he said, "All things were made through him" (John 1:3).

---

[42]Buchanan, To the Hebrews (Garden City, 1972). On Jesus as an agent, see also C. A. Wanamaker, "Christ as Divine Agent in Paul," SJT 39 (1986):517-28.

The Sent One. To realize how important legal agency was to the author of the Fourth Gospel it is necessary only to look up every use of the word "send" in that document. John was a man sent from God (John 1:6), and God was the principal who sent him to baptize (John 1:33). God sent his Son into the world (John 3:17). Jesus' "food" was to do the will of the one who sent him (John 4:34). The Father entrusted all judgment to the Son, so that all who honor the Son honor the Father who sent him (John 5:22-23). This does not mean they honor also the Father, but that they honor the Father through his agent whenever they honor the agent. Jesus did not seek his own will, but as a responsible agent he tried to do the will of the principal who sent him (John 5:30; 6:38-39; 9:4). The work Jesus did testified that the Father had sent him (John 5:36-37). No one could come to the Father if the principal who sent Jesus did not draw him (John 6:44). Just as the one who sent Jesus lived, so Jesus lived through the Father (John 6:57).

Jesus' teaching was not his but rather the teaching of the one who sent him; he did not seek his own glory but the glory of the one who sent him (John 7:16-18). Like other agents, Jesus was obligated to return to the one who sent him (John 7:33-34; 16:5). He judged no one, but if he did it would be valid, because he was a legal agent of the one who sent him (John 8:15-16). If anyone knew Jesus he would know also the Father who sent him (John 8:19). Jesus spoke nothing of himself but he said only that which his principal, the Father, had taught him. Although the Father had sent him, he was still with him (John 8:28-29; 12:49), that is, he was legally present. All of this means the apostle is not greater than the one who sent him (John 13:16). The one who received the agent whom Jesus sent received also Jesus and the one who sent Jesus (John 13:20). When Jesus was to be recalled, the one who sent Jesus would send a defense attorney in Jesus' name. This was the Holy Spirit who would come as Jesus' agent (John 14:26; 15:26; 16:8).

Moslems claim there have been six apostles of God: Adam, Noah, Abraham, Moses, Jesus, and Mohammed.[43] Because he was held to be an apostle, Mohammed was reported to have said, "Who obeys me, obeys God; who obeys the imam, obeys me; who does not obey me, does not obey God; who does not obey the imam, does not obey me."[44] This follows the normal laws regarding agency. Mohammed was a legal agent of God and the imam was a legal agent, or apostle, of Mohammed.

Christological Implications

Through Christ. The legal agent was the intermediary or the one in whom or through whom the principals acted and by whom the absent principal could be

[43]A. S. Tritton, Islam: Beliefs and Practices (London, c1957), p. 49.

[44]Ibid., p. 32.

legally present. The agent acted in the name of the one who sent him. When Christians offer prayers "through Christ our Lord" or "in Jesus' name," this means that Jesus is the agent through whom or in the name of whom they pray to the principal, the Lord. They do this because they believe that Jesus is God's authorized agent. It also means they believe they are legal agents of Jesus and have authority to speak in his name and with his authority. In a legally valid situation, Matthew said, where two or three [witnesses] are gathered in Jesus' name, there he will be in the midst of them, probably meaning they are legally authorized to act in his name (Matt 18:20). When the Pharisees claimed that Jesus was acting by the authority of Beelzebul, Jesus responded that they had committed the unpardonable sin of blasphemy. They could be forgiven for speaking against him, but when they spoke against the authority by which he worked, they were blaspheming God, the principal, of which he was the authorized agent (Matt 12:22-32). By sending their messages through the agent Christians are confident that they will reach the desired principal.

When Paul said, "God was in Christ, reconciling the world to himself" (2 Cor 5:19), he probably meant that Christ was God's legal agent through whom God worked and in whose authority he functioned. Physically, according to Paul, Jesus was a human being, "born of a woman, born under the law" (Gal 4:4), descended from David according to the flesh (Rom 1:3), but he was designated Son of God according to the spirit of holiness (Rom 1:4). Jesus had a natural body like the English kings, but at the same time he taught them "as one who had authority, and not as the scribes" (Mark 1:22). Like the legal body of the king he was above the law. The authority he claimed was legal authority--that due an apostle who spoke on behalf of the one who sent him.

When Jesus told his disciples that they could not know the times nor the seasons he said the Father had retained this under his own authority alone, but they would receive power when the Holy Spirit came upon them. The power he had in mind was the authority to act as his legal agents. When the Holy Spirit came upon them they would become authorized apostles (Acts 1:7-8). It was as he commanded them to receive the Holy Spirit that Jesus commissioned the disciples to become apostles, sending them just as the Father had sent him--with authority either to forgive or not to forgive sins (John 20:21-23).

The argument Paul had with the twelve was basically one of authority. Jesus, as the principal, had acknowledged them before their offices began. Since Paul did not become a Christian until after Jesus' death, they said he could not be a valid agent or apostle. The principal must acknowledge the agent before the agent can function in that capacity. Paul claimed that Jesus had appointed him, but he had no witnesses or documents to prove his apostleship. Rabbis did not give unqualified approval to voices from heaven. When Rabbi Eliezer differed with Rabban Gamaliel, Rabbi Akiba, and the other members of the court, he tried to prove his point by asking God to perform miracles for him. When these were done, the other rabbis refused to accept them as proof. Then he called on God to speak to them from heaven. When God said, "What do you have against Rabbi

Eliezer? The halachah is on his side in everything," Rabbi Yahoshua said, "It is not in heaven" (Deut 30:12), and Rabbi Eliezer was excommunicated (Baba Me zia 59b). The law even overrode a voice from heaven, because rabbis argued, the scripture was given to Israelites, and its word could not be refuted.

The argument was not that Paul's experience was spiritual and the other apostles had an objective, legal appointment that could be defended in court, as Käsemann claimed.[45] When the other apostles were appointed, the spirit descended upon them, also. Whenever disciples received the spirit, they became apostles. The spirit came with the authority. Paul had to argue on the basis of results. Just as prophets were not accepted as legal agents of the Lord until events proved that the Lord had fulfilled their predictions, so Paul could argue that God had prospered his ministry. This proved that he was a true apostle of the Lord. As an apostle, he was only an instrument through whom the Lord could act. Therefore he had no personal success; his boasting had to be in the principal, the Lord (2 Cor 10:17).[46]

The Incarnate Word. When the author of the Fourth Gospel said God's word had become flesh he meant that God had a human spokesperson who was his legal agent with authority to act in the name of the principal (John 1:14). Believers were no longer limited to the Hebrew Scriptures to learn what the word of God was, as they had been in Babylon.

Legal Incarnation. The incarnation of a word does not have to mean a human being has become a god, physically. The written word has a lot of authority. A person's name on a contract that has been adequately witnessed is binding in court. If the president of the United States sent a written message to some foreign power, bearing his or her stamp and signature, the legal power of the United States stands behind it. The foreign authority has a right to make plans on the basis of this written document. But there is another way of negotiating with foreign powers in absentia. The president could send the secretary of state to represent him in this communication. As the president's agent or apostle, the secretary is legally the president of the United States. He is authorized, within the defined limits, to discuss, negotiate, and sign an agreement in behalf of the president. Instead of the written message, the secretary of state is the president's human agent, who is the president's word in flesh or the incarnate word of the president of the United States. This does not mean that the secretary of state is the incarnate

---

[45]E. Käsemann, "Die Legitimität des Apostels. Eine Untersuchung zu II Korinther 10-13," ZNW 41 (1942):33-71.

[46]E. Käsemann, "Die Legitimität, 33-71. S. Hafemann, "'Self-Commendation' and Apostolic Legitimacy in 2 Corinthians: A Pauline Dialectic?" NTS 36 (1990):66-88, was basically correct in his analysis without realizing the significance of legal agency or the close relationship between spirit and legal authority.

president. Only the president is the president incarnate, but the secretary is the incarnate word of the president. Whatever the secretary of state finally settles and signs is understood legally as the very words that the president wanted said. They have legal authority as the ipsissima verba presidenti.

The Incarnate Christ. The author of the Fourth Gospel may have had something like this in mind when he said, "The word became flesh and pitched his tent in our midst" (John 1:14). The smoke and the fire from the tent of meeting constituted the real presence of the Lord who had condescended in this way to dwell with his people in the wilderness, and his word was stored there in the chest containing the contract. In the judgment of the author of the Fourth Gospel Jesus was the legal way in which God made himself present on earth. He was God's word in the form of human flesh, and legally he was God (John 1:1). The idea that incarnation is a legal concept was understood by a twelfth century A.D. legal doctrine that the prince was lex animata, "the animated" or "living law." This could also have been called the incarnate law or the law made flesh in the being of the prince.[47]

Ashton's idea that the Logos in John 1:1 was wisdom is less complex than he thought. God's word might be identified with God's wisdom.[48] It is his word or message. Both Jews and Christians have treated it as if it were the legal contract the Lord had made with his people. Therefore it has legal status, and God can be held to the terms given here. This is God's revelation through the scripture. When this word or wisdom became flesh, however, Ashton[49] thought this must be true as a myth, history, or theology, and he argued, "But there is no possibility of viewing incarnation (or resurrection, for that matter) as an event like any other."[50] He concluded that the Johannine prologue was a wisdom hymn and that it must be understood in some kind of ambiguity, like a myth.[51] It is possible, of course, for a written word to become incarnate in plain, ordinary history, in terms of events like any other. This happens whenever a written document is replaced by a legal agent.

By sending a human agent to bear his message, God arranged for his word to become flesh. Physically, Paul said Jesus was "born of a woman, born under the law" (Gal 4:4). He was of the posterity of David according to the flesh (Rom 1:3). Tertullian, in his argument against Marcion, insisted that Jesus was

---

[47]Kantorowicz, Two Bodies, pp. 128-29.

[48]J. Ashton, "The Transformation of Wisdom. As Study of the Prologue of John's Gospel," NTS 32 (1986):161-186.

[49]Ashton, "Transformation," p. 180.

[50]Ashton, "Transformation," p. 180-82.

[50]Ashton, "Transformation," pp. 180-81.

genuinely human; he had brothers and sisters; he was born of a human woman (Contra Marcion 3. 11). God could represent himself in any way he chose. He could use a pillar of cloud or a burning bush, but whatever he used to represent himself became worthy of himself. This is true because an agent is legally identical to the principal and therefore worthy of the principal. Since God chose Christ to be his agent or representative, Christ is a worthy representative of God (Contra Marcion 3.10).

Eternal Life. While he was physically still alive, Jesus, like other kings, had two bodies, a physical body that was born, lived, breathed, ate, studied, worked, and died, and a legal body which was eternal. This was the corporation or the body of Christ. This body had a legal structure organized around his apostles--all of whom were legally identical with Jesus. When Jesus was crucified, his suffering, pain, and death effected only the physical body. The corporate body is eternal. It never dies, and after the physical body of the deceased is buried, the corporate body continues with all of the legal clothing it had before.

When F. -M. Braun tried to explain the way in which Jesus was in the Father; the Father was in Jesus; Jesus was in his apostles; and the apostles were in Jesus, he said this was "the mystery of the incarnation."[52] Had he known the legal significance of agency, corporate identity, and the transference of legal clothing from the deceased to the heirs, this would not have seemed as mysterious to him as it did. Rengstorf's final chapter in his extensive and very useful study on apostleship, noted that Jesus is pictured as an ambassador in the Fourth Gospel, but Rengstorf strangely dropped his logic when it came to the conclusion and ended with an affirmation of faith, saying that the Gospel of John "derives its unique quality from the fact that Christ as ambassador is no man, not even Original or First Man."[53] This is not a necessary conclusion for one who understands the legal significance of incarnation. When Jesus appointed his apostles and gave them authority as agents, they constituted a corporate group, a legal entity, the body of Christ. Legally they were identical with Jesus. From the standpoint of legal authority, Jesus was in them, and they were in him. As the agent of God he commissioned them to go to all the nations, introducing others into the body of Christ by the legal ceremony of baptism and the reception of the Holy Spirit. This made the new initiates parties to the new contract and members of the body of Christ. This could all be done without the physical presence of Christ since his corporate, legal body, like other corporations, was eternal, and it was through this body that Jesus promised to be with them always (Matt 28:16-20).

---

[51]F. -M. Braun, Jean le Theologien (Paris, 1972), pp. 32, 176, 227, 236, 300.

[53]Rengstorf, "Apostleship," p. 66.

Acts of the Apostles. The significance of apostolic authority was taken for granted by the author of the Gospel of Matthew who structured his gospel accordingly. In chapters 5-7, Jesus preached; in chapters 8-9, he healed the sick, cast out demons, and cleansed lepers; in chapter 10, he appointed the twelve and gave them authority to be his legal agents--to preach, heal, cast out demons, and cleanse lepers (Matt 10:1-8) just as he had done. The author of Acts presumed that since these apostles had apostolic authority to be legally identical to Jesus they must also have performed the same kind of miracles Jesus performed. For example, the man who had been blind from birth was healed at once by Jesus. This caused a great furor among the religious people who tried to get the man to deny that he had been healed, but he refused (John 9:1-41). Likewise Peter healed a lame man at the temple gate. Afterward Peter and John were cross-examined by the high priest and other officials who tried to suppress Peter and quiet the excitement that had aroused the people (Acts 3:1-4:22). Paul also healed a lame man (Acts 14:8-10).

According to the report, Jesus raised a girl who had died by saying, "Talitha arise," "Little girl, arise" (Luke 8:49-56), and Peter did the same thing, saying "Tabitha arise" (Acts 9:36-43). Paul also raised the dead Eutychus (Acts 20:9-12). A woman touched the hem of Jesus' garment and was healed from her hemorrhage (Matt 9:20-22; Mark 6:56). People were healed by arranging for the shadow of Peter to fall on them (Acts 5:15). People brought scarves and other articles of clothing for Paul to touch. They then brought them back to the sick to touch and be healed (Acts 19:11-12). When they brought a lame man to Jesus on a mat, he ordered him to take up his bed and walk, and he did (Matt 9:1-8; Mark 2:1-12; Luke 5:17-26). Peter did the same (Acts 9:32-35).

At a certain point in Jesus' career, he set his face steadfast to go to Jerusalem, where he expected to be killed (Luke 9:51, 53). Paul, likewise set his face steadfast to go to Jerusalem and Rome, realizing that he would not return to see the people to whom he said, "Farewell" (Acts 19:21; 20:22; 21:15, 17; 23:11). Jesus appeared before the Roman governor, Pilate, who found no guilt worthy of death (Luke 23:4, 14, 22). Paul appeared before the Roman governor, Festus, who found Paul had done nothing worthy of death (Acts 25:25). Both were under accusation by the Jews.

These statements reflect more doctrine than factual history. The narrator, who believed Jesus had ordained these apostles to be his agents, reasoned that they must have done the things Jesus did, since an agent acts in behalf of a principal and in his name. In this conviction he composed examples of Jesus' actions and goals being fulfilled through the agency of the apostles. Along with all of this reconstructed, doctrinal history is an important basic truth. Jesus appointed legal agents to administer his program while he was still alive. This made it legally possible for the movement to continue after the death of Jesus.

Legal Perfection. It has been difficult for Christians to understand how Jesus could have demanded that they be perfect, when no one is ever actually perfect in terms of morality. Legally, however, anyone who observes the required laws is righteous or sinless.

There is an important distinction between legal and actual guilt. If, for example, a man came to a lawyer for defense and said he had just killed someone. He was admittedly guilty. His lawyer would probably tell him that the client was not a lawyer and therefore did not know whether he was guilty or not. He should just tell the lawyer what he did, and the lawyer would present the matter in court. Then the court would decide whether or not he was guilty. If the court decided he was innocent, he was not guilty, even if he knew he killed someone.

That which is actually true may be legally false, so it is important to know when a term is being used factually or legally. The concepts are not always the same. This is also true of theological doctrines that have been created on the basis of legal ideas. For example, Philo said that the high priest, when he entered the holy of holies, was immune to sin (Spec. 1.230, 293). Because he was required by liturgy to be legally perfect, at that time he offered a sacrifice of a bull for himself and his family before he entered the holy of holies. That offering cleansed him from all sins, legally, according to the ritualistic laws accepted at that time by Jews. This made him perfect, from a legal point of view, for the next ritual that required a sinless priest. It does not mean that he had never sinned or made any mistakes in his life.

Jesus was called the apostle and high priest of our confession (Heb 3:1). Since the term "apostle" is a legal term, it is quite likely that the author of Hebrews referred to Jesus' high priestly legal qualities when he said he was "without sin" (Heb 4:15). Having made his high priestly sacrifice, he was considered ritually "perfect." As a high priest, he was "holy, blameless, unstained, and separated from sinners" (Heb 7:26). This was not only true of Jesus, but also of others who had been made perfect through suffering (Heb 2:10). Their suffering had been adequate to pay for all their sins, so that they could no longer be prosecuted for anything. They were legally innocent. By the same token the pope is said to be infallible. Legally, like every monarch, the pope is infallible, because he cannot be taken to a higher court. Like Pope Leo III, every pope is authorized to cleanse himself from any presumed infraction, and no one has the authority to challenge his judgment. He is only infallible in a legal situation, namely, when he speaks from his cathedra, which is his throne or bench from which he could pronounce judgment. No one has the authority to challenge his judgment.

CONCLUSIONS

These comparisons show that there are many similarities between heavenly courts, as they were depicted mythologically in antiquity, earthly courts in antiquity, modern courts, and modern churches. These similarities are in the form of architecture and liturgical procedure. They also are carried over into traditional concepts and ways of thinking. The relationship of God to judges and clergy leaders; apostles and agents; contracts and treaties; legal and theological truth in relationship to actual fact; and the validity of the written word and the word made flesh in the form of an agent are all legal concepts and attitudes toward the written law. This law and the authority of traditional precedents is basic to Jewish and Christian interpretation of scripture, and they are not new. They were practiced by prophets, poets, and wisdom writers in the Hebrew Scripture.

Since Moses was God's agent or apostle who had legal authority to speak in God's behalf, it was understood that the books that were ascribed to him were the word of God and had the force of a contract. Those who wanted to know the terms by which they were under contract to serve God had to read the books of Moses. This is true not only of those who wrote New Testament documents and rabbinic literature, but it is the basis on which many prophets, Psalmists, and wisdom writers learned what the word of God was. These legal concepts that are still practiced in modern courts were found in the New Testament, the Hebrew Scripture, the early church fathers, and extra-canonical works such as the works of Josephus. Literature that was formerly thought to have originated charismatically can now be shown to have been based on legal analyses of earlier writings that the authors already considered sacred law to be treated as the legal word of God.

The close relationship shown between legal authority and the function of the Spirit sheds new light upon Christian spirituality. Whenever legal authority is given the Spirit is transferred. Oil was poured on the head of a citizen and he became a king or high priest. That was the precise moment when the Spirit descended on him. When hands were laid on Jews or pagans they received the Holy Spirit and became Christians. When Jesus breathed the Holy Spirit on his disciples they became his legal agents under commission to act for him, in his name, and at his responsibility. When they were commissioned as apostles the Spirit of Christ was in them. The Spirit of the principal could then speak through them. The so-called "in Christ mysticism" is a legal concept relating God to Jesus and Jesus to Christians.

When scholars take the legal significance of theological terms, like apostle, contract, and prayer, into account and recognize the frequency with which the scripture itself is a legal commentary on scripture already held to be the word of God, many new insights will become evident in its interpretation. For example, when Protestants learn the prominence of the treasury of merits in biblical thought, this should make relationships with Roman Catholics easier. When Christians learn that Jesus consciously functioned with the belief that he was an apostle of the Lord, this should bring Christians closer in communication with Moslems, who believe that Jesus and Mohammed were both apostles or legal agents.

Once it is understood that Daniel was not a prophecy but victory narrative, celebrating the success of the Hasmoneans, Christians should no longer be compelled to try to initiate international activity corresponding to the Hasmonean Revolt in the Near East under the erroneous belief that this will bring about the end of the world, the end of history, or the end of a pagan world. If this study is considered carefully and widely, it might make it easier for Christians and Jews to give up some erroneous and damaging doctrines that have been held. When Christians learn that the Bible was held to be only the legal word of God, we should not be under such a strong compulsion to fulfill the very words of the Bible, even though this action should lead nations into such militant activity as the Crusades, the Spanish Inquisitions, the Ku Klux Klan, and the Irish Republican Army. Many Christians today object to some of the historical behavior of Jews, Christians, and Moslems. They are frustrated by the apartheid teachings of the scripture. They would welcome an opportunity to reanalyze Jewish and Christian history with the idea of reform rather than perfect submission. Reformation without careful analysis is doomed to be superficial and only partially successful. This analysis does not offer solutions to all of the church's social, political, and ethical problems, but it provides a starting basis for further research and application.

GENERAL INDICES

WORDS

accuse 53, 57, 59, 69
adopt 15
Advocate . . 53, 59, 62, 72, 74
agent. . 8-10, 12, 13, 17-20, 27, 61, 62, 64, 65, 106, 111-116, 118-120, 122, 125, 127, 128, 130, 132, 133, 135, 137, 139, 142.
altar 1, 10, 22, 24, 26, 54
Amalekites 38
ambassador 116
Amen 43
American . . 3, 5, 19, 29, 53, 74, 114
angel 91, 106
apostle . .12, 13, 23, 30, 113, 117-120, 131, 132, 133, 134, 137, 139, 141, 142
architect 1, 24, 26, 27
attorney. . 3, 6, 19, 21, 24, 28, 34, 36, 39, 40, 44, 46, 48, 51, 53, 57, 59, 66, 72, 89, 90, 98, 119, 133 135
audit 88
authority . . 5-7, 9-13, 16-19, 21, 24, 30, 88, 94, 95, 102, 106, 111, 113, 114, 116, 118, 120, 122, 127, 131, 132, 133, 137, 140, 142
baptism 3, 15, 18
battle . . 89, 102, 105, 107, 111
Bible . . 3-5, 54, 74, 80, 84, 113, 118, 129
biblical. . 3, 4, 6, 23, 27, 53, 54, 62, 65, 69, 71, 74, 78, 79, 81, 82, 84, 88, 90, 111, 118, 120, 122, 142
blessing 74, 75, 77, 81
body 5, 12, 14, 15-16, 19
business 113, 116
canon. 121, 123, 129, 142
captivity 7, 21, 91, 111
chancel 1, 20, 25, 28
Chancellor 21, 23
Cheyenne 29, 31, 95
Christian . . 4-7, 14, 16, 27, 30, 33, 37, 38, 41, 43, 45, 48, 50, 53, 54, 63, 65, 67, 71, 77, 81, 84, 87, 111, 113, 115, 118, 128, 134, 136, 138, 142
Christianity 2, 16
church . . . 1-3, 7, 12-16, 18 22, 24, 25-27, 74, 81, 86, 113, 115, 118, 132, 133, 142, 143
clergy 2, 20, 24, 27
clouds . . 103, 106, 108-110, 112
Code Napoleon 5
commerce 115
complaint 29
confess 59, 60, 66
constitution 4-6, 10
contract. . 3, 16, 28, 30, 32, 39, 47, 69, 73-87, 114, 117, 120, 138, 142
corporation 12, 13
court . . 1, 3, 10, 16, 17, 19, 21-24, 26 30, 32, 34-35, 37-41, 43-48, 50, 53, 54, 56, 58-60, 62, 64, 66-69, 72-74, 80, 82, 86, 90, 92, 94, 95, 97-99, 102, 111, 115, 120, 141
covenant 74, 75, 80-82
crime 60
curse 42, 43
curses 74, 75, 77, 80, 81
Day of Atonement 88, 91
day of reckoning 88
day of vengeance 88, 91
day of vindication 88, 91
death . . 30, 32, 43, 45-47, 94, 99, 103, 107, 108, 110, 111, 120, 128, 129, 130, 136, 139, 140
debt 32
defendant . . 2, 19, 26, 31, 36-39, 46, 48, 53, 55, 57, 58, 61, 69, 70, 73, 88, 92, 94, 95, 98, 100, 111
defense 53, 58, 72
Deuteronomy. . 5, 21, 76, 81, 83,

84
doctrine . . 3, 14, 18, 20, 26, 113, 138, 140, 141, 143
emotion 53, 57
enemy 57, 70, 80, 89, 108
English. . 2, 6, 11, 10, 13, 14, 19, 74, 75, 81, 114, 136
evidence. . 35-37, 39, 41, 44, 45-48, 90
exegesis 3
fact 6, 7, 13
family 29, 31, 34
favoritism 71, 72
fiction 6, 7, 9, 11, 13
forgive 92, 111
garment 88, 91-93, 95
German 3
gospel 2, 14
Greek . . 2, 36, 38, 39, 47, 49, 51, 54, 74, 94, 99, 102, 111
guilt . . 33, 37, 44, 117, 129, 130, 140
guilty 53, 55, 56, 61
Hanukkah 103, 110, 111
Hasmonean . .90, 100, 102, 108, 111, 117, 134, 142
heaven . . 54, 56, 64, 67, 88, 90, 92, 99, 102, 104, 106, 107, 111, 115, 119, 122, 132, 136, 141
Hebrew . . 3, 4, 54-56, 74, 75, 79, 84-86
hostage 32, 33
incarnate 138
incarnation 138, 139
injure 53, 88
Indian 29
Israel. . 6, 11, 15, 23, 25, 27, 17, 23, 25, 26, 29, 56, 67, 72, 73, 75, 77-81, 83-89, 91, 98, 104, 111, 117, 119, 121, 123, 125, 128-129
Jew . . . 2, 7, 14, 16, 21, 26, 30, 33, 36, 41, 43-45, 48, 49, 60, 72, 76, 82, 83, 84, 86, 87, 91, 92, 94, 96, 98, 100, 103-106, 108, 115, 118, 119, 121, 127, 129, 140, 142, 143
Jewish 2, 5, 6, 16, 26, 30
Judaism 2, 7, 9, 16
judge . . 1, 3, 4, 9-12, 13, 15, 19, 21-25, 27-30, 32, 34, 36-37, 45, 47, 48, 51-54, 56, 57, 59, 60, 62, 65-67, 69, 71-73, 88-90, 94, 95, 97-99, 100, 103, 111, 116, 118, 120, 121, 122, 127-128, 131, 132
judgment. . 4, 9, 14, 21, 23, 25, 26,27, 32, 35, 36, 48, 53, 55, 56, 61, 62, 65, 67, 69-72, 77, 88, 90, 92, 94, 96, 106, 107, 111, 118, 120, 125, 127, 128, 135, 138, 141
Jurist 1, 2, 6, 12, 14
jury 30, 35, 39, 53
justice . .9, 14, 23, 26, 29, 31, 34, 51-53, 62, 67, 69, 70, 88, 90, 120
king . . 9-15, 18, 19, 21-23, 23, 26, 28, 30, 53, 65, 67, 75, 77, 79, 82, 85, 92, 93, 95, 99, 105, 107, 108, 111, 113, 116, 118, 121, 127, 128, 129, 131, 134, 136, 139, 142
kingdom . . 92, 98, 103, 104, 110, 120, 130
Latin . . 3, 38, 39, 47, 49, 51, 54, 65
law . . 2, 4, 6, 8, 12-14, 15, 18, 19, 21, 22, 24, 26, 27, 29, 30, 32, 36-38, 41, 44, 47-49, 115, 116, 130, 133, 136, 138, 141, 142
Laws of England 5
lawyer. . 2, 4, 6, 19, 24, 53, 54, 58, 62, 90
legal . . 3-5, 7, 10-18, 19, 21, 24, 27, 38, 44-47, 75, 77, 79, 82, 84, 87, 92, 94, 113, 115-117, 119, 120, 122, 127, 128, 130-132, 134, 137, 138, 140, 141, 142
liturgical . . . 1, 2, 30, 63, 65, 68
liturgy 117
love 74, 80, 82, 84-87
marriage 74, 78, 82, 84

messenger. . 115, 119, 122, 125, 128, 129
messiah . . 113, 117, 118, 127, 131-133
minister 1, 3, 15, 24
moot 29, 34
Muslim 29
myth . . 90, 92, 93, 98, 99, 100, 102, 103, 106, 108-112
Ndendeuli 29, 98
New Testament. . 4, 82, 84, 87, 133, 142
New Year's Day 88, 91
oath . . . 35, 41-43, 51, 74, 76, 78, 80, 87
offense 33, 36, 44, 45, 48
pardon 33
Passover 117
penalty 30, 33, 36
Pentateuch . . 4, 6, 120, 121, 129
perjury 42
Persian 4
Pharisee 131, 136
plaintiff . . 2, 19, 26, 29, 31, 36, 38-40, 48, 53, 55, 69, 88, 90, 98, 100, 107, 111
plead 53, 54, 59, 69, 71
politic 10, 14, 18
pope 134, 19, 42
prayer. . 1, 3, 26, 27, 53-57, 59, 62-65, 67-70, 72, 73, 90, 98, 116, 136, 142
precedent 4
priest. . 1, 3, 10, 15, 20, 26, 55, 68, 72, 76, 91, 92, 94, 111, 116, 117, 120, 134, 141, 142
principal. . 113, 114, 116, 119, 122, 128, 129, 132, 133, 135-137, 139, 142
prison 91, 92, 93
proof 41, 45, 49
prophet . . 4, 6, 15, 23, 29, 113, 118, 121, 122, 126, 129, 130, 133, 142
prosecute. . 36, 53, 59, 73, 89, 91, 98
Protestant 7
Proverbs 129
Psalm . . . 120, 127, 128, 129, 131, 142
Psalmist 95
Psalms 53, 56, 68, 70
punish . . 29, 31, 33, 36, 39, 41, 45, 50
Rabbi . . 33, 43-45, 51, 115, 117, 128, 136, 142
rebel 30
rebellion 100, 102
redeem 59, 60, 69
religion 31
religious 53, 54, 66, 74, 80
rhetoric . . 3, 4, 35, 38, 39, 49, 54, 57, 58, 61, 62, 64, 66, 72
righteous . . . 56, 67, 70, 72, 90
righteousness 23
ritual 1, 2, 24, 27
Roman . . 54, 58, 71, 89, 95, 94, 98, 101, 102, 105, 110, 115
Samaritan 119, 129
sanhedrin 23, 30, 93
Satan 37, 46, 59, 91
scripture . . 2, 4-7, 16, 21, 27, 30, 74, 75, 79, 85, 86, 88, 93, 117, 118, 122, 123, 127, 133, 138, 142, 143
sect 77, 84
sin . . 33, 77, 83, 85, 91, 92, 93, 111, 117, 141
Son of man. . 93, 98, 100, 103, 104, 106, 107, 110-112
sovereign 3, 79
spirit. . . 5, 15, 17, 118, 127, 130, 131, 135, 137-142
state . . 1, 10, 13, 15, 19, 19, 24, 30, 35, 52, 74, 81
synagogue 3, 16
temple . . .54, 61, 76, 84, 89, 91, 98, 99, 100, 108, 110, 111

testimony 2, 90
throne 58, 67
Torah 5
torture 99
tradition. . 1-2, 4, 6, 7, 21, 23, 25-28, 30
treaties 116
trial. . . 29, 30, 32, 34, 36-39, 45-47, 48
vengeance 31-33
verdict . . 55, 57, 59, 60, 89, 90, 92, 98, 99, 107
vindicate 59, 61, 62, 77
vizier . . 15, 18, 19, 25, 29, 62, 97
wilderness 138
witness . . 29, 31, 34, 35, 39, 41, 44-48, 74, 75, 76, 78
worship 1-3, 24
worshiper. . 53, 54, 57, 62-63, 66-68, 70, 71

ANCIENT NAMES

Aaron 72, 94, 117
Abel 38
Abimelech 38
Abraham . . 38, 62, 63, 67, 72, 76, 77, 92, 121, 135
Abram 38
Achilles 34
Adam 128, 135
Aesop 98
Akiba 136
Alexander 10, 11, 57
Amos 33, 46, 49, 88
Antiochus. . 76, 96, 99, 100, 103, 107-111
Antipater 57, 58, 68
Archelaus 58, 59, 89, 99
Aristotle. .4, 35, 38, 39, 47, 49, 50, 61, 62, 99
Athenagoras 133
Augustus 10
Barnabas 44
Barzilai 9
Bathsheba 9
Boaz 35
Caesar 58, 61, 89
Cain 38
Charlemagne 18
Chrysostom 133
Cicero 4
Clement 134
Daniel. . 6, 7, 88, 90, 98, 99, 102, 105, 107, 108-112
David . . 9-10, 17, 22, 23, 66, 77, 92, 93, 118, 127, 129-131, 133, 136, 138
Demosthenes 4
Diodorus 11
Eliakim 93
Eliezer 34, 136
Elizabeth 10
Enoch 90, 93, 98, 102, 107
Esau 63
Eutychus 140
Ezekiel 95, 121
Ezra 90
Gamaliel 136
Gideon 130
Hagar 38
Haggai 122
Halsbury 4
Hammurabi 8, 17
Henry VII 14, 18
Herod 57, 61, 93, 94, 199
Hippolytus 133
Hiram 85
Hosea 17, 129
Isaac 38, 64, 67, 72, 77
Isaiah 93, 131
Jacob . 38, 46, 62, 64, 67, 73, 77
Jehoiachin 93

Jehoshaphat 127, 132
Jephthah 130
Jeremiah . . 5-7, 47, 76, 83, 86, 121, 122, 123, 126
Jesus . . 5, 10, 13-14, 17, 25, 36-37, 43, 44, 45, 51, 94, 104, 112, 113, 118, 129, 131, 132, 134, 135, 136, 138-141
Jezebel 17, 47
Joab 129
Job 41, 53, 59, 60
John 44, 129, 138
Jonah 32
Jonathan 77
Jose 33
Joseph 46, 47, 51, 66
Josephus . . 57, 58, 63, 89, 96, 100
Joshua . . 47, 73, 91, 94, 95, 121
Josiah 76
Judas . . 44, 93, 96, 102, 103, 105, 107, 109, 111
Justin 133
Laban 38, 46, 77
Lot 38
Louis XIV 19
Malachi 60, 122
Marcion 133, 134, 138
Mark 44
Marqah 119
Matthew 16
Melchizedek 128
Mohammed 135, 142
Moses . . 94, 105, 106, 113, 118-121, 126, 130, 132
Nathan 10, 23
Nehemiah 90
Nicodemus 14
Nicolas 58
Nikolaus 10
Noah 135
Paul. . 5, 7, 17, 33, 37, 38, 44, 82, 82, 117, 120, 131, 134, 137, 138, 140
Peter 44, 140
Philip 11
Philo 43, 44, 48
Phineas 55, 56
Pilate 94
Plowden 14
Plutarch 11
Polybius 100
Pompey 103
Pseudo Philo 94
Quintilian. . 4, 22, 30, 34-35, 38-41, 44, 48-50, 53, 57-58, 61, 62, 68, 72, 91, 93, 95, 98
Rekh-Mi-Re 17-18
Rothair 130
Samson 16
Samuel 38
Sarah 38
Sarai 66
Saul 16, 23, 38, 128, 131
Silas 44
Socrates 35, 49
Solomon. . 10, 21, 22, 85, 118, 127, 129
Tertullian 133, 134
Theophilus 133
Thucidydes 63
Timothy 44
Uriah 9
Urshagga 64-65
Varus 58
Zechariah 92
Zedekiah 76
Zerubbabel 92
Zimri 56

MODERN SCHOLARS

Ackroyd 35
Aejmelaeus 53, 64
Aharoni 25
Ahlström 8, 89
Albright 25, 29
Andersen 47
Andrews 24
Aresto 114
Ashton 138
Balentine 72
Barton 75
Baumgarten 23
Beale 90
Bertholet 8
Bentzen 75
Boismard 126
Braun 139
Buchanan. . 5, 7, 8, 16, 25, 33, 42, 80, 85, 92, 95, 100, 117, 132, 134
Buis 75
Buss 122
Campbell 20, 21
Casey 101-102
Chernick 51
Clements 24
Coats 7, 118
Collins 103
Coppens 104
Cumont 106
Daremberg 106
DeLanghe 25
Dequeker 104
Derrett 120
Di Lella 103
Drew 130
Driver 61, 84
Engnell 20, 130
Ferguson 100
Finkelstein 75
Fitzmeyer 127
Forsyth 30, 66
Frankfort 23, 24, 130
Galinski 5, 20
Gerstenberger 54, 66, 68
Gerth 75
Ginsberg 78
Gnuse 118
Goetz 19
Gontard 18
Goodenough 58
Gray 61
Greenberg . . . 54, 57, 62, 63, 67
Greene 115, 122, 125
Gregory 114
Gulliver 29, 40, 98
Hafemann 137
Hallo 66
Hamilton-Kelly 24
Hamilton-Patterson 24
Hanhart 103, 104
Hartman 103
Harvey 36, 46
Hoebel . 1, 29, 32, 34, 61, 78, 95
Holdsworth 13
Holmes 31, 33
Hooker 8
Hunter 114
Kantorowicz . 9-13, 67, 130, 138
Käsemann 137
Kerschner 69
Klensch 114
Köhler 35
Kramer 64
Lacocque 103, 108
Lagrange 128
Leiser 1, 31
Levinthal 115, 117
Lightfoot 127
Lindbloom 126
Llewellyn . 1, 29, 32, 34, 78, 95
Lohfink 85
Long 7, 118
Lorenz 75
Lundquist 2

Martindale 75
Maine 2, 6, 8, 12, 13, 16, 78, 86
Mayle 3, 18
McCarthy 75
McKay 87
Meek 8, 41, 43
Mendenhall . . 2, 26, 30, 74, 75, 77, 79, 80, 105
Meyer 114
Meyers 37
Miller 106, 114
Moran 84
Morgenstern 89
Mosca 103
Most 79
Mueller 77
Nader 34, 61
Neyrey 128
Noth 103
Pellauer 103
Peters 102
Petersen 16
Phillipson 27
Pope 42
Porteous 103, 108, 112
Pritchard 8, 61, 75, 78
Proudman 103
Quell 84
Rengstorf 119, 139
Reuschlein 114
Rissi 106
Saglio 106
Sanders 121, 126
Saunders 14
Schiffman 16
Schnutenhaus 106
Seavey 114
Segal 89
Sell 113, 114
Sherwin-White 22
Simmons 115, 117
Smith 69
Speiser 55
Stauffer 85
Staunford 14
Thompson 75
Tigay 20, 22, 63
Trites 35, 38, 42, 74
Tritton 135
Tucker 7, 75
Vander Kam 91, 106
Von Rad 126
Wanamaker 132, 134
Weber 75
Weiser 75
Wenham 104
Westcott 128
Wigmore 80
Wilson . . 13, 17, 23, 26, 30, 41, 43, 52, 61

BIBLICAL REFERENCES

1 Chron 17:11-13; 22:30 21
1 Cor 1:1-7 11
1 Cor 5:1-5 17
1 Cor 6:1-19 7
1 Cor 6:9 120
1 John 3:18 85
1 John 5:16 15
1 Kgs 2:5-23 23
1 Kings 1:10 17
1 Kings 3:16-8 21
1 Kings 10:1-10 127
1 Kings 21:1-16 47
1 Sam 3:17 42
1 Sam 10:1-10 . . . . 16, 131
1 Sam 14:39, 45 42
1 Sam 15:10-33 38
1 Sam 16:18-23 128
1 Sam 18:3; 20:8, 16; 23:18 . 77
1 Sam 23:3 51
1 Sam 25:24-31 66

1 Thes 2:5, 10 44
2 Chron 3-4 24
2 Chron 19:5-7 62
2 Chron 19:6 127
2 Chron 23:1 75
2 Cor 1:23 44
2 Cor 3:4 134
2 Cor 3:4-6 117
2 Cor 5:11 96
2 Cor 5:17 95
2 Cor 5:19 136
2 Cor 10:17 137
2 Kgs 25:27-30 93
2 Sam 1:1-6 21
2 Sam 1:1-7 9
2 Sam 12:9 129
2 Sam 13:18-19 95
2 Sam 14:17 8
2 Sam 14:20 128
2 Sam 15:21 43
2 Sam 19:31-37 9
2 Sam 23:2 127
Acts 1:6-8 45
Acts 1:7-8 136
Acts 1:22; 2:32; 3:15; 5:32 . . 45
Acts 3:1, 11; 4:13, 19; 8:14 . 44
Acts 3:1-4:22 140
Acts 5:15 140
Acts 9:4; 22:7; 26:14 36
Acts 9:32-35 140
Acts 9:36-43 140
Acts 10:39-41; 13:31; 22:15, 20; 26:16 45
Acts 13:36 . . . . 23, 128
Acts 13:43, 46, 50 44
Acts 15:32 44
Acts 15:37; 23:27 71
Acts 15:39 44
Acts 15:40 44
Acts 16:19, 25 44
Acts 17:14-15 44
Acts 19:11-12 140
Acts 19:21; 20:22; 21:15, 17; 23:11 140
Acts 20:9-12 140
Acts 22:8; 26:15 36
Acts 25:25 140
Amos 3:3-6 49
Amos 3:12 46
Amos 4:6-11 33
Col 1:24 33
Col 2:11; 3:9-14 95
Col 3:18-19 81
Dan 7:10 97
Dan 7:10-11 90
Dan 7:11 . . . . 98, 99
Dan 7:14 100
Dan 7:22 100
Dan 9:1-2 5
Dan 9:2 6
Dan 9:4 6
Dan 9:27; 11:28, 30 77
Dan 11:14-19 109-110
Dan 11:40-45 109-110
Dan 11:41 108
Dan 11:44 108
Dan 12:1-13 110
Dan 12:7 43
Daniel 11:40 110
Deut 1:6 119
Deut 1:9-18 21
Deut 1:16-17 . . 36, 62, 118, 119
Deut 1:16-18 88
Deut 4:20 124
Deut 4:29 125
Deut 4:34 124
Deut 5:5 116
Deut 5:11 42
Deut 5:20 44
Deut 6, 11 77
Deut 6:5 85
Deut 6:7 5
Deut 7:9 87
Deut 7:12 . . . . 76, 124
Deut 7:13 85
Deut 9:9, 11, 15 76
Deut 11:1 84
Deut 11:19 5

Deut 12:2 123
Deut 15:12 125
Deut 15:12-13, 18 32
Deut 16:18 35
Deut 18:18 126
Deut 19:15 48
Deut 19:17-18 120
Deut 21:18-21 30
Deut 22:23-29 79
Deut 24:1 47, 79, 82
Deut 26:17 79
Deut 26:17-19 79
Deut 27-30 76
Deut 28:26 123, 124
Deut 28:49-51 123
Deut 29:20 80
Deut 30:1, 3 125
Deut 30:12 137
Deut 30:15 125
Deut 31:27 51
Deut 32:35 32
Deut 32:40 43
Deut18:21-22 121
Deuteronomy 18:18 120
Deuteronomy 19:15 44
Deuteronomy 24:1 83
Eph 4:22-24 95
Eph 5:25 82
Eph 5:25, 28, 33 81
Est 9:12 50
Exod 4:10 126
Exod 4:12 120
Exod 5:8-9 25
Exod 5:40 25
Exod 6:12 50
Exod 6:16-30 25
Exod 6:30 25
Exod 7:1 17
Exod 12:6 117
Exod 14:19 105
Exod 14:19-20 105
Exod 18:13 21
Exod 18:14-6 21
Exod 19:18-20 106
Exod 20:7 42
Exod 20:16 44
Exod 21:28-22:6 9
Exod 22:1 9
Exod 22:1-4 32
Exod 22:13 46
Exod 23:23-30 105
Exod 23:32; 34:12, 15 77
Exod 24:7 76, 83
Exod 24:8 79
Exod 24:15-18 105
Exod 25:22 47
Exod 28:38 94
Exod 28-29 94
Exod 31:18 47, 76
Exod 32:1-14 72
Exod 33:7-11 106
Exod 34:1 126
Exod 40:14 94
Exodus 21:8-22:6 10
Exodus 22:1 10
Ezek 15:5 51
Ezek 16:8 78
Ezek 23:5 85
Ezek 26:16 95
Ezek 33:11 43
Ezra 9-10 7
Ezra 10:14-30 7
Gal 1:13 36
Gal 1:23 37
Gal 3:15 75
Gal 4:4 136, 138
Gal 5:14 86
Gen 12:11-13 66
Gen 14:22 43
Gen 18:23 73
Gen 18:23-19:29 73
Gen 21:8-21 38
Gen 21:25-26 38
Gen 21:27, 32; 26:28 77
Gen 24:8-16 38
Gen 24:27 63
Gen 26:17-22 38
Gen 31:36-55 38

Gen 31:39 46
Gen 31:44 77
Gen 32:10-13 63
Gen 37:3-4, 23, 30-33 94
Gen 37:18-36 47
Gen 42:15, 16 42
Gen 44:4-8 50
Gen 47:18-19 66
Gen 50:24 43
Hab 2:20 97
Heb 1:3 . . . . 133, 141
Heb 1:5 5
Heb 2:2-4; 9:13-14; 10:28-29; 12:9; 12:25 51
Heb 3:1 141
Heb 3:7; 10:15 5
Heb 4:15 141
Heb 6:13 43
Heb 7:26 141
Hos 3:1 84
Hos 3:1-2 84
Hos 3:5 . . . . 17, 129
Hos 4:15; 5:5 129
Hos 7:11; 8:9-13 85
Hosea 10:4 76
Isa 4:20-24 43
Isa 6:4 26
Isa 8:1 17
Isa 22:12 95
Isa 22:20-23 93
Isa 28:15, 18 77
Isa 33:8 76
Isa 34:8; 61:2; 63:4 32
Isa 41:1-29; 43:8-13 38
Isa 41:1-29; 43:8-13; 43:22-28; 44:7-8; 45:20-21 . . . . 38, 89
Isa 41:21-22 41
Isa 43:9 43
Isa 43:10, 12 43
Isa 43:10, 12; 44:8 44
Isa 43:22-28; 44:7-8; 45:20-21; 48:14-16; 50:1; 50:7-9 38
Isa 48:14-16; 50:1-2; 50:7-9 . 89
Isa 53:7 107
Isaiah 40-50 89
Isaiah 40-55 38
Isaiah 42:1-4 131
James 5:12 43
Jer 1:7-8 126
Jer 2:20 123
Jer 2:22 123
Jer 3:8 . . . . 47, 82, 83
Jer 5:1 6
Jer 5:15-17 123
Jer 7:32-33 123
Jer 9:16 124
Jer 11:3-5 124
Jer 12:5 [2] 50
Jer 20:6 85
Jer 21:4 124
Jer 21:5 124
Jer 21:8 125
Jer 25:11-12; 29:10-11; 32:6-15 33
Jer 29:13-14 125
Jer 31:31-34 83
Jer 31:32 78
Jer 33:20, 25 77
Jer 34:8-18 76
Jer 34:14 125
Jer 36:28 126
Jer 46:10 32
Job 1:1-2:7 46
Job 1-2 37
Job 9:1 59
Job 9:14-15 59
Job 10:2-7 53
Job 11:5; 12:4 59
Job 13:3 60
Job 13:23 60
Job 19:25-27 59
Job 31:7-8 43
Job 31:21-22 43
Joel 3:1 26
Joel 3:2 26
Joel 3:16 26
Joel 4:14 89
John 1:1 138
John 1:3 134

John 1:6 135
John 1:14 137
John 1:33 135
John 3:1-5 14
John 3:17 135
John 4:34 135
John 5:15 36
John 5:22-23 135
John 5:30; 6:38-39; 9:4 . . . 135
John 5:36-37 135
John 6:44 135
John 6:57 135
John 7:16-18 135
John 7:33-34; 16:5 135
John 8:15-16 135
John 8:19 135
John 8:28-29; 12:49 136
John 9:1-41 140
John 9:29 119
John 10:33 129
John 10:34-36 128
John 13:16 135
John 13:20 . . . . 132, 135
John 14:9 . . . . 129, 134
John 14:26; 15:26; 16:8 . . . 135
John 14:28 . . . . 129, 134
John 17:20-26 134
John 20:21-23 136
John 20:22-3 17
Jonah 1:7-16 32
Josh 7:2-11 73
Josh 7:12-26 73
Josh 7:25 99
Josh 23:11 84
Judges 6:2 16
Judges 6:22 130
Judges 8:19 43
Judges 11:9 16
Judges 11:29 130
Judges 14:19; 15:14 . . . . 16, 130
Lev 6:4, 8 6
Lev 8:1-10 94
Lev 19:9-18 85
Lev 19:18 85
Lev 19:19 7
Lev 20:14; 21:9 99
Lev 26:23-33 80
Luke 1:8-25 116
Luke 1:30-35 131
Luke 1:73-75 43
Luke 3:21-22 131
Luke 3:38-4:1 131
Luke 4:18-21 131
Luke 4:30 132
Luke 4:36 131
Luke 5:17-26 140
Luke 9:34-35 106
Luke 9:51, 53 140
Luke 10:37 86
Luke 11:20 132
Luke 12:10 131
Luke 14:8-11 95
Luke 14:48 45
Luke 18:2-5 . . . . 36, 88
Luke 23:4, 14, 22 140
Luke 23:8-11 94
Luke 23:13-17 94
Mal 3:2 61
Mark 1:10 131
Mark 1:22 136
Mark 1:27 132
Mark 2:1-12 140
Mark 3:29-30 132
Mark 6:56 140
Mark 12:31, 33 85
Mark 12:35-36 131
Matt 3:16-17 131
Matt 5:20-26 44
Matt 5:34 43
Matt 5:34; 23:16 43
Matt 5:37 43
Matt 5:44 36
Matt 7:9-11; 12:11-12 51
Matt 7:29; 21:24 132
Matt 9:1-8 140
Matt 9:10-13, 14-15 38
Matt 9:20-22 140
Matt 10:1-8 140

Matt 10:8 16
Matt 10:20 118
Matt 10:40-42 132
Matt 12:14; 26:59 46
Matt 12:15-32 131
Matt 12:22-32 136
Matt 12:28 132
Matt 15:1 46
Matt 15:4, 8-9; 19:4-5, 18-19; 21:5, 13, 42 48
Matt 16:21; 17:22-23; 20:18-19; 20:28 104
Matt 18:15-17 44
Matt 18:20 136
Matt 19:3 46
Matt 19:8 23
Matt 19:17 15
Matt 19:19; 22:37 85
Matt 21:23 46
Matt 22:17 46
Matt 22:43-44 132
Matt 28:16-20 139
Matt 28:18 132
Matt 28:20 . . . . 130, 132
Micah 6:7 33
Neh 9:38 75
Num 3:4 117
Num 5 7
Num 5:11-22 65
Num 5:19-22 43
Num 6:24-26 36
Num 6:25-26 71
Num 12:14 50
Num 14:1-12 72
Num 14:13-19 72
Num 16:28 120
Num 16:48 116
Phil 1:8 44
Prov 2:17 77
Prov 6:34 32
Prov 12:31 50
Prov 14:20 85
Prov 31:23 35
Proverbs 2-7 5
Proverbs 7 5
Ps 17:1-2 56
Ps 17:6-7 57
Ps 17:13-15 57
Ps 17:15 . . . . 57, 59
Ps 19:15 68
Ps 31:7 53
Ps 31:24[23] 84
Ps 50:1-7 32
Ps 50:7, 21 35
Ps 50:16 77
Ps 69:6 54
Ps 70:1-2 69
Ps 70:6 69
Ps 70:6; 86:1-2 95
Ps 77:20 120
Ps 82:1 120
Ps 82:2-4 128
Ps 82:5 128
Ps 82:6-7 120
Ps 86:1-2 69
Ps 86:16-17 70
Ps 93:1 95
Ps 106:30-31 56
Ps 109:6 46
Ps 109:6-7 37
Ps 139:1 54
Ps 140:10-12 70
Ps 140:13-14 70
Ps 143:1-2 70
Ps 143:11-12 71
Ps 144:8 43
Psalm 82 129
Rev 2:11 15
Rev 2:13; 11:3-10 45
Rev 4:2-4 26
Rev 6:9-11 . . . . 33, 90
Rev 8:3-4 54
Rev 9:13 26
Rev 10:1 106
Rev 10:5-6 43
Rev 11:12 106
Rev 15:5-8 26
Rev 15:8-16:7; 19:5 26

Rev 20:6 15
Rev 20:11-12 26
Rev 20:14 15
Rev 21:8 16
Rom 1:3 . . . . 136, 138
Rom 1:3-4 132
Rom 1:4 136
Rom 1:9 44
Rom 5:8-9, 10, 17, 18, 21; 11:12, 15 51
Rom 12:14 36
Rom 13:8-10 85
Ruth 1:17 42
Ruth 3:9 77
Ruth 3:13 42
Ruth 4:1-2 35
Zech 3 37
Zech 3:1 46
Zech 3:1-10 91
Zech 3:3-6 46
Zechariah 3 93

NON-BIBLICAL REFERENCES

1 Clement 45:1-2 133
1QS 6:1 44
2 Macc 10:1 105
4QM 12:8 105
11QMelch 13 127
Aboda Zara 5a 128
Aboth 4:11 34
Aboth 4:29 44
Ad Autol. 2.9, 10 133
Ant 12.285-312 107
Ant. 12.131-54 108
Ant. 12.357-58 100
Ant. 12:354-59 99
Ant. 14.172-73 94
Ant. 14.173 58
Apoc. Abr. 13:1-14 93
Apologia Socratis 21 37
Apology 1.36 133
Asc. Isa 7:14, 4, 9, 33-34 . . . 26
B.K. 113b 132
Bar 2:11 67
Ber 4:4-5 91
Ber 5:4-5 116
Ber 6:5 117
Ber 6a 128
CD 9:2-4 44
CD 9:16-10:3 44
Comm. Isa. 29:9 133
Contra Marcion 3.11 139
Contra Marcion 3.10 . . 134, 139
Contra Marcion 3.2 134
Contra Marcion 3.2-4 133
De Antichristo 2 133
De Ps 88 133
Dec. 138-41 44
Decal 18.84-95 43
Enoch 45:1-48:10 90
Enoch 47:3-4 . . . . 48, 90
Enoch 48:1-10; 62:7-12 . . . 102
Enoch 50:3 21
Enoch 51:3; 55:4; 61:8; 6:, 5; 69:6-7 21
Enoch 62:13-16 93
Enoch 71:14 21
Ep. 70.7; 65.7; 82.7 133
ExodR 5.1 [4:9] 23
GenR 22:26, #78 132
Gerim 2:5 14
HE 6.14, 4 134
Hermas, Mand. 1-8 67
Herodotus, Hist. 6.82 . . . . 36, 37
Hom. in John 1.1 133
Iliad 18.497-508 34
JBer 4,5.8c 26
Jub 4:16-19 44
LamR 1:18-19 #53 133
Leg. pro Christ 9 133
Livy 37.39-45 112

Mekilta Kaspa 2:46-48 65
Mekilta Vayassa 4:432-45 . . . 51
Memar Marqah 2 #12; 3 #6; 4 #5; 5 #3; 6 #3, 11 119
Midrash Psalms 118:18 33
NumR 16:24 128
Polybius 31.17, 3 32
Polybius 31.9 99
Pseudo Philo 20:2-3 94
Quintilian 4.1, 14-16 39
Quintilian 4.1, 16-19 36
Quintilian 4.1, 17-19 40
Quintilian 4.1, 24, 40 40
Quintilian 4.1, 73-74 68
Quintilian 4.2, 1-45 40
Quintilian 4.2, 127 34
Quintilian 4.4, 8-9 41
Quintilian 4.7, 73-79 40
Quintilian 4.pr. 7, 6 39
Quintilian 5.6, 1-5 41
Quintilian 5.7, 1-6 39
Quintilian 5.7, 15-36 43
Quintilian 5.8, 7 49
Quintilian 5.9, 8-15 49
Quintilian 5.10, 17-27 49
Quintilian 5.10, 71-74 50
Quintilian 5.11, 3 49
Quintilian 5.13,6; 4.1,5-7 . . . 39
Quintilian 5.7,1-6 39
Quintilian 5.pr.4,1.2-4.2 61
Quintilian 6.1, 30 58
Quintilian 6.1, 33 58
Quintilian 6.1,34 58
Quintilian 6.3, 60-61 58
RH 1:8 44
RH 4:9 . . . . 91, 116
Rhetoric 1.2,1 39
Rhetoric 1.2, 14-19 50
Rhetoric 1.2, 17-18 39
Rhetoric 1.12, 4-9 35
Rhetoric 1.14, 6-7 50
Rhetoric 1.15, 14-26 . . . . 47, 61
Rhetoric 2:1, 2 35
San 3:4 98
San 4:3 23
San 5:2 44
SDebarim 6:5 #32 [73a] 85
Sheb 36a 43
Sifra, behuqqotai, perek 8:12; Lev 26:46 119
Sifre Deut 6:5; #31 33
Sifre Deuteronomy #5, 66b . 119
Sifre Piska 320 128
Sirach 45:17 47
Song of SongsR 1:2, #3 . . . 133
Song of SongsR 8:2, 5 14
Spec. 1.230, 293 141
Spec. Leg. 4.41-44 44
Spec. Leg. 4.59-61 44
Tanhuma, Shemot 9 23
Test Mos 11:17 119
TLev 3:4-5 26
TSan 7:11 51
War 1.452-54 57
War 1.627-39 58
War 1.656 100
War 2.24-25 89
War 2.37 58
War 6.383-84 72
Wars 2.135, 141-44, 152-53 . . 43
Wisdom 1:6 44
Xenophon, Hist. Graeca 7.3, 6 36
Yeb 48b 14
Yeb 88b, 115a 44
Yoma 5:1 . . . . 25, 91, 116

GEOGRAPHICAL LOCATIONS

Africa 29, 102
Babylon. . 5, 19, 67, 91, 93, 111, 121, 130, 137
Canaan 20
Egypt. . 62, 67, 72, 94, 105, 108, 110, 119, 124

Europe 30, 102, 115
Fertile Crescent 30, 99
France 18
Gerar 38
Great Britain 102
Horeb 76
Jerusalem. . 23, 26, 43, 45, 89, 100, 102, 106, 108
Jordan 63, 73
Judah 93, 123, 129
Kidron 89
Ligomba 29, 35
Lombard 130
Macedonia 11
Mesopotamia 31
Mizpah 38, 46
Near East . . 10, 29, 45, 59, 61, 65, 78, 87, 115, 116, 125, 142
New Mexico 61
North America 31
Palestine . . 102, 105, 107, 108, 110, 117
Persia . 90, 91, 94, 100, 102, 107
Rome 115, 117, 140
Shechem 121
Sinai 77, 80, 83
Tanzania 29, 34, 101
Tekoa 8, 128
U.S.A. 1, 81
United States . . 2, 4, 5, 19, 24, 31, 35, 37, 41, 68, 96, 137
Zion 32

STUDIES IN RELIGION AND SOCIETY

1. Anson D. Shupe, **Six Perspectives on New Religions: A Case Study Approach**
2. Barry Cooper, **Michel Foucault: An Introduction to the Study of His Thought**
3. Eileen Barker (ed.), **New Religious Movements: A Perspective for Understanding Society**
4. Christine Elizabeth King, **The Nazi State and the New Religions: Five Case Studies in Non-conformity**
5. David G. Bromley and James T. Richardson (ed.), **The Brainwashing/Deprogramming Controversy: Sociological, Psychological, Legal and Historical Perspectives**
6. Tom Craig Darrand and Anson Shupe, **Metaphors of Social Control in a Pentecostal Sect**
7. Judith Mary Weightman, **Making Sense of the Jonestown Suicides: A Sociological History of the Peoples Temple**
8. Barbara Hargrove (ed.), **Religion and the Sociology of Knowledge: Modernization and Pluralism in Christian Thought and Structure**
9. Niklas Luhmann, **Religious Dogmatics and the Evolution of Societies,** introduction by Peter Beyer (trans.)
10. Herbert Richardson (ed.), **Constitutional Issues in the Case of Reverend Moon: Amicus Briefs Presented to the United States Supreme Court**
11. Annette P. Hampshire, **Mormonism in Conflict: The Nauvoo Years**
12. Patricia Werhane and Kendall D'Andrade (ed.), **Profit and Responsibility: Issues in Business and Professional Ethics**
13. James H. Grace, **Sex and Marriage in the Unification Movement: A Sociological Study**
14. Rebecca Moore, **A Sympathetic History of Jonestown: The Moore Family Involvement in Peoples Temple**
15. Tommy H. Poling and J. Frank Kenney, **The Hare Krishna Character Type: A Study of the Sensate Personality**
16. Edward C. Lehman, Jr., **Women Clergy in England: Sexism, Modern Consciousness, and Church Viability**
17. Joseph H. Fichter, **Autobiographies of Conversion**
18. George B. Pepper, **The Boston Heresy Case in View of the Secularization of Religion: A Case Study in the Sociology of Religion**
19. Leo Driedger, **Mennonite Identity in Conflict**
20. Helen Ralston, **Christian Ashrams: A New Religious Movement in Contemporary India**
21. Martha F. Lee, **The Nation of Islam, An American Millenarian Movement**

22. James T. Richardson (ed.), **Money and Power in the New Religions**
23. Sharon Linzey Georgianna, **The Moral Majority and Fundamentalism: Plausibility and Dissonance**
24. Roger O'Toole, (ed.) **Sociological Studies in Roman Catholicism: Historical and Contemporary Perspectives**
25. Frank D. Schubert, **A Sociological Study of Secularization Trends in the American Catholic University: Decatholicizing the Catholic Religious Curriculum**
26. Hal W. French, **A Study of Religious Fanaticism and Responses To It: Adversary Identity**
27. A. D. Wright, **Catholicism and Spanish Society Under the Reign of Philip II, 1555-1598, and Philip III, 1598-1621**
28. Theodore Weinberger, **Strategies for Sustaining Religious Commitment: The Art of the Religious Life**
29. George W. Buchanan, **Biblical and Theological Insights from Ancient and Modern Civil Law**
30. James Thrower, **Marxism-Leninism as the Civil Religion of Soviet Society: God's Commissar**